P9-DXO-567

Anthropology of Contemporary Issues

A SERIES EDITED BY

ROGER SANJEK

# Farm Work and Fieldwork

## AMERICAN AGRICULTURE IN ANTHROPOLOGICAL PERSPECTIVE

EDITED BY

*Michael Chibnik*

*Cornell University Press*

Ithaca and London

First published 1987 by Cornell University Press.

International Standard Book Number (cloth) 0-8014-1978-6
International Standard Book Number (paper) 0-8014-9446-X
Library of Congress Catalog Card Number 86-19960
Printed in the United States of America
*Librarians: Library of Congress cataloging information*
*appears on the last page of the book.*

*The paper in this book is acid-free and meets the guidelines*
*for permanence and durability of the Committee on Production*
*Guidelines for Book Longevity of the Council on Library Resources.*

# Contents

# Acknowledgments

This book is the outgrowth of a symposium organized by Peggy Barlett at the 1982 meeting of the American Anthropological Association. Papers presented at the symposium by Peggy Barlett, Lisa Gröger, Susan Rogers, Sonya Salamon, Miriam Wells, myself, and others examined contemporary American agriculture from an anthropological perspective. Roger Sanjek, the editor of Cornell's Anthropology of Contemporary Issues series, was in the audience and saw a potential book. He later proposed that I edit a volume aimed at readers from a variety of disciplines. I solicited contributions from the participants in the symposium and from other anthropologists studying American agriculture.

Most of my work on this volume was done at the University of Iowa. University funds supported my writing in the summer of 1984. Shirley Ahlgren, Kathy von Peursem, and Joan Crowe of the Anthropology Department patiently typed portions of the manuscript and much of my correspondence with contributors.

In December 1985 I interrupted fieldwork in Peru to come to New York City, where I edited chapters, revised the Introduction, and wrote the Afterword. My sister, Katharine Chibnik, provided housing and access to a word processor. I am most grateful for her kindness, tolerance, and patience during this hectic period.

I returned to Peru in January 1986 and remained there until June. Peggy Barlett agreed to supervise the final copy editing during my absence. Her willingness to take on this task sped the book's publication.

Numerous people elucidated for me the subtleties and complexities of American agriculture. Maeve Clark's bibliographic assistance and

[7]

literature searches greatly facilitated my writing of the Introduction and Afterword. Susan Rogers provided useful information about policy issues. Peter Nowak, Mark Swanson, and Margery Wolf lent me clippings, articles, and books on midwestern agriculture, and Ralph Altmaier, Ralph Arnold, Les Betts, Barbara Craig, and Jim Huerter answered many questions about farming and rural life in Iowa.

Editing this book would have been much harder without the help of Roger Sanjek. Besides suggesting the theme of the volume, he made helpful comments about this book's organization and about individual chapters. His editorial help and logistical aid are most appreciated.

MICHAEL CHIBNIK

*Iowa City, Iowa*

# Farm Work and Fieldwork

# Introduction

## Michael Chibnik

The current economic difficulties of American farmers are well known. Magazines and newspapers run stories about mass meetings of angry rural residents caught in the credit squeeze. Television reporters interview farmers forced to declare bankruptcy because of huge debts, falling land values, and low commodity prices. Popular movies depict families fighting to save their land.

The widespread interest in the farm crisis stems partly from pragmatic concerns. Agriculture-related businesses are the mainstay of the economy in some regions, and the activities of American farmers affect the cost, availability, and quality of food throughout the world. The public reaction to increasingly capital-intensive agriculture and rural depopulation also demonstrates a recognition that a way of life is disappearing. The family farm is an important part of American folklore exalted by writers and politicians. The transformation of American agriculture represents more than economic change; it signals the obsolescence of social institutions and ideologies associated with farm life of earlier times.

Although many articles and books have examined the farm crisis, few have looked at it from an ethnographic standpoint. Some are dry, statistic-filled explanations of the underlying causes of the restructuring of American agriculture; others are emotion-laden human interest stories about individual farmers. Such accounts provide little information about the ways in which technological and economic changes have affected social institutions and cultural patterns in particular rural communities.

In the past few years, however, a number of anthropologists have conducted ethnographic studies of American farm life. These researchers have examined how farm families and communities have reacted to new technology, fluctuating commodity prices, changing land values, soil deterioration, and government incentives to adopt particular land use policies. This book presents some of the results of this research. My primary goal in compiling the volume is to demonstrate how anthropological methods can be used to study agriculture in an industrial society; an important secondary goal is to show how technological and economic changes have affected rural American communities.

## Anthropology, Agriculture, and Industrial Society

The social scientific study of agriculture has long been affected by a peculiar disciplinary division of labor. Anthropologists have dominated the study of nonindustrial farming systems. Working with tribal and peasant peoples, they have carefully analyzed the relationships among agricultural technology, population density, sexual division of labor, household composition, land tenure arrangements, marketing systems, and political organization (Netting 1974). Almost all social scientific examinations of agriculture in industrial countries, however, have been carried out by rural sociologists, geographers, and economists.

These self-imposed disciplinary boundaries have recently begun to vanish. To understand why this is so, it is necessary to examine the changing relationship between anthropology and other social sciences.

One of anthropology's distinguishing features has always been its panhuman scope. Introductory textbooks frequently begin by noting that anthropologists, unlike other social scientists, are explicitly concerned with the behavior and ideas of peoples from all places and times (see, e.g., Ember and Ember 1985:2). An examination of human societies in diverse geographic and historical settings is a necessary prerequisite for the anthropological tasks of documenting and accounting for cross-cultural similarities and differences.

Despite this commitment to studying a variety of societies, sociocultural anthropologists in the first part of this century conducted the majority of their research among non-Western peoples and racial and ethnic minorities in industrial countries. The few professionally trained anthropologists saw a pressing need for careful ethnography among these groups because their cultures were rarely studied by other social scientists and were often changing rapidly. The mores and behavioral patterns of the dominant groups in Western industrial countries, in contrast, had already been described extensively by psychologists, sociologists, economists, and historians.

In the past several decades more anthropologists have been studying "mainstream" cultures in western industrial societies. By 1970, 23 percent of doctoral dissertations in sociocultural anthropology granted by universities in the United States and Canada were based on fieldwork conducted in North America or Europe. This figure jumped to 42 percent in 1980 (Chibnik and Moberg 1983:33). Although some of these recent studies examine the culture and social organization of ethnic minorities, many others concern occupational subgroups.

This change in focus results in part from practical considerations. As the number of anthropologists working among tribal and peasant peoples has increased, some ethnographers have chosen to study people living in industrial countries. Opportunities for "salvage ethnography" have diminished as previously isolated groups have been integrated into the economies of nation-states. African, Asian, and Latin American countries now often impose restrictions on or completely forbid anthropological research by foreigners.

Theoretical concerns have also led anthropologists to examine industrial society. Ethnographers have become more aware that people in our own and other societies are greatly affected by inequitable power relationships between the poor and the elite and between Third World countries and the industrial nations. If important decisions in both developing and industrialized nations are made by the elite, then anthropological examinations of the powerful are as important as the traditional descriptions of the powerless (Nader 1972). Bureaucratic organizations in industrial nations thus become appropriate field sites for ethnographic investigation.

Anthropology is not the only social science expanding its horizons. Over the past three decades many sociologists, economists, and geographers have conducted research in Africa, Asia, and Latin America. The increasing involvement by anthropologists in research in the industrialized countries and by other social scientists in the Third World raises basic questions about the distinction between sociocultural anthropology and the other social sciences. Some writers note theoretical and methodological differences between disciplines (e.g., Ember and Ember 1985:3). In a phrase used so often that it has

[13]

become a cliché, anthropology is said to be the "most holistic of fields," showing functional interrelations between various aspects of culture. The methodology of anthropology is also somewhat different from that of other social sciences, often involving long-term personal relationships with the people being studied and collection of qualitative case materials as well as quantitative data. Clearly, the holism, methodologic electicism, and detailed ethnography characteristic of anthropology are adaptations to field situations in which one or two researchers are attempting to collect diverse data about a group with unfamiliar customs or language. Many anthropologists believe that these methods are also advantageous for research closer to home.

Except for a brief flurry of activity at the end of the depression and during World War II, anthropologists have traditionally neglected industrial agriculture. In the past decade, however, interest in this topic has grown. The 1982, 1983, and 1985 meetings of the American Anthropological Association included sessions devoted to ethnographic studies of American agriculture, and the association's 1984 Congressional Fellowship was awarded to an applicant (Susan Rogers) specializing in the analysis of farm problems in the United States and Europe.

This volume is one result of the recent spurt of interest among anthropologists in industrial agriculture. The topics examined and approaches taken by the contributors have been influenced by historical developments and anthropological theory and method. Before discussing the contents of the book, I will review some important recent changes in American agriculture and contrast anthropological studies of farm life in the United States with those done by rural sociologists.

## Twentieth-Century Changes in American Agriculture

Rural American life has undergone striking changes in the twentieth century, especially in the years since World War II. The driving forces behind these changes have been the technological innovations that have increased agricultural output and eased the transport of farm products to distant markets. These innovations have affected farm scale and type, given rise to new rural institutions, and caused the federal government to adopt complex, far-reaching agricultural policies. These technological, economic, institutional, and political changes have had profound effects on agrarian social organization.

The tractor has been described as "the harbinger of the technological revolution that set in motion the process that has led to modern agribusiness" (Shover 1976:49). Although tractors were not used much before World War I, their use spread in the 1920s and 1930s so much that by 1939 more than 1.5 million were in operation. There were still more than 15 million draft animals on farms in 1939, though, and it was not until after World War II that the tractors outnumbered the animals. Other labor-saving and output-increasing devices, including the combine and corn and cotton pickers, followed the development of the large, general-purpose tractor. Innovations in the use of fossil fuels also resulted in improvements in transportation and food preservation that allowed farm products to be sold many miles from their places of origin.

At the same time, developments resulting from scientific agricultural research enabled American farmers to increase their output. Higher-yielding hybrid corn seeds were developed in the 1930s; more recently, hybrid sorghum and new wheat varieties have become widely used. Chemical fertilizers, weed killers, and insecticides, all rarely used before the Second World War, have been adopted by most farmers. Scientific developments have resulted in much higher yields per unit of human labor and, for most crops, substantial increases per unit of land.

These technological innovations have transformed the microeconomics of farming. Although labor requirements have dropped as machines have replaced human and animal labor, capital expenses for farm equipment and chemicals have skyrocketed. Until the early 1980s land values were rising as well. One consequence of these changes has been a concentration of agricultural land into fewer hands. Farmers unable to afford large capital investments have lost out in competition with their wealthier neighbors able to take advantage of the economies of scale associated with new technology. As farms have become larger and more capital-intensive, they have become more business-like, less subsistence-oriented, and less diversified.

Economic and technological changes have led to the rise of new institutions and the growing importance of others. Large corporations have been established to manufacture and sell agricultural equipment and chemicals and to process and market food. Many such "agri-

[15]

businesses" are vertically integrated; that is, they control the production, processing, and marketing of certain crops and livestock.

In some places agriculture is now dominated by nonfamily corporations operating farms with hired managers and laborers. These corporate farms have tended to concentrate on risky, capital-intensive crops and livestock associated with vertically integrated agribusinesses. Such products include fresh and processed vegetables, cotton, cattle, and poultry. Nonfamily corporations cut costs by operating in areas with uniform soil and climatic conditions such as the irrigated West and humid South (Vogeler 1981).

Analysts disagree over the share of agricultural production controlled by nonfamily corporations. Such disputes hinge on the definition of "corporate farms." The United States Department of Agriculture, which consistently provides one of the lower estimates, reported in 1974 that more than 15 percent of all American farmland was controlled by nonfamily corporations. Although this figure is not enormous, the amount of corporate-controlled farmland is increasing. Moreover, even "independent" American farmers frequently find their production strategies controlled by agribusinesses. For example, some food-processing firms exerting virtual monopolies over products such as poultry and sugar beets sign contracts with farmers to deliver a certain quantity and quality of the product at a set price. These contracts commonly specify the methods farmers must use to raise the products (Vogeler 1981:11–34, 105–143).

Farmers expanding and modernizing their operations have been forced to rely increasingly on lending institutions. Banks have frequently favored large-scale producers, forcing some independent farmers to obtain loans under relatively poor terms. As Vogeler (1981:116) observes, "if family farmers receive credit, they quickly find they are on a treadmill of ever-increasing debt to finance production to pay this debt." When land values and farm prices fall, as happened in the 1980s, many farmers default on their loans and are forced to quit agriculture.

With the development of complex farming techniques, the land-grant universities have become more important in rural life. These institutions are centers for agricultural research and the dissemination of information about new farming methods. County agents associated with land-grant universities have become a source of information about agricultural techniques in the most remote rural areas. Critics of

[16]

land-grant institutions (e.g., Busch and Lacy 1983) have argued that the institutions' close ties with agribusinesses have led them to conduct a disproportionate amount of research on topics of interest to large-scale operators and to pay insufficient attention to the needs of small farmers and consumers.

The executive and legislative branches of government have also come to play a larger role in rural life. The technological innovations of the twentieth century have enabled farmers to grow enough food to meet domestic needs easily. As a result, the U.S. federal government since the 1930s has introduced a variety of policies designed to prevent flooding of domestic markets and consequent lower farm prices. Some policies, such as the Payment in Kind (PIK) program of 1983, have explicitly given farmers incentives for taking land out of production. Other less explicit policies have had the same fundamental goal. For example, legislation overtly aimed at preserving soil in the 1930s was actually designed to encourage farmers to reduce grain production. Similarly, programs designed to encourage the export of food have been motivated at least partly by a desire to prevent domestic oversupply.

The importance of federal policy has been so great that one historian has argued that "agriculture is the only economic sector in the United States where in any sense national planning may be said to have existed" (Shover 1976:237). Well-financed lobbying groups have been organized to represent the interests of various agricultural constituencies. Many writers (Hightower 1973; Britan, this volume) have argued that these lobbying efforts have resulted in policies favorable to agribusinesses and large farms and have shown a lack of concern for small farmers, tenants, and the food needs of the urban poor.

Community character, household economic strategies, and family organization have all been affected by the changing organizational structure and increasingly capital-intensive nature of agriculture. In most areas population densities outside of towns have dropped as farms have become fewer and larger. The number of people living on farms declined from 15.6 million to 8 million between 1960 and 1970 and is now less than 6 million. Improvements in transportation have enabled rural residents to rely less on their immediate neighborhood for shopping and entertainment and have led to the consolidation of school districts. Farm people have become less provincial with increased exposure to the outside world via television, radio, postsecondary education, and military service. While community ties and local institutions remain important in rural areas, many communities provide fewer services and seem less close-knit than formerly (see Salamon, this volume).

The monetary demands of modern agriculture have affected use of labor and land. Many men and women now must supplement their agricultural income with off-farm jobs (see Barlett, this volume); the substitution of machinery for human and animal labor has given them the time to do this. Increases in farm size and (until recently) land prices have made entry into agriculture very difficult for those without relatives with farms. Moreover, many farmers cannot afford to buy all the land they use and must rent some or all of their fields.

The sexual division of labor on American farms has also changed in recent years. Before World War II women worked on farms primarily in maintenance and subsistence activities quite different from the more cash-oriented tasks of men. Most contemporary farm women spend less time on these activities now that agricultural enterprises have become more specialized and electrification has given all but the poorest rural families access to labor-saving household appliances. Many married women have off-farm jobs or work with their husbands on agricultural tasks. Men's and women's on-farm tasks still differ greatly (Fink, this volume; Ehlers, this volume), but sometimes the differences are in degree rather than kind.

The rise of agribusiness, depopulation of the countryside, and increasing dependence of farmers on the federal government have led some writers to proclaim that the family farm is disappearing rapidly in the United States (see, e.g., Wessel 1983). Whether this is true depends to a certain extent on definitions. Most social scientists agree that on an ideal family farm, household members own the land, perform the labor, control the capital, and make the important economic decisions. Certainly there are still many American farms owned and worked by families, rather than corporations. However, many family farmers have limited choice about their use of capital and land because of constraints imposed by lending institutions, the companies that buy their products, and federal policy makers. Many writers arguing that the family farm is vanishing are not claiming that corporate-owned farms are coming to dominate American agriculture; instead they are noting that farm families are losing much of their control over capital and land management (e.g., Fink, this volume).

## Anthropological and Sociological Studies of American Agriculture

For many years rural sociologists working in the United States have been examining topics such as technological innovation, social relations, family organization, population movements, and religious beliefs. Nevertheless, anthropological research can provide insights into rural American life that are unlikely to be obtained by most contemporary sociologists. The limitations of rural sociology are related to that discipline's institutional setting and methodology, which differ greatly from those of anthropology.

Rural sociologists are strikingly concerned with the history and characteristics of their discipline. More than 10 percent of the articles published between 1966 and 1974 in *Rural Sociology,* the field's major journal, discussed disciplinary characteristics (Nolan et al. 1975). Rural sociologists discussing their field differ about perceived problems; some decry an alleged lack of theoretical and methodological rigor (e.g., Stokes and Miller 1975), while others deplore the paucity of policy-relevant studies (e.g., Nolan et al. 1975). Nevertheless, there is general agreement that the field's subject matter and methodology have been greatly influenced by the organizations within which rural sociologists have operated and by developments within general sociology.

### The Institutional Setting of Rural Sociology

Most rural sociologists working in the United States have been employed by either land-grant universities or federal and state agencies concerned with agricultural and economic policy. Many writers (e.g., Hooks 1983) argue that the topics investigated and analytic methods used by rural sociologists have been considerably influenced by political currents in their work places. During the New Deal, these writers say, the political climate allowed sociologists employed by government agencies to analyze rural class structure and the social effects of corporate control of agriculture. More recently, rural sociologists, now mostly employed by land-grant institutions intimately connected with agribusiness, have been less willing to conduct such critical research.

Although rural sociology was taught in many universities in the first two decades of this century, research funds were limited. Starting in the mid-1920s, a series of government acts increased funding for social studies by agricultural experiment stations and other government agencies. Rural sociologists and a few anthropologists were employed during the New Deal by agencies such as the Works Progress Administration and the Bureau of Agricultural Economics. Much of their research focused on rural socioeconomic stratification and took a critical view of existing class and social relations (Nelson 1969).

In the 1940s two studies funded by the Bureau of Agricultural Economics caused a tremendous uproar and were at least partly responsible for the reduction in funding by many government agencies for rural sociological research. The controversies surrounding these projects have been described in detail elsewhere (Nelson 1969; Goldschmidt 1978); here I will mention only the topics investigated. Frank Alexander, a sociologist, conducted a study in Coahoma County, Mississippi, in which he examined relationships between white landowners and black sharecroppers. Alexander (1944) described the methods the landowners used to maintain inequitable economic relations, noted differences between schools for blacks and for whites, and mentioned the fears of local whites that militant northerners might influence southern blacks. Walter Goldschmidt (1978), an anthropologist, compared two California communities, one consisting of many small farms, the other dominated by relatively few large-scale farms. Goldschmidt noted that the latter community had fewer social services and more socioeconomic stratification and in general seemed less cohesive.

The years since World War II have seen considerable changes in the topics examined by rural sociologists. In a content analysis of articles published in *Rural Sociology* prior to 1975, Nolan, Hagan, and Hoekstra demonstrated a steady decrease in articles concerned with social organization and stratification and a corresponding increase in articles classified as "social psychology." They noted there were very few articles on such important topics as agribusiness, farm specialization, land concentration, land tenure, and energy (Nolan et al. 1975). Although these criticisms have been echoed in recent years (Flinn 1982; Hooks 1983), political economic analyses of the sort advocated by Nolan, Hagan, and Hoekstra are still uncommon in *Rural Sociology*.

In a recent presidential address to the Rural Sociological Society, William Flinn (1982) attributed the uncritical stance of many rural sociologists to their affiliation with land-grant universities. He argued that most rural sociologists work for institutions that accept the basic trajectories and changes in rural society and the agricultural sector. The task of rural sociologists, he said, has been to provide information that will enable decision makers to manage these changes. Flinn also observed that rural sociologists often work in academic departments or government agencies with agricultural economists. He suggested that this proximity has led rural sociologists to see their domain as noneconomic and to cut themselves off from examining the political and economic forces affecting agriculture.

### Sociological Methodology

Although rural sociology has been institutionally somewhat separate from general sociology, methodological changes in the subfield have mirrored those of the discipline as a whole. An increased emphasis on "scientific method" has resulted in much quantification and statistical analysis of data collected systematically via interviews and questionnaires. In recent years there has been a decrease in the use of qualitative methods such as long-term ethnography, descriptive reporting, and "holistic" analysis.

While sociocultural anthropology has seen similar changes (Chibnik 1985), they have not been nearly as marked as those in sociology. Even the most quantitatively oriented sociocultural anthropologists (e.g., Johnson 1978; Pelto and Pelto 1978) regard statistical analyses of surveys as only one of many useful ethnographic research tools.

The growing emphasis on survey analyses in rural sociology has widened the gap between that field and anthropology. Research carried out by anthropologists examining rural America during the New Deal did not differ much from that of their sociologist colleagues. In contrast, the analyses presented in this volume are methodologically rather distinct from most (but not all) analyses by contemporary rural sociologists.

### Anthropological Research

Although several anthropologists (e.g., Miner 1949; Goldschmidt 1978) working for government agencies in the 1930s and 1940s examined American rural life, sociocultural anthropologists generally neglected the study of North American agriculture between the end of World War II and the mid-1970s. (The studies by Vogt [1955] and Bennett [1969, 1982] are notable exceptions.) Recently, though, there has been a rebirth of interest in the topic. Anthropologists can and do make distinctive contributions to this study of rural life in industrial countries in several ways.

First, anthropologists make an important contribution simply by presenting straightforward ethnography. Rural sociologists, with their emphasis on survey analysis, have largely abandoned giving descriptions of daily lives of country people. Readers wishing to find out about the texture of contemporary American farm life will learn more from examining some ethnographic descriptions (e.g., Bauer 1979; Kramer 1980) than by combing sociological journals.

Second, the holism and qualitative research methods characteristic of anthropology aid our understanding of rural economy and social structure. Many rural sociologists and agricultural economists seem reluctant to describe any complex interrelationships that cannot be analyzed using statistical techniques such as factor analysis. Anthropological studies, in contrast, often include qualitative analyses of relationships between technology, political economy, social organization, and individual decision making. Thus they show the link between microlevel processes (the social psychological studies of rural sociologists) and macrolevel data (the aggregate statistics of economists).

Third, anthropologists are able to present a critical outside view. Anthropologists, unlike most other social scientists, can place American farming in cross-cultural perspective. They are able to see what is unique about American farming and what is characteristic of industrial agriculture everywhere. Moreover, lacking sociologists' and economists' institutional connections to the agricultural establishment, anthropologists may feel freer to examine critically the effects of agribusiness and increased capitalization of farming.

**Organization of This Book**

The essays presented here examine the causes and consequences of changing agricultural technology, economic conditions, and government programs. These papers provide an overview of current anthropological research in rural America. Farmers described include corn, soybean, and livestock producers in the Midwest, strawberry sharecroppers in California, vegetable raisers in New Jersey, tobacco growers in North Carolina, and peanut and cotton planters in Georgia.

The book is divided into four parts, each preceded by a short introduction in which parallels and contrasts between the various papers are noted. In Part I, three authors describe the strategies American farmers in particular communities use to cope with economic and environmental changes. The issues discussed—the "cost-price squeeze," farm specialization, and soil degradation—are among the most pressing current agricultural problems. The authors of the two chapters in Part II discuss how changing economic conditions have affected the division of farm labor by gender. The two chapters in Part III describe racial and ethnic differences in rural household and community organization. The three chapters in Part IV examine legal and political aspects of American farming. The authors show how economic constraints and bureaucratic structures shape private contractual agreements and organizational policies. They also describe how these agreements and policies affect the daily lives of farmers.

In an afterword I explore some public policy implications of anthropological research and speculate about future trends and trajectories in rural American communities. I also suggest possible new research directions for anthropologists studying American agriculture.

Although their topics and approaches vary, the contributors to this book agree that ethnographic descriptions of farm life are meaningless without an understanding of the larger political and economic forces shaping rural culture. Thus their essays include considerable discussion of the political economy of agriculture. This approach reflects the contemporary anthropological rejection of "community studies," in which local events are described and analyzed with little reference to regional and national political and economic structures.

Nevertheless, I think that the unique contribution of the essays rests in the ethnographic detail they provide—for example, about the sexual division of labor on Iowa farms, attitudes toward land in North Carolina, and problems caused by trespassers in rural New Jersey. Sociologists, economists, geographers, and political scientists have examined trends such as land concentration, soil erosion, farm specialization, and rural depopulation. These social scientists, however, do not ordinarily attempt to describe the ways in which these trends affect local household economic strategies, interpersonal relationships, and social institutions. Anthropological research on American agriculture, in contrast, has the specific goal of providing close examinations of rural life at particular times and places.

# References Cited

Alexander, Frank B. 1944. *Cultural Reconnaissance of Coahoma County, Mississippi.* Washington, D.C.: Bureau of Agricultural Economics, Division of Farm Population.

Bauer, Douglas. 1979. *Prairie City, Iowa: Three Seasons at Home.* New York: Putnam.

Bennett, John. 1969. *Northern Plainsmen: Adaptive Strategy and Agrarian Life.* Chicago: Aldine.

———. 1982. *Of Time and Enterprise: North American Family Farm Management in a Context of Resource Marginality.* Minneapolis: Univ. of Minnesota Press.

Busch, Lawrence, and William Lacy. 1983. *Science, Agriculture, and the Politics of Research.* Boulder, Colo.: Westview.

Chibnik, Michael. 1985. The Use of Statistics in Sociocultural Anthropology. *Annual Review of Anthropology* 14:135–157.

Chibnik, Michael, and Mark Moberg. 1983. The Changing Research Interests of North American Sociocultural Anthropologists. *Journal of Anthropology* 3:25–35.

Ember, Carol, and Melvin Ember. 1985. *Anthropology.* Englewood Cliffs, N.J.: Prentice-Hall.

Flinn, William. 1982. Rural Sociology: Prospects and Dilemmas in the 1980s. *Rural Sociology* 47:1–16.

Goldschmidt, Walter. 1978. *As You Sow: Three Studies in the Social Consequences of Agribusiness.* Montclair, N.J.: Allanheld, Osmun.

Hightower, Jim. 1978. *Hard Tomatoes, Hard Times.* Cambridge, Mass.: Schenkman.

Hooks, Gregory. 1983. A New Deal for Farmers and Social Scientists: The Politics of Rural Sociology in the Depression Era. *Rural Sociology* 48:386–408.

Johnson, Allen. 1978. *Quantification in Cultural Anthropology: An Introduction to Research Design.* Stanford, Calif.: Stanford Univ. Press.

Kramer, Mark. 1980. *Three Farms: Making Milk, Meat, and Money from the American Soil.* Boston: Little, Brown.

Miner, Horace. 1949. *Culture and Agriculture: An Anthropological Study of a Corn Belt County.* Ann Arbor: Univ. of Michigan Press.

Nader, Laura. 1972. Up the Anthropologist: Perspectives Gained from Studying Up. In *Reinventing Anthropology*, ed. Dell Hymes, pp. 284–311. New York: Random House.

Nelson, Lowry. 1969. *Rural Sociology: Its Origins and Growth in the United States.* Minneapolis: Univ. of Minnesota Press.

Netting, Robert. 1974. Agrarian Ecology. *Annual Review of Anthropology* 3:21–56.

Nolan, Michael, Robert Hagan, and Mary Hoekstra. 1975. Rural Sociological Research 1966–74: Implications for Social Policy. *Rural Sociology* 40:435–454.

Pelto, Pertti, and Gretel Pelto. 1978. *Anthropological Research: The Structure of Inquiry.* Cambridge: Cambridge Univ. Press.

Shover, John. 1976. *First Majority—Last Minority: The Transforming of Rural Life in America.* DeKalb, Ill.: Northern Illinois Univ. Press.

Stokes, C. Shannon, and Michael Miller. 1975. A Methodological Review of Research in Rural Sociology since 1965. *Rural Sociology* 40:411–434.

Vogeler, Ingolf. 1981. *The Myth of the Family Farm: Agribusiness Dominance of U.S. Agriculture.* Boulder, Colo.: Westview.

Vogt, Evan. 1955. *Modern Homesteaders: The Life of a Twentieth-Century Frontier Community.* Cambridge, Mass.: Harvard Univ. Press.

Wessel, James. 1983. *Trading the Future: Farm Exports and the Concentration of Economic Power in Our Food System.* San Francisco: Institute for Food and Development Policy.

# PART I

# ECONOMIC STRATEGIES

Anthropologists frequently examine the extent to which generalizations made by other social scientists apply to particular places and times. Two famous examples of this type of investigation are Bronislaw Malinowski's research on family psychodynamics in the Trobriand Islands and Margaret Mead's study of sex roles in New Guinea.

The three chapters in this section examine some generalizations about changing economic conditions in rural America. Agricultural economists commonly assert that the capitalization of American agriculture has resulted in a decrease in "family farming" and an increase in farm specialization and soil degradation. Although the contributors to this section do not reject these generalizations, their studies of economic strategies in particular communities indicate that such sweeping statements are not entirely applicable everywhere.

Peggy Barlett's chapter focuses on the topic that dominates today's agricultural news, the fate of family farms faced with rising expenses and lower crop and livestock prices. Many writers have argued that large, capital-intensive farms inevitably drive out smaller, more family-oriented operations. Barlett presents ethnographic and economic survey data from Georgia demonstrating that this is not the case there. Barlett shows that "conservative" operators of medium-sized farms in Georgia are weathering the cost-price squeeze better than operators of larger farms, who have accrued tremendous debts. She also observes that nonagricultural income has enabled many smaller farms to survive.

Susan Rogers's paper closely examines an Illinois community that remains "an island of mixed farming in a sea of grain." Rogers explains why midwestern farmers are specializing and discusses some of the adverse consequences of specialization. Using ethnographic and econometric methods, she then shows why farmers in the Illinois community she studied have retained diversified farming. She argues that the purchase and rental markets for land are almost nonexistent because of the importance of farming and landownership to the German-American residents. Rather than acquiring more land for corn and soybeans, these farmers have expanded their operations by raising livestock. Rogers's article nicely demonstrates the complementarity of ethnographic and economic analyses.

My contribution to this section examines the experimentation by farmers in an Iowa county with no-till, an important soil conservation practice recently introduced to the Midwest. No-till is an especially attractive conservation measure for large farms, and the decision to use it would appear to be simple. Yet there are myriad social, economic, political, and ideological factors influencing the decision. Through an ethnographic analysis, we can better understand the problem of soil erosion and the complex decisions that must be made about it.

# [1]

# The Crisis in Family Farming: Who Will Survive?

**Peggy F. Barlett**
*Department of Anthropology*
*Emory University*

Family farms, once the backbone of the economy in colonial America, have dwindled in importance as the United States has become an industrial power. This chapter looks at the current situation of family farmers in one Georgia county in the midst of a national farm crisis. Long-term trends in the changing structure of agriculture seem to be reversed by the short-term cost-price squeeze, and the sudden decline in farm profits reveals which kinds of farms are more likely to survive.

The changing structure of United States agriculture refers to the declining numbers of farms in the United States and their increasing average size. Since World War II, the number of family-owned and -operated farms has become much smaller. Many of the family farms that remain are worked part-time and supported by off-farm jobs. "Industrial-type" farms in which ownership, management, and labor are carried out by different groups of people have grown in number and importance in some areas of the country. For the moderate-sized family farms that remain, farming conditions have also changed rapidly. As farms have become larger, capital costs have increased, and farmers have become dependent on machinery and on manufactured products such as chemicals and fertilizers. Until the OPEC oil embargo and the energy crisis of the early 1970s, experts predicted a continued concentration of United States agriculture into a smaller number of larger and more sophisticated farms. The family farm has been called "the disappearing middle," and some feel it is doomed to be replaced by agribusiness-owned, industrial-type farms.

The energy crisis and related international events in the first half of the 1970s set off important changes often referred to as "the cost-price squeeze." Inflation throughout the United States economy was felt keenly by farmers in the costs of their machinery, fuel, fertilizers, chemicals, and seeds. Land values soared, and to finance farm expansion, many families went deeply into debt. Inflation and tax policies encouraged expansion of both farm sizes and equipment. Then, in the late 1970s, the prices farmers received for their crops stagnated or began to fall. Income did not keep up with expenses, and interest rates climbed. Severe weather reduced harvests and compounded problems in certain regions. More and more farms were foreclosed or went bankrupt. Many commentators assumed that the moderate-sized family farm was hardest hit by the cost-price squeeze. Data from Dodge County, Georgia, suggest, however, that the cost-price squeeze actually has slowed the trend toward a more industrial structure of agriculture. The larger, more capital-intensive farms seem to face a more precarious financial situation than family farms that rely less on hired labor. The hardships of recent years have taken a heavy toll on all types of farmers—especially on newcomers to farming—but the family farm seems at present to be in a stronger position than would have been expected.

### The National Context: A Revolution in United States Farming

The difficulties facing farmers today must be viewed in the context of rapid changes in the agricultural sector. The changes in farm numbers and sizes in the United States since 1940 have been called "a revolution in agriculture" (Schertz et al. 1979). On average, 2,000 farms a week have been lost between 1950 and 1982, as the total number of farms in the country has declined from 5.6 million to 2.4 million (Coughenour and Swanson 1983:24; USDA 1983b). Farmland has been consolidated into ever larger units (Figure 1-1). With larger and more powerful tractors and harvesters, farmers now can handle more acreage, more quickly and with fewer workers. Thus the number of farm laborers has also declined.

The increasing overall average farm size in the United States, as seen in Figure 1-1, encompasses two different trends. On the one

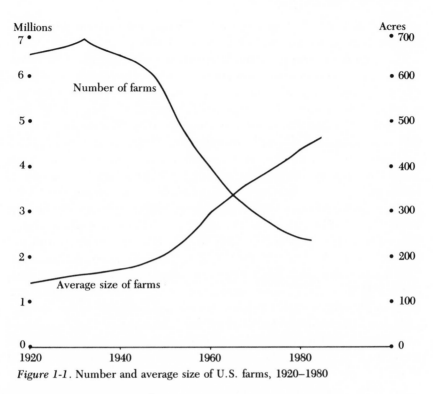

Millions                Acres

*Figure 1-1*. Number and average size of U.S. farms, 1920–1980

Sources: USDA 1981, 1983b.

hand, full-time commercial farms have become much larger, growing from an average of 276 acres in 1950 to 619 acres in 1982 (U.S. Bureau of the Census 1956:968; 1983:44). On the other hand, the vast majority of the total number of farms in the country continue to be small farms (Schertz et al. 1979:17). These farms are usually "part-time" in that the family depends mainly on jobs off the farm for their income. Such farms can be important in supporting local equipment dealers and farm supply companies, though their average acreage is small.

Between the large commercial farms and the small part-time farms is the so-called "disappearing middle" of moderate-sized family farms (Buttel 1983; Carter and Johnston 1978; Tweeten and Huffman 1980). This group is expected by some to continue to decline. Those who can increase their farm size may be able to remain in business as full-time farmers and achieve a rising standard of living competitive with that of nonfarm occupations (Peterson 1980; Tweeten 1981a). Other families will choose to make off-farm jobs their primary source of income and will cut back farm size (Fuller 1976; Kada 1980).

This predicted decline of the family farm and concentration of agriculture in fewer and fewer hands gives rise to a number of concerns. Many observers, farmers and nonfarmers alike, worry that if farming is dominated by a few very large producers, consumers may become vulnerable to rapid price increases (Vogeler 1981; Wessel 1983). Also, the large-scale, mechanized production of some crops may lead to a decline in quality and taste. And industrial-type production may drive local, small-scale competitors out of business (Buttel et al. 1983; Heffernan 1978; Hightower 1978). As ownership, management, and labor on United States farms become separated and are handled not by one family but by separate groups, the living and working conditions of those groups will inevitably become more unequal (Buttel and Newby 1980; MacLennan and Walker 1980). Owners of industrial-type farms may enjoy a much higher standard of living than the typical owner-operated farm family. In contrast, workers on industrial farms in the areas where such farms are common generally receive low pay and have little control over their working conditions. Thus, the trend toward industrial-type farms and increasing numbers of hired laborers has been linked to a decline in quality of life for the majority of those in agriculture (Raup 1978; Rodefeld 1979).

Inflation throughout the 1960s and 1970s has had an important role in the trend toward fewer and larger farms (Tweeten 1981b). Inflation fueled the demand for farmland as a stable investment, and land values increased sharply (Schertz et al. 1979). The value of farm real estate in Georgia, for instance, was more than 800% higher in 1982 than in 1961 (Georgia Crop Reporting Service 1982). This burden of higher costs for land (either purchased or rented) is an important part of rising real estate debt on farms in this country (USDA 1979). The rising cost of agricultural production inputs has fueled a heavy debt load, as more and more farmers borrow money to finance annual production as well (Figure 1-2).

Credit is costly; interest rates in rural Georgia in the early 1980s fluctuated between 13 and 16 percent. This interest payment means that farmers who use bank or government agency loans to pay for their annual expenses must give 13 to 16 percent of their profits to the lender. Thus although profits over 16 percent may seem to be high at first glance, only a profit level over the interest rate will leave a farmer with anything to show for the year's work. These interest rates also

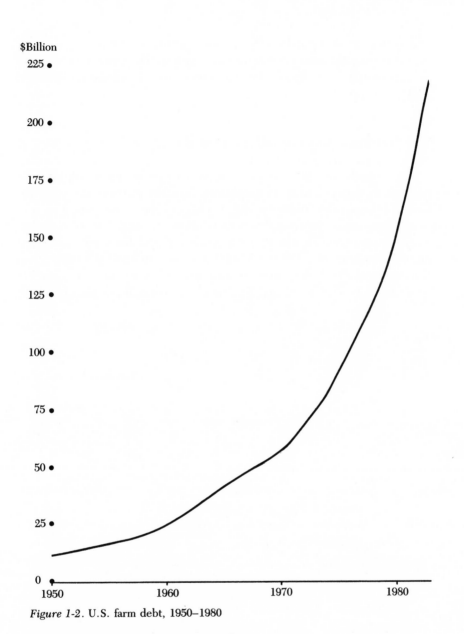

*Figure 1-2*. U.S. farm debt, 1950–1980

Sources: Schertz et al. 1979, USDA 1983b.

add to the farmer's risk because a poor year means the payments must be deferred, and interest continues to mount. The sums involved can be substantial; one Georgia farmer interviewed in 1983 said he owed $130 a day in interest.

## The Cost-Price Squeeze and the Drought

For roughly the last decade, the cost-price squeeze has brought farmers to depression-level conditions in many parts of the country. Costs of the inputs farmers need—fertilizer, chemicals, gasoline, and machinery—have increased rapidly (Figures 1-3 and 1-4). In Georgia, for example, farm production expenses jumped from an average of $4,900 per farm in 1959 to $53,000 per farm in 1983 (Georgia Crop Reporting Service, personal communication). One farmer said that when he started farming in 1972, fertilizer cost $80 per ton. By 1982,

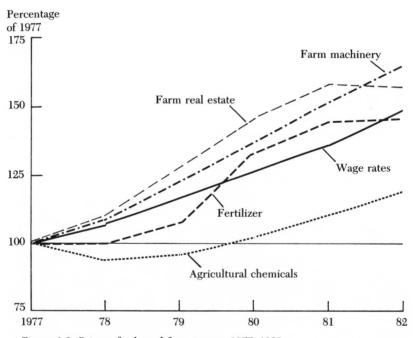

*Figure 1-3.* Prices of selected farm inputs, 1977–1982

Source: USDA 1981:11.

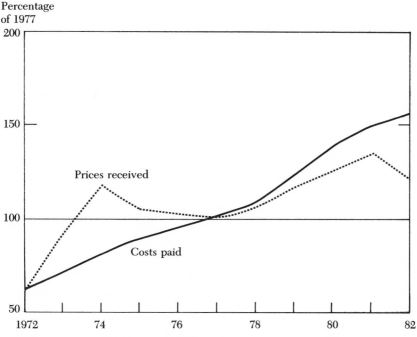

Percentage
of 1977

*Figure 1-4.* Prices received and costs paid by farmers, 1972–1982

Source: USDA 1983a:11.

it was up to $230, but corn prices declined in the same period. Diesel fuel jumped from $0.22 to $1.05 per gallon. He was able to buy his tractor and all the attachments for $15,000 in 1972, but today it would cost him $40,000 just for the tractor. As Figure 1-4 shows, the prices farmers receive for their products have not kept pace over the last ten years. Together with soaring interest rates, rents, and land prices, the squeeze on farmers' profits has left many in critical financial shape.

Weather conditions in the Southeast compounded the financial problems faced by farmers all over the country. Most of the agricultural areas of Georgia were hit by successive years of drought in the late 1970s. Many farmers who sustained weather losses borrowed extra money to expand their operations the following year—"doubling up to catch up." Then 1980 saw the worst drought of the series, and dry weather continued in some parts of the state in 1981. By 1984, five or six out of the seven previous years (depending on location) had

[35]

been dry, a pattern previously unknown to farmers in the area. The losses to the farmers were huge, and loan default rates—more than 40 percent were the highest since the Great Depression.

The rest of this chapter will explore how these double shocks to Georgia farmers—the cost-price squeeze and the drought—have changed the trends in farm size and organization. Of particular interest is how the strategies used by farmers to get through the crisis are accelerating, slowing, or reversing the long-term trends in the changing structure of United States agriculture.

Specifically, this chapter will address three issues:

1. Are large commercial farms increasing their use of hired labor and moving toward a more industrialized pattern of separate ownership, management, and labor?

2. Are large-scale farmers cannibalizing less successful, smaller family farmers during this crisis period, speeding the concentration of landownership in fewer hands?

3. Are moderate-sized family farms less able to survive during these difficult economic times, accelerating the process of "the disappearing middle"?

## Research Setting

The data to answer these questions were gathered using a combination of anthropological, sociological, and economic techniques. Anthropologists often take a single community as their unit of study, but in rural Georgia, the county is the primary unit, with its own identity, local government, educational system, and agricultural patterns. Because government programs such as price supports and disaster loans are also administered at the county level, it was decided to do an in-depth study of one county and to interview half the farmers in that county.[1]

The choice of county is especially important if the results are to

1. The research reported here was done in three stages. The researcher and three student assistants surveyed half the farmers in the county in the summer of 1982. The sample was drawn randomly from the master list of farm operators provided by the Agricultural Stabilization and Conservation Service. In open-ended discussions with farmers during these interviews, the research team gathered qualitative information on farmers' decision making, opinions, and recent histories. The team also attended local churches, crop and livestock sales, and farmers' meetings.

contribute to understanding nationwide trends in agriculture. Dodge County is located in the coastal plain region—a large belt of low, rolling hills running from North Carolina across South Carolina and the southern half of Georgia, Alabama, and Mississippi. The coastal plain is the primary agricultural area of the southern states, an area of row crop and livestock production. In the choice of research site, heavily industrialized counties as well as counties emphasizing specialty crops such as pecans, peaches, or vegetables, were eliminated. Dodge County is typical of the coastal plain and contains farms of all sizes. While cotton, peanuts, and tobacco are grown throughout Georgia's coastal plain, Dodge County farmers do not rely heavily on any one of those crops. Corn, soybeans, winter wheat, cotton, peanuts, and tobacco are the main crops in the county, and hogs and cattle are also produced.

Conditions in Dodge County are similar to those of other areas in the United States that specialize in row crop and livestock production. The commodities produced are mostly the same as in the grain belt of the Midwest and many areas of the South and Northeast as well. The cost of inputs, machinery, and capital are affected by nationally based corporations and agencies, and crops are sold in national markets as well. Though the Southeast has less favorable soils and climate than the Midwest and hence yields are lower, land values and rents are also lower, and farmers benefit from these lower costs. New varieties of winter wheat allow a harvest of wheat and soybeans on the same plot each year, and federal programs for tobacco, cotton, and peanuts all tend to balance the less favorable agricultural potential of the Southeast.

The 1982 *Census of Agriculture* shows that Dodge County is a good place to start to understand the national picture. The average U.S. farm size is 440 acres, and the Dodge County average is 414 acres.

---

The second phase in the fall of 1982 involved follow-up studies by the author and one assistant on part-time farming, land sales, and timber ownership. Individuals who had left farming were also interviewed. The third phase, the following summer, focused on full-time farmers, their farm histories and backgrounds. Additional information on debts, assets, and gross sales were obtained from the entire sample. An active farm was defined as ten acres or more from which crops or livestock were sold in the previous year (see Kada 1980). One hundred thirty-nine out of 148 farmers in the sample were interviewed (94 percent). These cases represent 152 households since some farms are multi-household partnerships. No absentee-owned corporations appeared in the sample.

[37]

Though Dodge County has a lower proportion of very small farms than the national average, its proportion of farms over 1,000 acres (6 percent) is similar to the 8 percent in the whole country. Annual farm sales in the study sample are only slightly higher than the national average: $61,000 versus $59,000. The proportion of farmers with full-time jobs is 34 percent in Dodge County, and nationally 36 percent of farm operators work 200 days or more off the farm. In age, Dodge County farmers are a bit younger than the national average: 47.3 years versus 50.5 years. As would be expected in the South, there are more black farmers in Dodge County (11.3 percent) than is typical of the country as a whole (1.5 percent), but the figures for women operators are quite similar (3.2 percent versus 5.4 percent nationally). Though no one county can possible mirror the conditions of the country as a whole, these figures suggest that the findings from Dodge County may apply to a significant sector of row crop and livestock farms in the United States.

## The Diversity of Farms

In Dodge County, there are three main kinds of farmers—retired/disabled farmers, part-time farmers, and full-time farmers—each with different goals and activities and each responding differently to the current crisis.

The *retired/disabled* category makes up 21 percent of the farmers in the county. In this group are two kinds of small-scale farmers. Most of these are people who call themselves "retired" from full-scale farming, though many still do considerable farm work. Often, they receive a pension or social security from a former job. Any farmers over sixty-five and receiving social security are automatically placed in this category, whether or not they define themselves as retired. The disabled farmers are operators under sixty-five who are unable to work full-time because of a health problem (such as a heart condition). They operate a small farm in addition to receiving disability payments or some other financial assistance.

*Part-time farmers* are operators (male or female) under sixty-five who have full-time, off-farm jobs or part-time jobs that provide more than $75 per week and that seriously reduce the amount of time available for farming. Thirty-seven percent of the Dodge County farmers are part-time.

[38]

*Table 1-1.* Dodge County sample farms, acres, and sales, by type of farmer (percentage)

| Type of farmer | Farms | Acres operated | Total sales |
|---|---|---|---|
| Retired/disabled (N = 26) | 21 | 8 | 2 |
| Part-time (N = 46) | 37 | 22 | 18 |
| Full-time (N = 52) | 42 | 70 | 80 |

*Full-time farmers* are primary farm operators who work full-time on the farm. They are the largest group in the county, 42 percent. In half of the full-time farms, the wife has an off-farm job, and in 20 percent the husband has a part-time job as well (such as school bus driver or crop duster). In these cases, the family does not depend solely on the farm for income.

Because these three types of farms vary greatly in size and sales, they contribute quite differently to the overall agricultural economy (Table 1-1). Though full-time farmers are often seen as the "real" farmers in the county, they operate fewer than half of the total farms. In contrast, they control the vast majority of the land in farming (70 percent) and sell most of the agricultural products (80 percent). Retired/disabled farmers operate 21 percent of the farms and therefore make up a significant group, but they control only 8 percent of the land and sell 2 percent of the products. Although part-time farmers also tend to have small farms, their role in the local economy is more significant. Part-time farmers control over one-fifth of the land (22 percent) and sell 18 percent of the crops, livestock, and timber produced in the county.

Some full-time farmers and other farm commentators tend to dismiss part-time and retired/disabled farms as "just pasture and a few cows." The Dodge County research suggests otherwise, however. Of the four main crops (corn, soybeans, wheat, and peanuts) common in the county, full-time farmers typically grow three or four, while part-time farmers typically grow two. Retired/disabled farmers commonly grow one or two of the four crops; this group concentrates slightly more on livestock (cattle and hogs) than on crops. Retired/disabled farmers resemble full-time farmers in the frequency with which they

[39]

raise livestock. Although part-time and retired/disabled farmers work on a smaller scale, they nevertheless participate actively and produce a variety of crops and livestock.

The differences between these types of farms can be seen in the following three examples. To protect the identity and privacy of individual farmers interviewed, these examples are composites of a number of cases, and the names used are pseudonyms. The quotations are the actual words of Dodge County farmers, and the facts are drawn from the actual results of the study. Black and white farmers are included in these figures and quotes, but the composite cases reflect the majority of farmers and are assumed to be white.

### Jim and Judy Bailey—Retired Farmers

The Baileys have always been farmers, and though they are both nearly seventy, they remember well the "Hoover days," when farming was done "with mules and boys." Their families were both sharecroppers during the Great Depression, and after their marriage, Jim and Judy continued to rent farms. After World War II, they were able to buy a farm of 103 acres. Judy worked at the local shirt factory for many years, and slowly they paid off the farm and built a new house to replace the original farmhouse that came with the land.

At their peak of activity, the Baileys rented an additional 200 acres, grew a variety of row crops, and raised hogs. When Jim reached sixty-five, he was suffering from arthritis and decided to retire and cut back his operation. They now keep a few hogs and cows and sell livestock to pay bills. They grow about fifty acres of corn in the summer and some wheat in the winter, both for feed. They plant a good-sized garden, and Judy spends a month each summer freezing vegetables for the family's use for the rest of the year. In the fall, they join with neighbors to have a calf and some hogs butchered at the local slaughterhouse, and they keep the meat in their freezer. Their total sales of crops and livestock is less than $5,000 a year.

When the first dry years hit Georgia in the late 1970s, the Baileys were already cutting back their operation and did not suffer too much from the loss of profits. But when the disastrous droughts came and they harvested almost no crops, they had to dip into savings to live on and to pay for feed for their hogs and cattle. By the time the Baileys were interviewed, the low prices for farm products and the rising prices for fertilizer, fuel, and replacement parts had wiped out much of their savings. Fortunately, their farm is all paid off, and they do not borrow money for operating expenses each year, so they are not in danger of losing their farm. The cost-price squeeze, however, has removed their comfortable retirement cushion and left them fearful that any heavy medical expenses will not be covered by their remaining savings.

The Baileys are typical of the retired/disabled group in that the farm is an important part of their economic survival. They would have difficulty maintaining their current standard of living on social security without the food and income from the farm. Both of them find the work on the farm helps keep them fit, and Jim thinks much of his current good health comes from being active every day. Judy says that during these discouraging years of losses they have often thought of selling their farm, but Jim jokes, "I'd have to dig holes then and fill 'em up, just to keep busy."

The Baileys get social security, but neither has an off-farm job at present. In about a third of the retired/disabled group, the husband or the wife has a job of some kind to bring in extra income. In other cases, the couple receives a pension, food stamps, disability payments, or income from investments. Only 8 percent have no extra income from any of these sources.

Jim and Judy have one son who works in town and lives nearby. He and his children occasionally help out on the farm, and when Jim and Judy can no longer keep up with the daily farm tasks, they expect their son may be interested in renting it as a part-time farm. The Baileys also have a daughter, but she has married and moved out of the county. Neither she nor her husband has any interest in farming or living on the family farm. Eventually, the farm will be inherited equally by the Bailey's two children, and probably their son will buy his sister's portion to keep the farm in one piece. Meanwhile, Jim and Judy hope to keep farming as long as possible. They love farming and the good food and health it brings, though the losses and droughts in recent years have brought new risks they did not anticipate.

## *Howard and Helen Morton—Part-time Farmers*

Howard and Helen farm "because we love it." "I grew up on a farm," said Howard. "I love the magic of growing things and the personal

[41]

satisfaction of creating something." After finishing high school, Howard chose to work on a military base several counties away because the salaries were high and the benefits good. "You can't make any money in farming, so I never intended to try to farm full-time." Shortly after Howard settled into a career in quality control on the base, Howard and Helen married, and Helen continued her work as a bookkeeper for a local company. Today, their two jobs give them a combined income of just over $30,000. Helen has kept her job through most of the years of raising their three children. When interviewed, the Mortons were in their early forties and had been in farming about fifteen years.

Shortly before turning thirty, Howard was able to realize his dream of buying a farm. Land from Helen's family came up for sale, "but I would have gotten into farming, even without family land available; I always wanted to farm," he said. Helen had her doubts about adding the expenses and hard work of a farm to their already busy lives, but "I just knew Howard wouldn't be happy unless he was farming." Like most part-time farmers, the Mortons see the farm as an important source of extra income that allows them to live the kind of middle-class lifestyle they want. The farm is also a long-term investment for their children. Howard plans to expand the farm operation and become a full-time farmer when he retires; in his civil service job, he can retire with a comfortable pension substantially before age sixty-five.

Both the Mortons love "country living . . . the peace and contentment. It's so quiet and still at night around the place." Howard appreciates the exercise that lets him wind down from the frustrations and tensions at his daytime job. "It's a different kind of tired when I come in from riding a tractor," he said. They also value the experience for their children—"It's good for them to grow up on a farm, having responsibilities." The Mortons, like the Baileys, appreciate the high-quality food they can have by raising it on their own place.

Howard does most of the farm work, using the headlights of his tractor by night and working long hours on Saturday. Like most farmers in Dodge County, the Mortons avoid work on Sunday and often go to church both in the morning and in the evening. Howard grows about fifty acres of corn, soybeans, and winter wheat, and though he would like to grow peanuts (whose price is kept high by a government program), his farm does not have an "allotment," a right to grow peanuts that goes back to the depression-era federal crop programs. The Mortons raise hogs and cattle, though small numbers of both; they have cut back on livestock since the drought years hurt feed supplies. Their farm is 125 acres, including 30 acres of timber and 45 acres of pastures. Between crops and livestock, the Mortons gross about $15,000 in sales.

One of the financial advantages of farming is the reduction of taxes. In order to sell $15,000 worth of products, the family invests money in equipment, vehicles, land, and production expenses. Though the costs of farming are over ten times the tax savings, the Mortons count the tax benefits as one of the pluses of being in part-time farming.

The economic slump in farm prices and the successive drought years put considerable strain on the Mortons' preference to farm part-time. They have lost money in a number of recent years and have had to cut back in their daily living expenses. There have been bad years before, says Howard, who remembers the drought of 1953. "But back then, you lost only hundreds of dollars. Now it's thousands, and it takes so much longer to catch up after a bad year." Today, the Mortons struggle to take enough out of their paychecks to meet the mortgage and farm expenses. They are not behind on any of their loans, but meeting their obligations has been "real tough" at times. Helen is bitter about the losses—"I can't take enough aspirin to get over the headaches farming has caused us." When asked how he would change his farm if he had a son to join him, Howard was emphatic: "I would strongly discourage him from going into farming."

The Mortons are typical of about half of the part-time farmers in Dodge County in having two salaries to help see them through the farm losses of recent years. Their income from jobs is therefore a bit more than the average for the whole group, which is $25,000. They are also typical in that they sell both crops and livestock from their farm. Roughly one fourth of the part-time farmers sell just livestock (though they grow crops for feed), and one-fourth sell just crops. Most part-time farmers, like the Mortons, never intended to be full-time farmers, but a few farmers in this group are newly part-time, having decided to cut back from full-time farming and take jobs off the farm to get through the crisis period.

## Cab and Carol Ann Streeter—Full-time Farmers

The Streeters are in their early fifties and operate a farm of 320 acres, growing the four major crops of the area—corn, soybeans, wheat, and peanuts. They raise hogs and cattle and sell between

[43]

$40,000 and $100,000 worth of products a year, depending on prices. They earn more from crops than from livestock, but use the income from sales of hogs every few weeks to pay bills and meet household expenses. The Streeters own most of their land, but rent 120 acres, in two pieces, from neighbors. Several years ago, they rented a third farm of 200 acres to try to make some extra money to "catch up" on the debts they owe. Instead, they lost more money than ever and cut back to the 300 acres or so they feel they can operate well. They also cut back on corn production because it costs so much to grow and is more susceptible to drought. Soybeans rotated with winter wheat are a cheaper and less risky crop mix. In 1982, though, many farmers made these same crop shifts, and large harvests drove prices down. The Streeters have a good-sized peanut allotment on the land they own, and one of the farms they rent also carries the right to grow peanuts. The costs of peanut production are very high, but the "peanut program helps a lot," says Cab. The worst part of the 1980 drought year was that they harvested almost no peanuts at all and lost a huge investment in fertilizer, seed, and chemicals.

Cab has been demoralized by the current crisis. "It *hurts*," he says. "The farmer is just overloaded now." "Being a farmer today is just like being a mule in the old days—you work and work all day with that carrot dangling right out front of you, but you never get it." Equipment breakdowns forced Cab to replace his tractor in the middle of the drought years, when prices were very high and he could least afford it. When the dry years continued and again he watched the corn "burn up in the fields, it got so discouraging, I just didn't want to go on farming. I love farming; it's all I know, but when year after year you can't get fair prices for what you produce and the prices you pay just keep going up, it's just not right. But I can't just get out. There's not a job I could get that would let me make the payments I owe."

Like many full-time farmers, the Streeters have gotten behind on their loan payments. Their debts have stayed the same or built up every year since the drought started. Their banker says they are better off than a lot of farmers, but they find his words to be little consolation. The debts cause them considerable worry, and Carol Ann says she lies awake at night. "It's the mental anguish of owing so much. But, you know, we don't go on like this all the time—you have to put it out of your mind at times, so you can go on."

The Streeters are typical of older, full-time farmers in that neither of them has a job to provide extra income off the farm. Carol Ann provides important help on the farm tasks, caring for hogs and cattle, doing part of the bookkeeping, shopping for spare parts in town, and helping to move machinery and haul loads. Although almost half of the women in full-time farming families do have jobs outside the home, the Streeters appreciate the efficiency of having two workers.

The Streeters have two children, a son, Paul, who has completed junior college and is now an accountant, and a daughter, Sandy, who completed a B.A. and is a social worker at a nearby government agency. Paul and his wife have no interest in farming for a living and are glad their jobs have let them escape that life. His wife grew up in town, and they both feel the high costs and risks of farming outweigh the benefits. One of Paul's high school friends, a neighbor near the Streeter farm, has talked with both Paul and Cab about buying the Streeter farm someday. Cab is not interested in selling, but Paul has said he might be willing to rent his share of the farm, if the land is left to him and his sister. Because it is possible that Cab and Carol Ann will need to sell the farm or even will lose it in the current crisis, no firm plans can be made for the future.

The Streeters' daughter is married to a farmer who is in partnership with his father. About one-third of full-time farmers in the county are in partnerships, usually involving two households, but sometimes connecting as many as three or four households. Sandy's father-in-law's farm has become one of the largest in the county. He and his son operate over 1,000 acres and benefit from the larger base to support new equipment and other investments. They recently bought a new combine and also purchased irrigation systems for half their cropland. Just before the bad years began, they bought a 300-acre farm to add to the 450 acres they already owned. It was a risky decision to grow so fast, especially after just adding a new hog facility, but the land came up for sale adjacent to their property—a once-in-a-lifetime opportunity. Also, with inflation pushing land values up, they felt it was a sound investment to buy in before prices soared further. Unfortunately, the drought years have stalled land prices, and the land they bought would probably sell for less today than what they are paying for it.

Sandy's husband and father-in-law also rent four small farms, from retired or widowed neighbors. They plant the same crop mix as the Streeters, but have a larger cattle herd and considerably more hogs.

They hire two full-time hands to help with the livestock maintenance and fieldwork. Sandy's father-in-law handles most of the "town work" at banks, government offices, and suppliers. He also does most of the marketing for the partnership, while Sandy's husband does much of the "mechanicking" of the farm equipment. Sandy's mother-in-law coordinates the workers and machines at "central," where they base their truck radios. Sandy's job has been an important contribution in keeping household expenses paid so that the farm income can be used to pay the high debts they are facing. Like many large-scale farmers who use hired hands, this partnership faces a crippling debt load, and though they sell over $150,000 worth of crops and livestock each year, profits have been nonexistent in some years, and interest has compounded their losses.

Sandy's father-in-law is sorry he expanded when he did and is rueful that bankers and farm experts alike encouraged him to do so. Sandy and her husband used to talk of taking over her father's farm when Cab retires, but now they are unsure they can handle the additional risk of so large an operation. "Maybe if things get better . . . we just take it one year at a time now."

Sandy's husband got his start as many full-time farmers do—in a partnership with his father. Sometimes, rather than entering into a partnership, a father will help a son get started in farming by lending equipment, renting land, or even lending land for free. Some father-son partnerships last until the death or retirement of the father; others are transitional, lasting only a few years. When a young farmer has built up sufficient experience to farm on his own, he will often look to parents and relatives for land to purchase, although, of course, family land is not always available. It is not unusual for several sons to begin farming with their father and then to continue their partnership when their father dies. Some brothers' partnerships last indefinitely; some break up quickly if the brothers don't "see eye to eye." Farmers reaching retirement age with no son or daughter interested in farming may rent out the farm and live off the rental income. Others prefer to sell the farm and invest the proceeds, living off the earnings. In either case, the land becomes available to neighboring farmers, allowing them to expand or begin farming. Most Dodge County farmers plan to leave their land equally to all their children, though some choose to sell more land to one heir in farming, rather than force that heir to buy it from his or her nonfarming siblings.

## Responses to the Cost-Price Squeeze and the Drought

How have these farmers responded to the difficult economic conditions over the last five years? Figure 1-5 shows four strategies adopted by the farmers in the five years prior to this 1982 study: changes in farm size (increasing or decreasing acres operated), labor (increasing or decreasing use of hired labor), capital (taking or giving up off-farm jobs), and technology (by adding or expanding irrigation systems).[2] As the figure shows, more retired farmers have cut back farm size than other farmers, though some of them probably would have cut back anyway. Of the part-time farmers, about one-third have expanded their farms, one-third contracted, and one-third stayed the same. More full-time farmers expanded than cut back the size of their farms during this crisis period. Rather than purchase new land, however, almost all of the farmers who expanded did so by *renting* additional farmland. Land was rented mostly from people who no longer wish to operate their own land (usually retired farmers or nonfarmers who inherited farmland). Some rentals come from full-time or part-time farmers who have cut back.

The prediction that owners of larger farms would be able to take advantage of owners of smaller farms in this difficult period has not proven true in Dodge County. Land sales are at a virtual standstill in the county (except for purchases by timber companies), and even the wealthier full-time farmers say they are not in a financial position to expand their farms. The evidence suggests that the economic crisis has slowed the trend to larger farms, and there is no data to show that owners of large farms have an advantage over owners of smaller farms in obtaining land to rent.

Figure 1-5 shows that all three types of farmers cut back more often than they increased hired labor over the last five years, while half or more maintained the same level of hired help. Even among the full-time farmers, only 15 percent increased hired labor, while 35 percent cut back. These cutbacks in hired labor in part reflect the use of larger, more efficient equipment and some reduction in labor-intensive crops, such as tobacco. But given that 42 percent of full-time farmers increased their farm size during this period, the decreased

2. Although there have been other changes in technology over the last five years in Dodge County, the increase in irrigation has been more widespread and expensive than the others, and it requires more adjustment of farming practices.

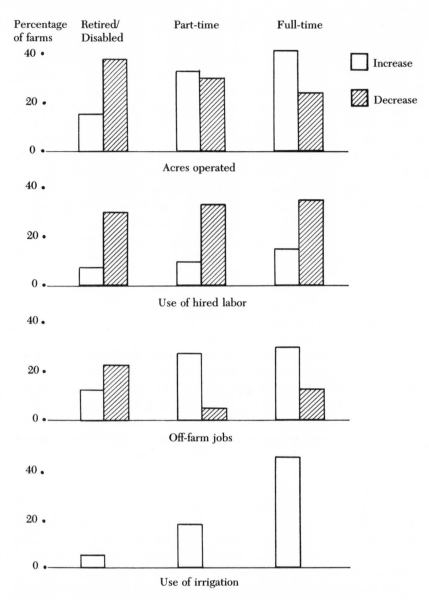

*Figure 1-5*. Changes in farm operation by type of farm, 1978–1982

use of hired labor also suggests that in response to economic conditions, farm families have had to work themselves harder to manage a larger farm.

The declining use of hired labor in Dodge County suggests that the economic crisis is also slowing the trend toward a more industrial structure of farming. Some farms are returning to a pattern of family operation in which the family provides most of the labor. The costs of hired help are a heavy burden in low-profit or no-profit years and are a drain on resources that makes it hard to cut costs to weather these difficult times. There is no evidence that farm ownership is becoming more separate from farm management either; the number of absentee-owned corporations in Dodge County has not increased.

Figure 1-5 shows two other kinds of changes in farming as well. To increase the flow of capital to get the farm through this bad time, some farmers in all three groups have increased the amount of off-farm work that brings in income to support the family. Understandably, more farmers in the retired/disabled group reduced than increased off-farm work over this time, but nearly 30 percent of farm families in the other two groups increased off-farm work. In many full-time cases, the wife's job "provides the living," while the family uses the farm income to try to keep up with farm expenses (and debts). The few families that cut back off-farm work during this period cited personal reasons such as health or child care as the cause.

The purchase of irrigation equipment has become important during these drought years. Irrigation is one of the most expensive technological investments a farmer can make. Simpler "cable-tow" systems pump water from a well or pond through movable pipes to a rotating "gun." A stationary tractor reels in a cable that pulls the gun across the field. The more sophisticated "center-pivot" irrigation systems require permanent installation of underground electrical cables to power a pump that feeds water to a large pipe on wheels that travels in a slow circle over the field. Almost half of the full-time farmers use some kind of irrigation system. The more expensive center-pivot systems can cost as much as $100,000. These investments have saved some farmers' crops from drought, but other farmers claim the high cost of operating and paying for the system has worsened their financial condition. The retired/disabled and part-time farmers are understandably reluctant to add such expensive facilities to their smaller farms, but, as Figure 1-5 shows, a few in each group have done so. Irrigation increases the risk of farming in precarious economic times though it decreases the risk of low yields. With higher electricity costs and unknown ecological consequences, it is unclear whether the sharp increase in the use of irrigation in Georgia over the last ten years will continue.

## Debts, Bankruptcy, and Farm Survival

What is the outlook for survival for the moderate-sized, full-time family farm? The biggest threat to this kind of farm is heavy debt. During interviews with farmers in Dodge County, data were collected on number and types of debts, whether they were overdue, debt-to-asset ratios, and the farmers' own assessments of their situations. The three kinds of farms in the county show very different patterns in their financial conditions. Table 1-2 shows the proportion of farms that have no farm debts, those with severe or critical debt loads (usually 75 percent or more of assets), and those in between. Only 12 percent of the retired/disabled farmers face possible financial crisis. Like the Baileys, most (65 percent) have no farm debts at all, though many have sustained losses from the drought years. Only 22 percent of part-time farmers have no debts; about the same number face a serious or critical financial situation. Many more of the full-time farmers are in danger of losing their farms; 38 percent face serious or critical financial difficulties while only 4 percent have no farm debts.

The precarious debt situation faced by farmers all over the country has resulted in increasing rates of foreclosure and bankruptcy. Some farmers, discouraged and unable to make a profit, have voluntarily left farming. "I don't want to gamble that big," said one. In Dodge

*Table 1-2.* Financial condition of Dodge County sample by type of farmer, 1982

| Type of farmer | No farm debts | Some farm debts | "Serious" or "critical" farm debts |
|---|---|---|---|
| Retired/disabled | 17 | 6 | 3 |
| (N = 26) | (65%) | (23%) | (12%) |
| Part-time | 10 | 26 | 10 |
| (N = 46) | (22%) | (57%) | (22%) |
| Full-time | 2 | 30 | 20 |
| (N = 52) | (4%) | (58%) | (38%) |

*Table 1-3.* Financial condition of full-time farmers in Dodge County sample by structural groups, 1982

| Structural group | No farm debts | Some farm debts | "Serious" or "critical" farm debts |
|---|---|---|---|
| Newcomers | 0 | 7 | 9 |
| (N = 16) | | (44%) | (56%) |
| Large-scale farmers | 0 | 6 | 5 |
| (N = 11) | | (55%) | (45%) |
| Established family | 2 | 17 | 6 |
| farmers (N = 25) | (8%) | (68%) | (24%) |

County, interviews were carried out with most of the farmers who left farming either voluntarily or involuntarily since the late 1970s. Seven of the twenty-five families about whom information was gathered had been forced out of farming by illness or death. Of the remaining eighteen, most left farming voluntarily because of financial difficulties. Some left with considerable outstanding debts to lenders, while others were able to pay off their debts, often by selling land or equipment. The people who left farming for financial reasons fall into two groups. The majority were newcomers to farming who had been in operation for five years or less. Starting up farming during the drought years and having to buy new equipment or land during a time of high interest rates had proven too difficult. The other group of farmers were older—all had been farming ten years or more—and had relatively large farms and used full-time hired hands. All of the bankruptcies and foreclosures in the county fall into one of these two groups, but neither group includes the established, moderate-sized family farm.

Following the pattern presented by these cases, all of the full-time farmers in the sample were divided into three groups: the *large-scale farmers* (defined as all full-time farmers who hire 50 percent or more of the labor used on the farm), *newcomers to farming* (defined as all full-time farmers who use less than 50 percent hired labor and who have been in farming for ten years or less), and the *established family farmers* (who use less than 50 percent hired labor and who have farmed full-time for more than ten years).

Table 1-3 shows that the established family farmers are much better off than the other two groups in facing the current crisis. Only 24

[51]

percent of them face serious or critical debt loads compared with 56 percent of the newcomer farmers and 45 percent of the large-scale farmers. Their average farm size is 305 acres per household, and fewer than half of them have bought irrigation systems. They have generally been quite conservative over the last decade, as their comments indicate: "I've always been afraid of debt and never really wanted to buy much on credit." "I never liked to pay interest; that's the way I made it." "You have to struggle and do without; we always saved instead of spent." "The big farmer is not the successful one—the average farmer, with 300–400 acres, is the man who will survive, who knows how to cut corners."

"Cutting corners" is hard for the large-scale farmers, who must maintain considerable equipment and meet their payroll regardless of profits. They operate an average of 1,346 acres per farm—over four times the size of the established family farms. Three-fourths of them have irrigation systems, and many have made other expensive investments in equipment and facilities. Said one large-scale farmer, "The danger of getting too big in the good times is that you can't get through the bad times." Many large-scale farmers expressed a desire to cut back in order to supervise their operation more closely and improve the efficiency of the resources they use. Their heavy debt loads make cutting back impossible, however. "Lots of farmers around here are bigger than they should be," said one such large-scale farmer. "If they'd cut back, they'd farm better, with higher productivity, and they could work on a timely basis." One farmer, who operates a very large farm, admitted that the "old-time farmers" who operate only the land they own without using hired hands are "using a safer strategy." "But they don't need a high income," he said. "You can't put kids through school on 300 acres—you need 600 acres, I figure."

The newcomer farmers have the smallest average farm size—256 acres, almost the size of the established family farmers. About one-third of them have bought irrigation systems. They are trying to build up their farms by buying land and buildings and by developing expertise. But more than half are in danger of losing their farms. "The biggest mistake I made was to start farming in debt. . . . I had no cushion at all," said one. But another young farmer said, "My orientation is different from your typical older farmer who used the good years to pay debts and sit on their money instead of expand. I grew up poor and wanted to be middle-class—you can do that in farming now, but you couldn't back in the fifties and sixties." Said one part-time farmer: "A farmer can make a living these days, but it's impossible to start new." His pessimism is not entirely correct. While many of the newcomer farmers are struggling, almost half are getting through this crisis period as well as many of the older farmers. Some experts have worried that these difficult times would prevent a whole generation of young farmers from getting started. Young farmers certainly have a much harder time now than those who started fifteen or twenty years ago, but not all are facing disaster (Barlett 1986a). As Table 1-3 shows, substantial portions of each of the three groups of full-time farmers are making it through this crisis without the threat of losing their farms.

The reasons farmers find themselves in financial difficulties are complex. Decisions about land or equipment purchases, marketing, crop choices, and production techniques all affect profitability. Rainfall in the county is erratic, and not all farmers suffered equally in the drought years. Farmers with more eroded soils are also more vulnerable to poor weather conditions. The amount of land rented cheaply or inherited from family members, the quality of hired labor and family help, the luck of animal production and market price cycles, the farmers' own health—all of these things affect full-time farmers in the current crisis.

It seems, however, that the decision to expand the farm, to double or triple the average for full-time farmers, and to work that operation with hired labor, is a strategy that carries with it considerable risks. Large-scale farming may allow the use of sophisticated new technology, and in good years it may provide a higher income, but the heavy debt load creates a serious burden. It remains to be seen whether an improvement in the overall economic situation in agriculture will allow these farmers to pull out of this critical financial state and whether with their large-scale, high-technology farming, they will have an advantage over the established family farmers with their more conservative strategies.

## Conclusions

These data from Dodge County suggest that predictions of the demise of the family farm are premature. These one-family farms are the backbone of agricultural production in the county, comprising more land and producing more food than the large-scale farms. Their conservative strategies during the good years have left them in a

[53]

stronger financial situation to survive the drought and the cost-price squeeze. The farming unit that combines ownership, management, and labor in one family seems to have a competitive advantage in these difficult times.

Newcomer full-time farmers face an uphill battle to establish their farms. Some experts have said that the current crisis will eliminate the inefficient operators and that only the best managers will survive. Though skill and hard work are crucial to survival, the age of the farm operation is also important. As one farmer said, "Farmers used to build up equity over the life of their farms—paying off land, building new buildings, establishing timber stands and savings. All of that's been eroded by the bad times." In years when farm losses are common, it is impossible for new farmers to build up the necessary equity in their farms. The debt loads shown in Table 1-3 are the result. It is not necessarily greater efficiency but the time at which the farm was established or the property inherited that may give one farmer a better chance for survival.

Though the overall picture is bleak in this crisis period, the patterns are not uniformly gloomy. The majority of farmers in the county are retired/disabled farmers and part-time farmers. These groups have suffered losses, but most are surviving without danger of losing the family farm. They continue to receive the investment, tax, income, health, and psychological benefits they seek in farming. Not just "pasture and a few cows," these operations show substantial diversity in crop and livestock production, and most are supported by additional off-farm income. These small part-time and retirement farms are an important market for machinery, parts, and inputs and help sustain the local agricultural economy in the county. Equipment dealerships and supply stores all over Georgia are facing hard times too, and these small-scale farmers play an increasingly important role in their survival.

Full-time farming has seen major changes in recent decades. Until recently, land values have soared, and the prices farmers receive for their products have not kept pace with their costs. Off-farm income has become increasingly important in subsidizing the full-time farm, and especially in helping it through the cost-price squeeze. Sophisticated technology as well as some favorable tax laws and government programs have helped push the average farm size ever larger. The gap in size between the larger, full time farms and smaller, part-time and retirement farms is greater than ever before. But the full-time family farm is not doomed. Rather, family farms are typically larger than they used to be, and there are fewer of them, but they generally enjoy a higher standard of living.

The data from Dodge County, Georgia, suggest that the current drought and cost-price squeeze have brought to a halt several trends in the changing structure of agriculture in the United States. With land concentration at a standstill and the use of hired laborers on the decline, the future of the highly indebted, large-scale farm is unclear. In contrast, the smaller, more conservative, established family farms are alive and well and seem to have an advantage in surviving the current crisis.

Several national and international trends may threaten the viability of family farms in row crop and livestock production in the future. Large corporations have come to dominate the marketing of many commodities and, in some areas, have begun to penetrate production as well. Near-monopoly control of markets, plus the tax and capital advantages enjoyed by large conglomerates, could rapidly change the economic context in which family farms must compete. Vertical integration of food-processing companies and grain dealers with implement and chemical manufacturers and seed suppliers could also tighten the squeeze on farmers' costs and prices. Some government programs have also been found to support the trend to large-scale operations, and tax laws in particular can have profound impacts on the viability and survival of the family farm. These trends in the agribusiness and legal environment surrounding agricultural production in the United States need to be watched carefully, and it may be that the predictions challenged by this study will yet become true.

## Acknowledgments

This material is based upon work supported by the National Science Foundation under Grant No. BNS-8121459. Any opinions, findings, conclusions or recommendations expressed in this publication are those of the author and do not necessarily reflect the views of the National Science Foundation. An earlier version of this paper was published in the *American Journal of Agricultural Economics* 66(5): 836–843. I gratefully acknowledge the hard work of my three assistants, Gregg Cochran, Paul Dark, and Barbara Sigman, and the cooperation and helpful advice from the Dodge County Cooperative Extension Service, the Agricultural Stabilization and Conservation Service, county officials, and experts at the University of Georgia

[55]

College of Agriculture and the Rural Development Center in Tifton. Special thanks are also due to Debra Fey of the Emory University Department of Anthropology, Maurice H. Hammer of the Georgia Crop Reporting Service, Dean Duncan of the Emory University Computer Center, Elaine Ellerbee for preparation of the figures, the Statistics and Biometry Department of Emory University, Sonya Salamon, Christina Gladwin, Frederick Buttel, and Michael Chibnik. I also thank the farmers of Dodge County, whose generous cooperation made this study possible.

## References Cited

Barlett, Peggy F. 1986a. "The Disappearing Middle" and Other Myths of the Changing Structure of Agriculture. In *Agricultural Change: Consequences for Southern Farms and Rural Communities*, ed. Joseph Molnar. Boulder, Colo.: Westview.

————. 1986b. Part-Time Farming: Saving the Farm or Saving the Lifestyle? *Rural Sociology* 51(3): 290–314.

Buttel, Frederick H. 1983. Beyond the Family Farm. In *Technology and Social Change in Rural Areas*, ed. G. F. Summers, pp. 87–107. Boulder, Colo.: Westview.

Buttel, Frederick H., and Howard Newby, eds. 1980. *The Rural Sociology of the Advanced Societies*. Montclair, N.J.: Allanheld Osmun.

Buttel, Frederick H., Martin Kenney, and Jack Kloppenburg, Jr. 1983. *From Green Revolution to Biorevolution: Some Observations on the Changing Technological Bases of Economic Transformation in the Third World*. Cornell Univ. Rural Sociology Bulletin no. 132 (August).

Carter, Harold O., and Warren E. Johnston. 1978. Some Forces Affecting the Changing Structure, Organization, and Control of American Agriculture. *American Journal of Agricultural Economics* 60:738–748.

Cochrane, Willard W. 1979. *The Development of American Agriculture: A Historical Analysis*. Minneapolis: Univ. of Minnesota Press.

Coughenour, C. Milton, and Louis Swanson. 1983. Work Statuses and Occupations of Men and Women in Farm Families. *Rural Sociology* 48(1):24–43.

Fuller, Anthony M. 1976. The Problems of Part-Time Farming Conceptualized. In *Part-Time Farming: Proceedings of the First Rural Geography Symposium*, ed. Anthony Fuller and Julius Mage, pp. 38–56. Norwich, England: Geo Abstracts.

Georgia Crop Reporting Service. 1982. *Georgia Agricultural Facts: 1982 Edition*. Athens, Ga.

Heffernan, William D. 1978. Agricultural Structure and the Community. In *Can the Family Farm Survive?* pp. 27–37. Special report no. 219. Agricultural Experiment Station, Univ. of Missouri, Columbia.

Hightower, Jim. 1978. *Hard Tomatoes, Hard Times: The Original Hightower Report.* Cambridge, Mass.: Schenkman.

Kada, Ryohei. 1980. *Part-Time Farming: Off-Farm Employment and Farm Adjustments in the United States and Japan.* Tokyo: Center for Academic Publications.

MacLennan, Carol, and Richard Walker. 1980. Crisis and Change in U.S. Agriculture: An Overview. In *Agribusiness in the Americas,* ed. Roger Burbach and Patricia Flynn, pp. 21–40. New York: Monthly Review Press.

Peterson, Willis. 1980. *The Farm Size Issue: A New Perspective.* Dept. of Agriculture and Applied Economics staff paper no. P80-6. Univ. of Minnesota, St. Paul.

Raup, Philip M. 1978. Some Questions of Value and Scale in American Agriculture. *American Journal of Agricultural Economics* 60:303–8.

Rodefeld, Richard D. 1979. *The Family-Type Farm and Structural Differentiation: Trends, Causes and Consequences of Change, Research Needs.* Staff paper no. 24. Dept. of Agricultural Economics and Rural Sociology, Pennsylvania State Univ., University Park.

Schertz, Lyle P., et al. 1979. *Another Revolution in U.S. Farming?* Agricultural Economic Report no. 441. Washington, D.C.: U.S. Dept. of Agriculture.

Tweeten, Luther. 1981a. Agriculture at a Crucial Evolutionary Crossroads. *Research in Domestic and International Agribusiness Management* 2:1–15.

———. 1981b. *Farmland Pricing and Cash Flow in an Inflationary Economy.* Research report no. P-811. Agriculture Experiment Station, Okalahoma State Univ.

Tweeten, Luther, and Wallace Huffman. 1980. Structural Change. In *Structure of Agriculture and Information Needs Regarding Small Farms.* Paper no. 7. Washington, D.C.: National Rural Center, Small Farms Project.

U.S. Bureau of the Census. 1956. *1954 Census of Agriculture.* Vol. 2. Washington, D.C.

———. 1983. *1982 Census of Agriculture.* Vol. 1. Pt. 51. Washington, D.C.

U.S. Department of Agriculture. 1979. *Structure Issues of American Agriculture.* Economics, Statistics, and Cooperative Service. Agricultural Economic Report no. 438. Washington, D.C.

———. 1981. *A Time to Choose: Summary Report on the Structure of Agriculture.* Washington, D.C.

———. 1982. *Handbook of Agricultural Charts, 1982.* Agriculture Handbook no. 609. Washington, D.C.

———. 1983a. *Handbook of Agricultural Charts.* Agriculture Handbook no. 619. Washington, D.C.

———. 1983b. *Agricultural Statistics.* Washington, D.C.

Vogeler, Ingolf. 1981. *The Myth of the Family Farm: Agribusiness Dominance of U.S. Agriculture.* Boulder, Colo.: Westview.

Wessel, James. 1983. *Trading the Future: Farm Exports and the Concentration of Economic Power in Our Food System.* San Francisco: Institute for Food and Development Policy.

# [2]

# Mixing Paradigms on Mixed Farming: Anthropological and Economic Views of Specialization in Illinois Agriculture

**Susan Carol Rogers**
*Department of Anthropology and*
*Institute of French Studies, New York University*

The farms of central Illinois, in the heart of the Corn Belt, are an assault on the senses for anyone whose primary experience with agriculture is with farms that produce a variety of goods, including at least some for home consumption. In most of central Illinois, there are none of the sounds or smells one expects on a farm: the odor of manure spread on the fields, the sounds of roosters crowing and of cows shifting about in their stalls. Old people talk nostalgically about the days when everyone sold eggs at the local store and raised at least a few hogs for fresh sausage. On some farms, milk cans are still found, but now they are gaily painted and used for decoration only. Farmyards contain a house and one or several machine sheds; outbuildings that once housed animals have been torn down or converted to shelter for farm equipment. Corn and soybeans are raised here, just corn and beans.

As in other commercial agriculture regions of the United States, farming in Illinois has become increasingly specialized over the last several decades. Here, specialization on most farms has meant that farmers have abandoned diversified production of both livestock and crops (mixed farming) and replaced it with the production of only one or two crops, destined exclusively for the market (cash grain mono-cropping). Maps 1 through 3, based on U.S. Department of Agri-

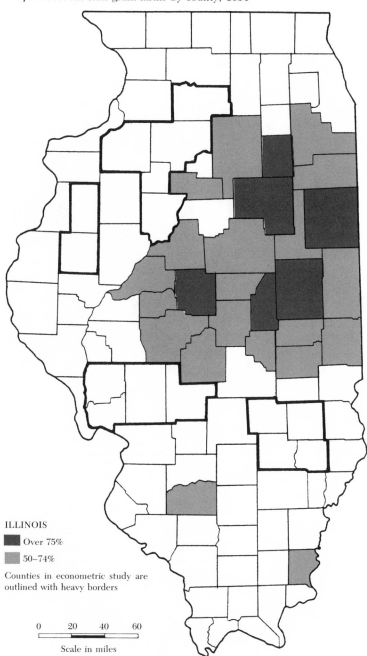

*Map 1*. Percent cash grain farms by county, 1954

ILLINOIS

Over 75%

50–74%

Counties in econometric study are
outlined with heavy borders

0    20    40    60

Scale in miles

*Map 2.* Percent cash grain farms by county, 1964

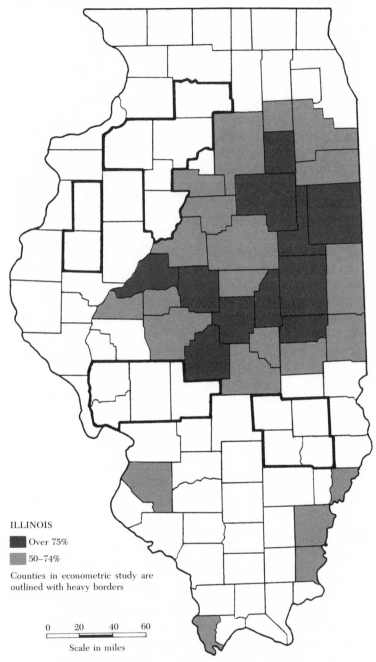

ILLINOIS

■ Over 75%

■ 50–74%

Counties in econometric study are
outlined with heavy borders

0    20    40    60

Scale in miles

*Map 3.* Percent cash grain farms by county, 1978

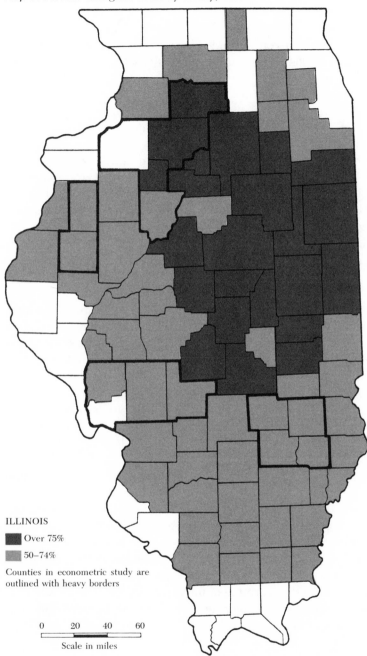

ILLINOIS

◼ Over 75%

▨ 50–74%

Counties in econometric study are
outlined with heavy borders

0    20    40    60

Scale in miles

culture census data, reveal the spreading "grain desert" in Central Illinois over the twenty-five years since 1954. The census also indicates that in 1954, cash grains and livestock/dairy accounted for equal proportions of the value of Illinois agricultural products sold (48 percent each). In contrast, by 1978 cash grains accounted for nearly two-thirds (63 percent) and livestock/dairy for barely one-third (33 percent) (cf. Finke and Swanson 1973; Dovring and Yanagida 1979; Breimyer 1978).

In this chapter, I explore the causes and ramifications of this trend. I begin by outlining some of the arguments that are conventionally used to explain this increasing specialization of agricultural production and that are easily taken to imply that it is logical, virtually inevitable, and generally beneficial. These arguments are drawn from the economics paradigm that dominates current discussions of American agriculture. I then raise some questions about the underlying premises of these arguments and about whether increasing specialization is necessarily beneficial.

Next, using two contrasting approaches, I examine whether this specialization is inevitable. First, I present ethnographic material on the exceptional case of "Freiburg,"[1] a farm community on the southern edge of central Illinois's sea of grain, which remains an island of mixed farming. Ethnographic analysis of this community's resistance to cash grain monocropping suggests that the decision whether to specialize or diversify is systemically related to an array of social and economic considerations. Second, I present the results of an econometric analysis designed to test some of these hypothesized relationships. Data for this analysis was drawn from business records of 179 farms (including several in the ethnographic study community) in fifteen counties around the edges of Illinois's cash grain region.

I have several purposes: to describe some of the far-flung implications of specialization and diversification in farm production in American commercial agriculture and to show how anthropological methods and analysis can address a problem that has, for better or worse, been defined in economic terms. Realizing that newcomers to a foreign land are well advised to learn to communicate in the dominant language, I am interested here in exploring some ways in which anthropology can use and respond to the kinds of analyses produced by economists.

---

1. "Freiburg," like the names used to refer to individuals living there, is a pseudonym.

[62]

## Explanations for Agricultural Specialization

At first glance, there is nothing particularly remarkable about the kind of evolution Illinois agriculture has undergone. In general terms, increasing specialization has long been seen as a cause or reflection of economic development, growing labor productivity, and enhanced efficiency of production. American agriculture—and Illinois agriculture in particular—can be seen as simply following a path of inexorable economic logic. Several plausible explanations have been offered for the kind of increasing specialization observed in Illinois:

1. The drive to adopt costly, enterprise-specific technologies favors specialization. Land- and labor-saving technological innovations such as hybrid corn, chemical fertilizers, and mechanical equipment have led to increases in productivity (conventionally defined as output per unit of land or labor input) and in production efficiency (measured as production cost per unit of output). Farmers have had to adopt these technologies to remain competitive on the market. They are then apt to specialize because in general these technologies are enterprise-specific (directed to only one kind of production), require considerable capital investment, and have cost advantages only when the relevant enterprise is large enough (Swanson and Sonka 1980; White and Irwin 1972; OTA 1985). The replacement of human labor with mechanical equipment illustrates how this works. Human labor is highly versatile: the same farm laborer can milk a cow, load hay, and harvest corn. In contrast, labor-saving equipment is much more specialized: no single piece of equipment can handle all these tasks. Because any one piece of equipment—a milking machine, say—is apt to be both specialized and costly, it reduces the cost of production only if its own cost is spread over many quarts of milk. A farmer with two cows would be foolish to invest in a milking machine, while a farmer with enough cows to warrant buying a milking machine can produce milk more cheaply and drive the two-cow farmer out of the market. As capital—embodied in specialized technologies—has replaced more versatile labor or land, farmers have had to select one or a few enterprises in which to invest and have had to abandon those in which their inability to invest makes them unable to capture technology-induced cost advantages and therefore noncompetitive on the market. Having made such a decision, the farmer may be locked into it. He or she cannot move in and out of, for example, hog production from year to year if the available capital is invested in buildings and equipment that cannot be used for any purpose other than hog production. In the drive

[63]

for increased productivity and efficiency, Illinois farmers have tended to invest in technologies associated with cash grains and to abandon livestock production.

2. Institutional and technological innovations have reduced farmers' risks, making profit-maximizing more attractive to them than loss-inhibiting diversification. It is conventionally assumed that farmers make decisions only partly in response to market conditions. They are also concerned with managing the risks inherent in agricultural production, keeping them at an acceptable level. Specialization may maximize potential profits, but is also increases risk in that the farmer places all eggs in one basket. In the past, this has been a particularly important barrier to agricultural specialization because both yields and prices are determined largely by factors that are beyond the farmer's control and that affect various commodities differently. For example, weather conditions may be disastrous for winter wheat without affecting the corn harvest; low prices for corn may be offset by strong hog prices. Diversification is a way to hedge bets; it limits the potential losses as well as the potential profits of specialization. The attractiveness of this strategy, however, has declined with the development of innovations that have helped reduce farmers' risks of failure due to natural causes or low prices. These include institutional innovations such as crop insurance and price and income supports, which shift inherent risks away from the farmer, as well as chemical and mechanical innovations that reduce risk by increasing mastery of natural forces. These innovations have replaced diversification as a way to manage risk, clearing the way to the potentially higher profits of specialization (Johnson et al. 1979; White and Irwin 1972).

3. A declining labor-to-land ratio favors specialization in non-labor-intensive enterprises. Illinois's shift toward cash grain specialization has occured at the same time as a sharp drop in the number of farms in the state (175,000 in 1954 to 110,000 in 1978). Meanwhile, the amount of farmland has remained about the same, and farms have continued to be operated with family labor. This means that the labor-to-land ratio has declined considerably, with the decrease in the size of the farm labor force most frequently attributed to the lure of higher wages off the farm. In response to these exits from farming, relatively labor-intensive mixed farming was abandoned in favor of more land-extensive cash grain production (Colyer and Irwin 1967; Van Arsdall and Elder 1969; White and Irwin 1972). (Note that this line of reasoning rests on the premise that reductions in the farm labor force were a cause, not an effect, of shifts in production strategies.)

4. Growing dependence on rental land shifts risks so as to favor specialization. As farmers and children of farmers have left the land, they have often maintained ownership of their land, renting it to those who continue to farm. Increasingly, commercial farms in Illinois are composed of some land owned by the farmer and some rented from nonfarmers, as the rental market has become the main source of land for farm expansion (Reiss 1971; Bray 1963). Rental arrangements in Illinois are almost always on a crop-share basis; that is, the rent is a fixed percentage of the crop produced or its sale value. This arrangement further reduces the risks to the farmer of specializing in cash grains, because overall risks are shared with the landlord. For instance, if the harvest is poor or prices are low, then the rent is relatively low as well. At the same time, a farmer heavily dependent on rentals may have less security of tenure than one who owns most of his land. Unsure of his land base from one year to the next, the former may be reluctant to make the heavy investments in equipment and buildings required for livestock production. Shifts in tenure patterns therefore contribute to a changing balance of the risks associated with diversification and specialization (Willet and Hinman 1981; Timmons 1972; Boehlje and Durst 1982; Hottel and Harrington 1979).

5. Specific events in the mid-1970s made cash grain production attractive and prompted subsequently irreversible decisions to specialize. Largely as a result of the "Russian grain deal" and general fears of grain shortages, grain prices shot up in the mid-1970s. The prevailing wisdom at the time, among farmers and other experts, was that these high prices were part of a new era in farming and would remain at this level for some time. This created a strong incentive for farmers to expand their grain production and to abandon livestock, a move strongly encouraged by both policy makers and the scientific community. Insofar as these decisions were irreversible, farmers continued to specialize in cash grains even when the precipitating cause disappeared and prices fell to a new equilibrium at low levels (cf. Dovring and Yanagida 1979).

The most obvious conclusion to be drawn from explanations of this sort is that the observed evolution of agriculture is both inevitable and generally positive. However, leaving aside for the moment the question of the inevitability of these changes, some rather serious doubts can be raised about their beneficial nature. Certainly the current crisis and disarray in the agricultural production sector, especially in the midwestern breadbasket—suggest that this sector has become alarmingly fragile. More specifically, in order to read many of the justifications listed above in a positive light, one must assume that ever-increasing productivity and efficiency are necessarily a good thing. This assumption underlies a great deal of behavior in the agricultural sector, including that of decision-making farmers, technology-developing scientists, and behavior-assessing economists.

A drive to increase the productivity of agricultural land and labor is, however, a positive force only under certain conditions. It indeed makes good sense in a context in which there is a shortage of labor for agricultural production relative to the land and/or capital resources available, a need to free labor from subsistence production in order to provide a work force for infant industrial or service sectors, and an expanding market for food to feed a rapidly growing nonfarm population. All of these conditions characterized the United States in an earlier era. None of them do today. We now have a shortage of credit and land relative to the number of people who wish to farm, a "normal" rate of unemployment, which periodically climbs considerably higher than normal, and a saturated domestic market for food. Under these conditions, the continued drive for ever-increasing land and labor productivity in agriculture only creates economic problems generated by chronic surpluses and human problems generated by continual reductions in the number of farms and farmers able to earn a living from agriculture. There is nothing absolutely good about increasing agricultural productivity; while it is undoubtedly a good thing under certain economic conditions, after a point it becomes neither beneficial nor, beyond the blind logic of inertia, especially rational.

It could still be argued that increased productivity has gone hand in hand with increased efficiency, that is, declining cost of production. And that, it is said, is unambiguously beneficial to "society." On closer examination, however, it becomes clear that these benefits are not distributed evenly among all actors in the food chain, but rather that they accrue only to those segments of society with the most market power.

For farmers, the per-unit reductions in production costs have not resulted in increasing profits, but rather in a decline in the prices they receive for their products. This trend is seen most clearly in the parity ratio, defined as the prices received divided by prices paid by farmers (reflecting, for example, the amount of gasoline that can be bought for the price of a bushel of wheat). This ratio has generally declined throughout most of this century, dropping by 40 percent between 1950 and 1976 (Vogeler 1981:102). Consumers, meanwhile, have not experienced a sharp decline in food prices. Over the last several decades, there has been a growing discrepancy between the retail cost of food and the prices paid to farmers, with the difference going to food-processing companies and distributors. Today, only about one-third of the total retail value of food goes to farmers (Parlett 1983:706). This means that prices paid to farmers (farmgate prices) as well as related per-unit food production costs have less and less influence on consumers' food costs. Consumers receive at best only a small part of the benefits of reductions in the cost of food production, and farmers are unlikely to receive any at all.

If it is not assumed that increasing specialization of agricultural production is necessarily a good thing, then the question of its inevitability becomes an interesting one. In Illinois, as elsewhere, the trend toward specialization has been strong, apparently justifying the kind of universalistic explanations outlined above. But there remain pockets of diversified commercial farming in Illinois, which suggests that under some conditions the constraints and forces acting on commercial farming may provide an impetus for diversification rather than a drive for specialization. The case of Freiburg offers an example of how this might work.

## Mixed Farming in Freiburg: Ethnographic Analysis

The township of Freiburg[2] is located about 200 miles south of Chicago, on the edge of central Illinois's rich, flat prairie land. Its "gray prairie" soils are good, though not as productive as those in the "black prairie" to its north. Just south of Freiburg begins the rolling, wooded terrain of southern Illinois. Freiburg is heavily agricultural. There are about sixty-five working farms scattered about the township, as well as a small village. The village includes a Catholic church and a few professional offices and businesses (mostly bars) serving the area. For the most part, the professionals and businesspeople there belong to the same families that have provided these services to the area for

2. Research in Freiburg was undertaken in 1982 as part of the Ethnicity and Family Farming project directed by Sonya Salamon. Freiburg was chosen for study as a contrast to the six "black prairie" communities studied earlier by Salamon and her students. I lived in Freiburg from February through August 1982, administering the survey used in the other communities included in the Salamon project, and conducting more informal participant observation research.

generations. The village is also home to a number of retired farmers who have moved in from the countryside, leaving farm and farmstead to the next generation.

In some ways, Freiburg is typical of farm communities in Illinois, and indeed much of the Midwest. Its farms are commercial, family operations. That is, all labor and management is provided by the farm household, the farms are major consumers of purchased inputs, and virtually all production is ultimately destined for market. There is little class stratification within the community; resources are distributed fairly evenly, with farm size and income for full-time operators tending to cluster around the average for the community.

Freiburg was founded in the 1830s by a North German land settlement company and later became an important German Catholic mission center, attracting large numbers of German immigrants to the area. Today the population of the entire county is predominantly of German origin. Freiburg's residents make frequent and proud reference to their German identity, ascribing a variety of characteristics to it. Because of their German roots, they say, they are good, highly dedicated farmers, strongly committed to maintaining family ties to the land, stubborn, tight-fisted, family-oriented, and clannish as a community (cf. Salamon, this volume; Rogers 1982, 1985).

Freiburg farms stand out from those elsewhere in central Illinois in several ways. First, unlike the majority of farms in the state and the overwhelming majority in central Illinois, they are engaged in mixed farming. Nearly all Freiburg farms include a sizable hog or dairy enterprise and also produce feed grains, and about half the farmers raise beef cattle as a supplementary source of income. These farms are relatively small for the area, averaging about 275 acres. Central Illinois farms are generally considerably larger than those elsewhere in the state, but average farm size in Freiburg is identical to that for the state as a whole. An unusually large proportion of Freiburg's farmland is operator-owned: about 70 percent compared to about 45 percent for the state as a whole (the percentage for central Illinois is generally slightly lower than the state average). Finally, land prices have been unusually high in Freiburg's area, sometimes surpassing those of the more productive farmland to the north. These high prices suggest that the demand for Freiburg farmland is greater than that for farmland elsewhere in central Illinois.

These interrelated features—mixed production, small farm size, predominantly owner-operated tenure pattern, and high land prices—

are generated by local sociocultural traits in combination with more general economic pressures. First, most Freiburg farm families are deeply attached to their family land and strongly committed to the long-term viability of their family farm. Their notion of long-term is long indeed. One farmer, for example, noted: "I want to see [my farm] stay together. It's something from the past, and what I really want is to make sure it keeps going. I'd like to come back in five hundred years and see what my great-great-great grandchildren've done with it and see if maybe they've built it up two or three times what it is now." Not all Freiburg farmers have a planning horizon extending to the year 2400, but they do generally think well beyond their own lifetimes, doing what they can to ensure that their children and grandchildren will inherit a farm from which they can make a reasonable living. Freiburg farmers assume that this assurance requires that farm production be continually expanded. Like commercial farmers elsewhere, they have been caught in the cost-price squeeze—mounting total costs of production and unstable farmgate prices—and so have had to increase their volume of production to maintain an adequate income in the face of narrowing or uncertain profits per unit produced. They see this economic pressure and the resulting imperative to expand production as a long-term trend, not simply as a temporary disequilibrium that will eventually disappear. Their perception of current economic pressures is projected into a future that is of no less concern to them than is the present.

The strong commitment of all Freiburg farmers to farming and to the future of their own farms means that there is very little opportunity for any of them to expand their acreage. Land rarely comes up for sale, and the rental market is virtually nonexistent because those who own farmland work it themselves and plan to pass it on to their children to farm in turn. "Once land gets into a family, you can bet it'll stay there a good long time," said one farmer. As a result, Freiburg farmers cannot pursue a strategy of expansion through increases in cereal production, which would require more land. Rather, their only option is to expand vertically, adding livestock enterprises to the fixed amount of land available for feed production. This intensive land use optimizes the income generated and labor absorbed per unit of land, allowing cultural values to be honored in the face of economic realities.

To understand the economic choices made in Freiburg, then, it is necessary first to look in more detail at the social and cultural processes influencing the availability and use of farming resources there.

[69]

The matter of land is a major preoccupation among Freiburg farmers and a key element in their social as well as economic system (Rogers 1985).

In Freiburg, having title to land is considered virtually synonymous with farming and with one's identity as a farmer:

> Your land is really part of you. Selling it would be like cutting off your arm. Like Eddie Schmidt, when his wife died, the estate wasn't quite in order, so he had to have his land appraised. Some relative who's a lawyer did the papers, and he told Eddie it was appraised at so much. But Eddie told him there's no way he'd sell any of it. He told that lawyer, "It'd be just like if you took your college education and sold it. Then how'd you make your living or be who you are?" That's kind of how I see it too.

> It used to be, landowners were better off than laborers and that used to be one reason why people wanted to own land. But anymore, that's not true. Heck, I could probably make more money in town than I do here. But that's not the point. It's something else.

One is a farmer not just by virtue of working the land, but by virtue of owning it too. Renting land is acceptable as a way to supplement the farm's acreage or as a temporary arrangement in anticipation of eventually inheriting. Ownership, though, is what counts. One farmer, for instance, had, like his brother (who also farms in the area), purchased some land from his father and expected that the remainder of the father's land would be bequeathed to the two of them. He considered it reasonable that the two farmers in the family should split the inheritance, but was incensed by the father's recent talk of dividing the land equally among all six of his children. I asked if the nonfarming siblings would not simply continue to rent their shares to the two farming brothers, as the father currently does. He punctuated his answer with slams of the fist: "Well I don't know. I guess so, but I want to *own* it. When it's yours, you're sure of it, and you can do what you want with it. And it's *yours*." My question was a naive one, and beside the point: usage is not the issue—ownership is.

The inextricable link in Freiburg between landownership and farming is, in turn, very much bound up with farmers' strong commitment to the intergenerational continuity of their farms. They farm not only because it is the occupation they have chosen, but also because they feel considerable responsibility as stewards of the family patrimony,

[70]

seeing themselves as part of a family line extending into the past and into the future. Farming successfully is not just an end in itself, but is a way to fulfill one's obligation to the past by providing for future generations. In fact, a few Freiburg farmers say they would have preferred to leave farming, but their sense of obligation to the family line prevented them from doing so. One retired farmer whose son has now taken over the farm says: "I was all set to leave, but then Dad put it in his will that I was supposed to get the farm. I was supposed to take care of Mother as long as she lived and the farm would be mine. I guess I could've sold it or rented it, but really I couldn't do that. My brothers had all left by then, and it was up to me to carry on—said so right in Dad's will. So I stayed after all."

Landownership is crucial in this context, partly because, as the passage above suggests, the obligation to the past is secured only with title to the land and partly because one can be sure of passing on only what is owned. A farm composed primarily of rental land may be very successful at present, but its success is hollow if its transfer to the next generation is not assured. By the same token, it is title to the land, not simply usage rights, that must be transferred. One cannot be a true farmer or a proper steward of the family patrimony without both owning and working the family property.

Usually the family farm (homeplace) is transferred intact to the designated successor (most commonly the youngest son), and other children are given money or other property. In the old days, farmers tried to buy a farm for each of their sons. Each farm would then be resold at preferential prices to a son as he married, with the home-place finally going to the youngest, together with the obligation to care for the elderly parents. One retired farmer in Freiburg, one of the last to follow this practice and set up each of his six sons with a farm, reports with considerable pride that the joke in Freiburg was that "every time another son is born on the Schneider place, old man Schneider's out looking to buy another farm." At present, land is too scarce and expensive for this practice to be feasible even as an aspiration. The homeplace continues to go most frequently to the youngest son (or to the son most interested in farming), while the others are unlikely to receive any farmland. Commenting on this change, one farmer said: "People used to give land to all their sons, but now you need more land and you need it all together, so people are getting away from passing it around like that. They're less anxious to get all their sons in. Wanting to farm is something you learn, like you learn a religion, so parents just don't teach that to all their kids anymore."

[71]

Under the present system, as under the old, land is generally not considered to belong in the hands of nonfarmers. Anyone who owns land is expected to farm it, and conversely, no one is expected to farm unless he owns at least some of the land he works. For this reason (especially when there is some question about whether the successor is willing to stay on the farm), transfer of title usually begins as soon as the son reaches adulthood. Most commonly, title is transferred through a series of purchase contracts under favorable terms (for example, the son may agree to pay whatever he can manage each year). Retired farmers often retain ownership of a small amount of land, which is rented to the successor and will eventually be inherited by him. Generally, little or no rent is charged, and the operator is free to use the land as he wishes. It would appear that for these older farmers, continued ownership of at least one small tract is important for continuing to "be who you are."

Because farmland is imbued with deep emotional significance and also because it is very scarce and valuable property, it can be a source of bitter and long-lived conflict. People are willing to go to considerable lengths to obtain it or to prevent others from obtaining it, and few families succeed in avoiding disputes over its management or transfer. One Freiburg patriarch took the unusual step of refusing to write a will, reportedly telling his children that they were bound to fight over his property after he died in any event. If there were a will, he said, it would be too easy to blame him for the ill feelings. Without a will, they could fight all they wanted, and he would not be responsible.

Often those who do not inherit farmland believe that they have been cheated out of a fair share of the parents' wealth. At the same time, those who take over the homeplace are apt to resent having full responsibility for the care of the elderly parents and resent even more having to contribute to the monetary inheritance provided for their brothers and sisters. "Why should I have to help support city people when I do all the work here? This farm wasn't a gift, you know. And anyway, they make more money than I do."

An endless variety of conflicts may be triggered at any time over land. In one family, two brothers became farmers, and the family land was divided between them. One later became disabled and had to quit farming, so he rented his land to his brother. After a number of years, the disabled brother, strapped for cash, sold part of his land to a neighboring farmer. The other brother felt robbed, the whole extended family was furious that the land had been sold outside of the family, and the guilty seller was left on speaking terms with no one in his family. He knew very well what social costs he would incur by selling the land, explained at great length that he never would have done it had he not been in desperate straits, and was prevented from moving away from the area only by his wife's reluctance to live elsewhere.

In another family, a series of disputes culminated when an elderly widow was persuaded by some of her children to sell on the open market the small amount of land she still owned. She had been renting it to the son who had taken over the homeplace. In the ordinary course of events, he would have inherited the land at her death. Instead, his only alternative to seeing it pass out of the family (which was an option he could not even consider) was to pay full market value for it. Close to retirement age himself, he found himself burdened with a mortgage, and, believing he had been double-crossed by spiteful brothers and sisters, he cut off all relations with them.

These incidents illustrate the strong sentimental ties asociated with family land. They also explain why bequeathing the family land to the heir who farms is thought to be the best way to keep the land in the family. Everyone in the community has an impressive repertoire of similar stories—some of them no doubt apocryphal—illustrating what can happen otherwise.

The virtual absence of purchase and rental markets for land in the area, then, may be attributed to the inheritance system in Freiburg as well as to the meanings given to farming and to landownership. When land does come up for sale, it is sold at a very high price. During the spring and summer of 1982, for example, several small tracts were sold, each at between $3,000 and $3,500 per acre. Much more productive land farther north never cost more than $4,000 per acre when the market peaked (1980–1981) and was worth only about $2,800 in 1982. Freiburg farmers say that land there has always been more expensive than elsewhere in the region. One often hears it said that "any land in sight of the church steeple is going to cost you." One farmer said that no matter what the price, "if you can stand on your porch and throw a stone in it, it's a good buy."

They offer several explanations for the scarcity and high cost of land in the Freiburg area. Freiburg families are generally much larger than those of the neighboring Yankees ("Yahoos") and Lutherans, so there is nearly always at least one son who wants to stay and farm. Also, Freiburg farmers are fond of pointing out that "those Yankee farmers"

[73]

are not nearly as committed to farming and care little about keeping land in the family, so Yankee farmland finds its way to the auction block much more frequently. In Yankee territory, entire farms are often put up for sale, something that virtually never happens anymore in Freiburg. In fact, a few Freiburg farmers have bought land in the Yankee area. None of them is willing to consider living there, though, and hauling farm equipment back and forth between there and Freiburg is an unattractive prospect for most.

Freiburg farmers are able to pay high prices for land in their own area partly because only small tracts are ever sold. Also, they are likely to hold clear title already to most of their land and to have obtained it through family transactions at prices well below market value. Most of those entering the land market have saved enough money to be able to pay cash and therefore need not be concerned with the added expense of interest payments or finance charges.

They are willing to pay such prices for two reasons:

> One is if you've got a boy coming into the operation so you need the extra ground, and a lot of them buy because of that. The other one is you know if you don't get it, somebody else will, and it won't be sold again in a hurry. It's a once-in-a-lifetime chance for that piece of ground. And you'd rather see yourself get bigger than see your neighbor do it. There's lots of competition for land around here.

Either reason seems to be worth the investment of a great deal of money, and those individuals for whom the sky is not the limit stay out of the market. The bits of land reaching the market are usually sold by sealed bid auction. This method has the advantage of allowing the seller to choose who will get the land and thus to prevent it from falling into the hands of nonfarmers or Lutherans. (The neighboring Lutheran community has prevented Catholic incursions by the same method.) Some say that sealed bidding tends to increase prices; everyone is afraid that someone else will submit the high bid, so the tendency is to offer the highest imaginable price. On several occasions, however, land has been sold at open auction, which has become a type of arm wrestling match between feuding neighbors. They outbid each other with a vengeance until one is finally forced to abandon the bidding, long after a price considered exorbitant by everyone else has been reached. When this happens, no one is quite sure who lost: the one who failed to get the land or the one who had to pay for it.

Under these conditions, demand for rental land as a less costly way of augmenting operation size is quite high. Very little rental land is available, however, for the simple reason that little land is owned by nonfarmers. The purchase market, such as it is, is virtually closed to nonfarmers. And the result of local inheritance patterns is such that anyone who is not planning to farm himself is unlikely to obtain land through family transactions. The high market value only reinforces this tendency; those who are not committed to farming the family land are considered all too likely to succumb to the temptation of mammon and sell it out of the family. Most rental land is leased within families, usually by a retired farmer to his son, and is not made available to any other potential tenants. In general, the only land on the rental market is that owned by retired farmers who have no heirs planning to farm. These individuals are apt to be actively courted by farmers in the neighborhood, and the misfortune of not having a successor in the family seems to be compensated at least partially by the considerable power the owner wields over potential tenants.

This system of attitudes and behavior with respect to land has generated a high rate of operator-ownership (low tenancy rate) and a relatively large number of active farmers, virtually all of whom have a strong commitment to farming and to passing the farm on to future generations, but very little possibility of expanding acreage to honor these commitments. The solution is to make intensive use of the land available through livestock husbandry combined with feed grain production. On individual farms, livestock enterprises are added, abandoned, expanded, or reduced in accordance with the labor available or expected to be available for the future. In the community as a whole, livestock plays an important role in maintaining a maximum number of families on a limited amount of land.

Local attitudes toward livestock are less complex than those toward land. Most farmers take considerable pride in their animal husbandry skills. Some are quite attached to the animals they raise and often strongly dislike other kinds of livestock. Said one farmer, "Every night, last thing before I go to bed, I like to go out to the hog barn one more time, just to make sure everybody's OK. Sometimes I just sit out there with them for quite a while. . . . My Dad, though, he had some bad luck with hogs during the depression, and after that he never wanted to see another hog as long as he lived." One farmer (who has no sons) earns most of his income from grains, but buys some cattle to fatten each winter "just to keep busy." When I commented that there

[75]

has not been much money in cattle recently, he grinned and said, "Well, some people play golf, even though they don't get any money out of that. I guess you just do it for the pleasure." Livestock are not, however, generally considered to be mainly a source of pleasure. Complaints about the demanding work they require are much more common than expressions of affection for them. A farmer who gave up all animal husbandry when his son left the area said, "I was telling the guys, I thought when I gave up dairy for beef cattle that I'd be in heaven. But I wasn't in heaven, I was in purgatory. Now that I got rid of the cattle, too, and don't have any livestock at all, now it's heaven."

While the choice of particular livestock enterprises may be based at least partly on personal preferences and skills, the decision to raise livestock is usually seen as the only way to maintain the viability of the farm and to assure that there will be a working operation to pass on to the next generation. These ends are generally considered worthy of a great deal of trouble and expense. (By the same token, livestock are likely to play a relatively minor role on farms that, for one reason or another, will not be taken over by a child of the current operator.)

Decisions regarding livestock production, then, are generally made with an eye to the future. In particular, they are made as a function not only of the labor currently available, but also of that anticipated in the future. For example, several farmers have gradually expanded their hog enterprises in anticipation of the day when their children will be old enough to help and later to take over part of the operation. In the meantime, hired help is used to supplement the operator's labor. One farmer considered abandoning his dairy enterprise, but decided to expand it instead when his adolescent children agreed to help out and several of them expressed serious interest in later taking over the farm. Another family abandoned dairy farming when it became clear that they would never have any sons. Still another dairy farmer is postponing modernization of his dairy and expansion of the herd until his son decides what he wants to do. The son will probably take over the farm, but claims to dislike dairying, although his father says he may change his mind once he starts collecting part of the milk check.

It is taken for granted that the long-term viability of a farm requires that the operation expand with each successive generation. Furthermore, the transfer process may require absorption of an additional increment of labor, at least temporarily. That is, the father does not necessarily retire immediately when his son begins working full-time on the farm. Indeed, one justification given for turning the farm over to a particular son at low cost is that he has already contributed a great deal of low-cost labor to the operation. We have seen that farmers occasionally purchase additional tracts of land in preparation for transferring an expanded farm operation, but the opportunities to do so are limited. Much more commonly, either in addition to or instead of adding acreage, a livestock enterprise is added to the operation to "make room for a boy coming up." A few years before the son finishes school, a farrowing or cattle-feeding enterprise, for example, may be added and gradually built up. Sometimes this enterprise is absorbed into the operation as a whole, and sometimes it remains the particular responsibility of the son. In either case, it is likely to be financed, at least initially, by the father. Alternatively, an existing livestock enterprise may be expanded.

By the time the son marries, the father is likely to retire. Some livestock enterprises may then be eliminated or cut back. At the same time (or instead), the retired farmer may continue to contribute some labor to the operation, now run by his son. More commonly, the young farmer's wife is expected to help out with farm work, until they have children old enough to take her place. Thus, in general, the relative importance of livestock on a farm varies with the farm family's domestic cycle, but appears to be increasing over time.

The direction of change in Freiburg, then, is contrary to that suggested by the propositions listed earlier. Economic pressures in this social environment favor diversified livestock and grain production, not specialization in cash grains. Before returning to these propositions, we must consider whether Freiburg is not simply an extremely odd case, interesting for itself, perhaps, but not particularly representative of important processes underlying agricultural evolution in Illinois or elsewhere. Conclusions drawn on the basis of observations in one small community seem rather shaky ground on which to challenge general notions of economic inevitability. Ethnographic analysis of Freiburg suggests a number of hypotheses about farmers' behavior, but this method of analysis is not a very convenient one for assessing how widespread such behavior may be. A different analytical method was therefore used to check whether the processes observed in Freiburg might legitimately be assumed to occur elsewhere as well.

## Mixed Farming in Illinois: Econometric Analysis

To test hypotheses developed in the analysis of Freiburg on a larger area of Illinois, I turned to econometric (regression) analysis. This

[77]

method, while less useful than ethnography for generating hypotheses, is a powerful tool for testing certain kinds. The data from Freiburg did not include the kinds of information suitable for econometric analysis or a sufficient number of cases. In any event one purpose was to see if the relationships observed in Freiburg existed more generally in the state. Therefore I used as a data base annual farm records from the Farm Business Farm Management (FBFM) association at the University of Illinois, a record-keeping service in which some 8,000 Illinois farmers are enrolled (Wilken et al. 1982). A sample of records was selected according to the following criteria:

1. All the records are from farms located in one of the fifteen counties (including Freiburg's county) on the periphery of the long-established cash grain area of east central Illinois. The sample counties have a physical environment suited to either mixed livestock and grain production or cash cropping, but have moved increasingly to the latter over the past fifteen years (see Maps 1 through 3).

2. The records were coded as usable by the staff of the record-keeping service, that is, they were considered complete, coherent, and free of "abnormalities" (about 50 percent of all records).

3. For each farm included in the sample, usable records were available for each of the five most recent years recorded at the time of the study (1977–1981).

A total of 895 (179 farms × 5) records were included in the analysis.

A further selection criterion was imposed by the use of this data source. Farms participating in the record-keeping service do not represent a random sample of all farms in Illinois. For example, about 10 percent of all Illinois farms under 500 acres participate in the service, while about 20 percent of those over 500 acres do. Average farm size in the state is 275 acres, but about half of all the farms participating in the record-keeping service have more than 500 acres. The farms considered in this analysis, then, are primarily technologically sophisticated, full-time, commercial operations with larger-than-average acreage. They are the kinds of farms that dominate Illinois agriculture economically, if not demographically.

While the use of ethnographic methods was limiting, due to the small size of the group that could be studied, the use of econometric methods was no less constraining, due to the small number and limited types of variables that could be considered. A great deal of data that might have been relevant to the analysis could not be included for the simple reason that it had not been reported in the farm records.

[78]

These records are meant primarily as an accounting tool for individual farm businesses and therefore exclude information of a personal sort (for example, farmer's age, family size) and data about the community in which a farm is located (for example, the nature of local land markets). Also, construction of a statistically adequate econometric model requires that each variable pertain to a discrete phenomenon, that each be translatable to a specific numerical value, and that the number of variables in the model be fairly small (theoretically, less than the total number of cases in the sample, but in fact elegance requires many fewer).

The model specification and results of this analysis have been reported in some detail elsewhere (Rogers 1983). Briefly, the results were as follows:

1. A major purpose of the analysis was to see if the relationship between mixed farming and a high degree of operator-ownership of farmland, as observed in Freiburg, obtains generally in Illinois. In fact, a very strong relationship was found. The rate of tenancy (measured as percentage of rental land in an operation) varies directly with the degree of cash grain specialization (measured as percentage of the value of total farm production represented by grains). This does not necessarily mean that the specific kind of relationship observed in Freiburg between land tenure and production exists elsewhere, but it suggests that it might.

2. The labor-to-land ratio was found to decline with the degree of specialization. This confirms the well-established idea that mixed farming is more labor-intensive than cash grain production.

3. Contrary to expectations, farm size was not found to vary significantly with the degree of specialization. That is, in the sample of farms analyzed, cash grain farms were no larger than mixed farms. In Freiburg, it was argued, mixed farming is practiced both because land is not available to allow for expansion sufficient for a cash grain farm and because farmers wish to absorb available labor. Elsewhere, the latter consideration may be relatively more important than the former.

4. A strong negative relationship was found between degree of specialization and total investment in farm equipment. In part, this finding simply reflects the obvious fact that more equipment is needed on a farm producing both livestock and grains. However, the picture is somewhat more complicated. A strong negative relationship was also found between farm equipment investments and the percentage of rental land in the operation, even when the lower rates of

[79]

investment attributable to specialization were statistically removed. This suggests that farmers paying rent for much of their land have less capital available to invest in equipment. Alternatively, they may be unwilling to risk large investments in equipment if their dependence on rentals makes their security of tenure uncertain.

5. While mixed farming appears to require a larger non-land capital investment than cash grain production, it also generates a higher rate of return on investment. Total rate of return, calculated as total value of production minus production expenses (including unpaid labor) divided by total capital investment, was found to vary inversely with the degree of specialization. In other words, a given sum invested in a mixed farm can be expected to generate more net income than if it were invested in a cash grain farm. This finding implies that mixed farms can absorb more labor, not only in the sense of generating more work, but also in the sense of generating enough income to support a larger work force. It also means that more capital may be available on mixed farms to continue to invest in diversified enterprises. The apparent trend in Freiburg toward further diversification, therefore, may not be unique.

While these results do not conclusively prove that the complex social reality described in Freiburg is typical of other Illinois farm communities and farmers, they do suggest that the processes observed in Freiburg are not unique. A number of hypothesized relationships between variables could be abstracted from the ethnographic analysis, and a few of these were amenable to econometric testing. The results of the econometric analysis, interpreted in part with the aid of ethnographic insights, yield an incomplete picture of the processes at work in Illinois agriculture. This partial picture is, nonetheless, generally consistent with the more fleshed out patterns identified in Freiburg.

## Mixed Farming in General: Economic Analysis

We may now return to the propositions listed at the beginning of this paper, purporting to explain an inevitable trend toward increasing agricultural specialization. Having described in some detail the processes favoring diversification in Freiburg, and having developed evidence that these processes are at work elsewhere as well, we are ready to examine the discrepancy between these propositions and the behavior actually observed in Freiburg.

1. *The drive to adopt costly, enterprise-specific technologies favors specialization.* Freiburg farmers are as technologically sophisticated as any in Illinois and are, to some degree, forced to choose among a number of enterprises in which they might invest. Their decisions are, however, largely constrained by land scarcity and by their commitment to absorbing available labor. Thus, faced with a choice between buying a new combine for the existing grain enterprise or investing in facilities for a new hog-farrowing enterprise, for example, they may very well choose the latter, knowing the unlikelihood of expanding grain acreage and wishing to assure income and work for the next generation. The grain enterprise will not be abandoned as a result; rather the farmer will look for less expensive ways to gain access to relevant technologies (for example, by hiring a combine owner to harvest the crop or by making do with used equipment).

In Freiburg, capital constraints are perhaps less potent than elsewhere as a force limiting the number of investments that can be made. First, because most land is operator-owned and obtained through low-cost family transactions, little of a farmer's available capital need be used for land (either purchase or rent) and is therefore free for other uses. Second, it has been argued that large capital investments in an enterprise are economically efficient only if they are spread over many units produced. The "many units" may be perceived as implying a very large enterprise at any one point in time, but, alternatively, may be perceived as implying a smaller enterprise over a long period of time. For example, a farmer nearing retirement may not expect to produce enough piglets to recoup his investment in a new, modest-sized hog-farrowing facility before he retires, but if his planning horizon extends beyond his own career, then the investment may be an attractive one. The economic returns on his successor's pig production, combined with his own, may be expected to make the investment pay off in the long term. We have seen that Freiburg farmers do generally look beyond one generation; they may therefore be expected to invest more capital in more enterprises than would otherwise be the case. This is all the more true insofar as the social returns on investments—in the form of seeing the farm continue into the next generation—may be at least as important to Freiburg farmers as short-run economic returns.

2. *Institutions and technologies have shifted risks of specialization away from the farmer and made profit-maximizing specialization more attractive than loss-inhibiting diversification.* Most Freiburg farmers describe their farm management style as conservative, in the

sense of avoiding undue risks. They enjoy pointing out, for example, that (because of their German heritage) they resisted pressures in the mid-1970s to borrow heavily and to build up their farms on credit and that as a result they are much less vulnerable than many midwestern farmers to the current farm crisis. Because they see themselves as stewards of a family patrimony, which should extend beyond their lifetimes, they are less concerned with maximizing current profits than with minimizing risk of present *and future* failure. With or without existing risk-shifting institutions, loss-inhibiting diversification remains a more attractive strategy to them. Furthermore, the advantages of specialization appear to exist only in the short run. In the long run, diversification appears to be the best strategy for maximizing profit (higher rates of return on investment) as well as for inhibiting losses. Because Freiburg farmers have a long planning horizon, they are more likely to be attracted by the greater long-term profits of diversified farming than the short-run profits of specialization.

3. *A declining labor-to-land ratio favors specialization in non-labor-intensive enterprises.* This appears to have been the case in the neighboring Yankee area, where commitment to farming is purportedly lower and out-migration has been much greater. Nearly all farms there have indeed shifted to specialized cash grain production, apparently at least in part as a response to labor shortage. In Freiburg, however, resistance to cash grain specialization can be seen as part of a conscious strategy to maintain a high labor-to-land ratio. The example of Freiburg begs the question whether increased specialization has been an effect or a cause of exits from farming and of the resulting drop in labor-to-land ratios.

4. *Growing dependence on rental land shifts risk so as to favor specialization.* The social and cultural systems in Freiburg are such that rental land has not taken on the importance it has elsewhere. As a result, the vagaries of grain yields and prices are not generally shared with a landlord. Also, the tenure security associated with operator-ownership of land together with limited opportunities for expansion due to the very small purchase and rental markets for land mean that Freiburg farmers can predict the size of their farms far into the future. This situation facilitates the kind of long-range planning favoring diversification.

5. *Specific events in the mid-1970s made cash grain production attractive and prompted subsequently irreversible decisions to specialize.* It is difficult to reconstruct decisions made in the past, but the

fact remains that the high grain prices of the mid-1970s were insufficient to make Freiburg farmers abandon their livestock enterprises. In retrospect, they say that grain prices in those years were abnormally high and were obviously a bubble bound to burst. Whether or not they were really so clear-sighted, their inclination toward wariness and risk aversion apparently did prompt them to wait and see before shifting their grain production from on-farm feed to market sale, even if it meant forgoing immediate profits. By the time they might have been convinced that the future did indeed lie in cash grain specialization, grain prices had dropped again and they had every reason to continue mixed farming.

In relation to these five economic propositions, we can look at Freiburg as an exception that is nonetheless consistent with the rule (point 4), as a variation on the terms of the rule (points 2, 3, 5), or as an exception that suggests that the terms of the rule be rethought (point 1). In each case, the fact that Freiburg is exceptional can be explained with reference to its social or cultural characteristics. Such factors are likely to result in exceptions to economic explanations for the simple reason that cultural and social variables are generally removed from economic explanation in two ways. First, underlying much economic theory is the assumption that all individuals operate according to the same motives, respond identically to the same pressures, and so on. Patterned variation in behavior can be reintroduced into economic models if the universe observed is partitioned into contrasting categories, each assumed to be composed of individuals behaving in a similar way. Anthropological analysis can suggest meaningful criteria for defining categories relevant to a given problem—criteria which, with a simple shift in vocabulary, may be built into economic models. "A strong commitment to intergenerational continuity," observed by the anthropologist, for example, makes sense to the economist as "a planning horizon extending beyond one generation"; "unwillingness to jeopardize the farm's future" may be roughly translated as "risk aversion." Behavior that theoretically should not exist can thus be made perfectly explainable; trends that appear inevitable can be turned into trends that occur only under specifiable conditions. In this way, anthropological analysis can be used to make economic analysis more nuanced and, oddly enough, more precise.

The second way in which sociocultural factors are left out of economic explanations is less easily dealt with. Individuals or individual production units are apt to be treated as if they were operating in isolation from other individuals or units, responding in a one-on-one way to price signals, risks, opportunities for profit, and so on. We can fit the behavior of a Freiburg farmer into this mold by describing him as being risk-averse, having a long planning horizon, and the rest. But an important key to the behavior of Freiburg farmers is that they cannot expand their land base significantly. The reason they cannot is that they live in a community in which everyone has a long planning horizon, is risk-averse, and so on. Any one Freiburg farmer might, without changing his own motives, values, and beliefs, behave quite differently if he were operating in a different social context. The explanatory power of economics fails altogether to take into account the interaction between particular social environments and individual behavior, the ways in which patterns of individual behavior create a social context, which in turn impinges on individual decision making. Anthropological insights in this domain may be presented most productively not so much through accommodation to the terms of dominant economic paradigms, but as a challenge or corrective to those paradigms.

## Conclusions

Although midwestern agricultural production has generally moved toward increased specialization over the past several decades, this pattern is not an inevitable one, generated strictly by universal laws of economics, but is contingent in part on particular social and cultural factors. Conversely, the interplay between current economic conditions and some sociocultural contexts can be expected to favor production diversity, not specialization.

The analysis leading to this conclusion is characteristically anthropological rather than economic in that it is premised on the notion that cultural values and social constraints are at least as influential on human behavior as factors such as price signals and market conditions. It also betrays the anthropologist's greater interest in identifying variable conditions underlying patterned behavior than in discovering universalistic laws or explanations.

This contrast in approach to the problem is clearly reflected in the differing limits and potentials inherent in ethnographic and econometric research methods. The ethnographic enterprise involves deciphering relationships between a very wide range of factors impinging on behavior in a natural setting. Toward this end, the ethnographer is likely to focus on a relatively small group of individuals, becoming personally involved in local conditions of life in a research process in which data collection (fieldwork) is intimately connected with data analysis. This type of research lends itself to consideration of intangible and unmeasurable factors, as well as more readily quantifiable variables. At the same time, though, the ethnographer is likely to avoid collecting data (such as income and yield data among Illinois farmers) if doing so might jeopardize the rapport between the ethnographer and the individuals in the study group. Because, relative to most other methods, ethnographic analysis seeks to retain a more realistically complex view of social life, it is a particularly powerful method for generating hypotheses about real human behavior. For the same reason, however, it is generally possible to study only relatively small groups. While the intricacies elucidated by ethnographic analysis may be presumed to have implications beyond the study community, the ethnographic method itself is not very useful for either establishing or measuring the generality of its results. Furthermore, the painstaking work of conducting ethnographic research frequently leads the ethnographer to become so absorbed in the local study setting that he or she either neglects to ask how it compares with others in the larger context or is inclined to emphasize its specificity.

Econometric analysis is a fundamentally different enterprise. A more formal method of analysis, it involves modeling a highly simplified version of reality and using data series to test the model's strength. It seeks to abstract out the "noise" of a wide range of disturbances, peculiarities, and imponderables, allowing a clear view of the relationships between a relatively few behavioral traces of a particular kind. Econometrics requires the use of data that is translatable into precise numerical values, with each variable measurable independently of the others. It also requires that equivalent information be available for all "observations" (for example, the farm operations in the analysis above) and that each be treated as a discrete case, unrelated to the others. The econometrician therefore uses a much narrower range of data than the ethnographer and operates several steps removed from the complexities and distractions of the "on the ground" behavior that is of such interest to the ethnographer.

These characteristics of econometric analysis have a number of implications. For example, a distinctly asocial perception is built into this method of analysis, not only because social variables are apt to be beyond the range of data that can be treated, but also because results refer to an essentially asocial universe, composed of "observations" (for example, firms or other economic actors), supposed to be unconnected. While the ethnographer defines his or her study group in social terms and immerses himself in its social life, the econometrician abstracts out the social and does not include data collection as an integral part of the research process. Indeed, data sets constructed for entirely different purposes are frequently used in econometric analysis. While much of the data used in ethnographic analysis is neither accessible nor usable for the econometrician, the econometrician can use data that is unlikely to be obtainable in a form usable by the ethnographer (for example, price and income information from a depersonalized series of farm records). The smaller number of variables used, greater level of abstraction from "real" complexity, and the use of standardized, quantified data sets frequently assembled by someone else, mean that the econometrician is able to analyze a much larger universe and make higher-level generalizations than can the ethnographer. The usefulness of these generalizations, however, is limited by the quality of the data used, usually beyond the econometrician's control and often considered of no major interest to him or her, as well by the narrow range of information that can be included. The kinds of data amenable to econometric analysis necessarily define the types of hypotheses tested and conclusions drawn. Furthermore, while econometrics is a powerful tool for testing measurable relationships between specific variables, it generates only statistical results (slope coefficients, t-values, and so on); it cannot, in itself, provide explanations for these relationships, nor can it necessarily distinguish between spurious or artifactual (but statistically significant) relationships in a poorly specified model and those that are true reflections of real behavior. (Some economists argue that this is not a problem, because models are meant to predict behavior, not necessarily portray it accurately.) Finally, high levels of generalization—imposed to some extent by the requirements of statistical rigor—may simply reflect an amalgam of very different behaviors, failing to give an accurate picture of any one pattern (the "aggregation problem").

Ethnography and econometrics thus reflect and generate very different—and necessarily incomplete—views of reality and of the dynamics of human behavior. Each is only one of several research methods within its discipline, but both are central to their disciplines, playing key roles in shaping and reflecting anthropological or economic thought.

Because the study of American agriculture has been dominated by economics, agricultural problems and dynamics are largely perceived and understood, by scholars, farmers, and policy makers alike, in terms strongly colored by the parameters inherent in econometric analysis. Therefore the ethnographer can hardly afford to ignore or dismiss the body of knowledge developed by economists or to be unaware of its strengths and weaknesses. At the same time, by offering a specifically anthropological view of agricultural issues, the ethnographer can introduce quite a different slice of reality, potentially correcting, complementing, or rendering more precise conventional wisdom in this domain.

## Acknowledgments

This paper is based on research and study supported by National Institutes of Health Postdoctoral National Research Service Award MHO8514 from the National Institute of Mental Health, held from May 1981 through May 1983. The economic analysis was carried out as part of a master's thesis project in the Department of Agricultural Economics at the University of Illinois, Urbana-Champaign, and owes much to the encouragement and support of John Braden, Folke Dovring, and Earl Swanson. The ethnographic research was undertaken as part of a larger project directed by Sonya Salamon, Department of Human Development and Family Ecology, University of Illinois, Urbana (see footnote 2). I am grateful to her for introducing me to the world of Illinois agriculture.

## References Cited

Boehlje, Michael, and Ron Durst. 1982. Getting started in Farming Is Tough. In *Food from Farm to Table: Yearbook of Agriculture*, ed. Jack Hazes. Washington, D.C.: U.S. Dept. of Agriculture.

Bray, James O. 1963. Farm Tenancy and Productivity in Agriculture: The Case of the U.S. *Food Research Institute Studies* 4:25–38.

Breimyer, Harold F. 1978. Agriculture's Three Economies in a Changing Resource Environment. *American Journal of Agricultural Economics* 60:37–47.

[87]

Colyer, Dale, and George D. Irwin. 1967. *Beef, Pork, and Feed Grains in the Cornbelt: Supply Response and Resource Adjustments.* Missouri Agricultural Experiment Research Bulletin no. 921.

Dovring, Folke, and John Yanagida. 1979. *Monoculture and Productivity: Study of Private Profit and Social Product on Grain Farms and Lifestock Farms in Illinois.* Report no. AE-4477. Dept. of Agricultural Economics, Univ. of Illinois, Urbana-Champaign.

Finke, Jeffrey, and Earl R. Swanson. 1973. Diversification in Illinois Crop Production, 1938–1970. *Illinois Agricultural Economics* 13:8–11.

Hottel, Bruce, and David H. Harrington. 1979. Tenure and Equity Influence on the Incomes of Farmers. In *Structure Issues of American Agriculture.* Economics, Statistics, and Cooperative Service. Agricultural Economic Report no. 438. Washington, D.C.: U.S. Department of Agriculture.

Johnson, James D., et al. 1979. Price and Income Policies and the Structure of Agriculture. In *Structure Issues of American Agriculture.* Economics, Statistics, and Cooperative Service. Agricultural Economic Report no. 438. Washington, D.C.: U.S. Dept. of Agriculture.

Miller, Thomas A. 1979. Economies of Size and Other Growth Incentives. In *Structure Issues of American Agriculture.* Economics, Statistics, and Cooperative Service. Agricultural Economic Report no. 438. Washington, D.C.: U.S. Dept. of Agriculture.

Office of Technology Assessment (OTA), U.S. Congress. 1985. *Technology, Public Policy, and the Changing Structure of American Agriculture: A Special Report for the 1985 Farm Bill.* Publ. no. OTA-F-272. Washington, D.C.

Parlett, Ralph. 1983. The 1984 Outlook for Food Prices and Consumption. In *Proceedings: 60th Annual Agricultural Outlook Conference.* Washington, D.C.: U.S. Dept. of Agriculture.

Reiss, Franklin. 1971. *Growth and Ownership Patterns among Large Illinois Farms.* Publ. no. AERR-112. Dept. of Agricultural Economics, Univ. of Illinois, Urbana-Champaign.

Rogers, Susan Carol. 1982. The Illinois Family Farm Project: Ethnicity and Family Farming in the Corn Belt. Paper presented at Wingspread Seminar on Women's Roles on North American Farms, Racine Wis.

———. 1983. Land Tenure and Cash Grain Specialization in Illinois: The Significance of Farmland Ownership and Rental. M.S. thesis. Dept. of Agricultural Economics, Univ. of Illinois, Urbana-Champaign.

———.1985. Owners and Operators of Farmland: Structural Changes in U.S. Agriculture. *Human Organization* 44:206–214.

Swanson, Earl R., and Steven T. Sonka. 1980. *Technology and the Structure of U.S. Agriculture.* Report to the Committee on Agriculture, Nutrition, and Forestry, U.S. Senate.

Timmons, John F. 1972. Tenure and Size. In *Size, Structure, and Future of Farms,* ed. Gordon Ball and Earl O. Heady. Ames: Iowa State Univ. Press.

Van Arsdall, Roy N., and William A. Elder. 1969. *Economies of Size of Illinois Cash Grain and Hog Farms.* Univ. of Illinois Experiment Station Bulletin no. 733.

Vogeler, Ingolf. 1981. *The Myth of the Family Farm: Agribusiness Dominance of U.S. Agriculture.* Boulder, Colo.: Westview.

White, T. Kelley, Jr., and George D. Irwin. 1972. Farm Size and Specialization. In *Size, Structure, and Future of Farms,* ed. Gordon Ball and Earl O. Heady. Ames: Iowa State Univ. Press.

Wilken, D.F., et al. 1982. *1981 Summary of Illinois Farm Business Records.* Univ. of Illinois, Urbana-Champaign. Cooperative Extension Circular no. 1024. (Previous years' reports were also consulted.)

Willet, Gayle S., and Herbert R. Hinman. 1981. A Method for Analyzing the Farmland Lease or Purchase Decision. *Journal of the American Society of Farm Managers and Rural Appraisers* 45:37–45.

# [3]

# Saving Soil by Abandoning the Plow: Experimentation with No-Till Farming in an Iowa County

## Michael Chibnik
*Department of Anthropology*
*University of Iowa*

No-till is an important soil conservation measure recently introduced in the Midwest. Farmers using this technique plant corn or
soybeans in previously unprepared soil by "opening a narrow slot,
trench, or band of sufficient width and depth to obtain proper seed
coverage" (Choi and Coughenour 1979:1). The use of herbicides
makes it possible to control unwanted weeds and grasses without
turning the soil.

Many midwestern farmers have been experimenting with no-till
because technological and macroeconomic changes have led them to
become dissatisfied with older soil conservation practices. Huge new
tractors cannot be operated easily on fields with intricate systems of
contours, terraces, and shelterbelts. During the 1970s expanding markets and soaring land values (with consequent higher taxes and rents)
caused farmers to shorten crop rotations and plow under pastures and
woodlands.

In this chapter I describe recent experimentation with no-till by
farmers in Kirkwood County, Iowa.[1] In doing so, I show why a seem-

---

1. "Kirkwood County" and all personal names used in this chapter are pseudonyms.
The bulk of my research was carried out in June through August, 1982. I made several
short visits to Kirkwood County in 1983 and 1984.

ingly simple decision about a soil conservation technique is in fact complex, involving consideration of a host of social, economic, and environmental factors.

## Soil Conservation in the Midwest

When settlers of European descent came to the Midwest of the United States in the nineteenth century, they found the land very well suited for agriculture. An important reason was the exceptionally deep topsoil layer, on average about 15 inches, in what is now called the Corn Belt. Topsoil, inherently more productive than subsoils, is only a few inches deep over much of the earth's surface.

The Midwest is still noted for its enormous agricultural productivity. In 1984, 59 percent of the corn and 54 percent of the soybeans grown in this country came from five Corn Belt states—Illinois, Indiana, Iowa, Minnesota, and Ohio. This efficient production of animal feeds has enabled midwestern farmers to be among the nation's leaders in raising cattle and hogs.

Serious soil erosion problems threaten this agricultural preeminence. By 1980 many farms in the Midwest had lost half their original topsoil. Despite deteriorating soils, midwestern farmers have been able to increase corn and soybean yields by applying massive amounts of fertilizers, herbicides, and pesticides. These energy-intensive practices, however, have become less cost-effective as the price of fossil fuels has soared, and gains in productivity have started to level off. The extensive use of chemical fertilizers and pesticides, moreover, has caused soil damage that may eventually adversely affect productivity in some areas. Besides these on-farm costs, soil erosion causes off-farm environmental problems such as silting of reservoirs, streambeds, and other water bodies and the deterioration of water quality by suspended sediment.

Although agronomists generally agree that midwestern farmers can prevent long-term land degradation by adopting appropriate soil conservation measures, recommended practices such as terracing and crop rotation are often not in a farmer's short-term economic interest. For the past fifty years, therefore, federal and state governments have offered a variety of incentives to farmers to use soil conservation techniques. But the continuing soil losses in the Midwest suggest that the adverse short-term economic consequences of soil conservation

[91]

have influenced farmers' decision making more than the long-term benefits of and governmental incentives for preserving the land.[2]

The practical importance of soil erosion has led researchers from diverse disciplines to examine why some midwestern farmers are willing and able to use particular conservation measures while others are not. Agricultural scientists and geographers have shown that conservation measures appropriate for some cropping systems and ecological zones may not be feasible for others. Economists have calculated the short- and long-term financial consequences of different conservation strategies under conditions specific to particular farms, places, and times. Sociologists have studied the psychological and socioeconomic characteristics of early adopters, late adopters, and nonadopters of conservation practices and the channels of communication farmers use to gather and evaluate information about new measures.

Social scientists and historians have also written extensively about the political economy of soil conservation. Economists have described how technological innovations and changing world market conditions have led midwestern farmers to engage in increasingly capital-intensive, land-extensive farming, which causes soil erosion and discourages the use of certain conservation methods. Historians and political scientists have examined the circumstances that have influenced the government to offer particular incentives to farmers and have described the development and operation of government agencies created to promote and provide information about soil conservation. Critics of the "agricultural establishment" have argued that land grant universities, influenced by their connections with manufacturers of farm machinery and supplies, have overemphasized research designed to increase yields and have underemphasized research on methods to avoid erosion and other environmental dangers.[3]

Although these studies have provided much useful information about the causes and consequences of erosion, researchers have rarely presented detailed accounts of why particular soil conservation tech-

2. The preceding four paragraphs draw on these sources: Berg 1982; Brown 1981; Crosson 1982; Napier and Foster 1982; Soil Conservation Service 1977; Timmons 1980; United States Department of Agriculture 1983.

3. Some books and articles by agronomists, historians, and soil scientists that include material on soil conservation are: Cosper 1983; Dallavalle and Mayer 1980; Ervin and Washburn 1981; Gersmehl 1978; Hightower 1973; Hudson 1971; Jolly, Edwards, and Erbach 1983; Nowak 1983; Pampel and van Es 1977; Rasmussen 1982; Simms 1970; Taylor and Miller 1978; Vogeler 1981.

niques are selected. Such "ethnographic descriptions" are essential in providing a full picture of soil conservation problems in the Midwest. Members of farm households (not necessarily individual farmers acting alone) adopting a conservation practice usually must make a whole series of "microdecisions." These include the scale on which the measure will be used in the first year of experimentation; where, when, and on which crops to try out the practice; where to find any relevant information; and whether to abandon or decrease the use of other conservation techniques. The extent to which the advantages and disadvantages associated with different conservation measures affect these decisions depends on a specific combination of farm family attributes that are unlikely to be shared completely with any other household. Decisions about soil conservation, moreover, must be considered in the context of overall farm management planning and short- and long-term household economic strategies.

## No-Till Farming

The search for better conservation methods has led many farmers to attempt to control erosion by using "reduced tillage systems." These systems minimally disturb the soil during seedbed preparation and subsequent weed control (Swanson 1981). Although some writers (e.g., Faulkner 1943) in the 1940s recommended that farmers reduce or abandon plowing to preserve soil, such a change was not practical at that time because of the absence of effective nonmechanical means of weed control. Postwar research in chemistry, however, led to the development of more effective herbicides and pesticides. These new metabolic compounds were more effective than older herbicides and pesticides in distinguishing between crops and weeds and were much more efficient in terms of effect per gram of material applied (Gersmehl 1978:67). No-till, the most radical of the various reduced tillage systems, essentially consists of the substitution of chemicals for plows. This technique has been used in the United States primarily on corn and soybeans.

The equipment required for no-till differs somewhat from that used in conventional midwestern farming. Because of the absence of plowing in no-till farming, there are barriers of dead organic material between the soil and the atmosphere. Special planters or attachments to conventional planters are needed to penetrate the residue and

[93]

place seed in the soil. The absence of plows, disks, harrows, cultivators, and other heavy equipment used in turning the soil enables no-till farmers to use considerably smaller tractors than those used in conventional tillage.

Despite the substantial change in farming methods that no-till represents, increasing numbers of American farmers in recent years have been trying it. Although no-till was tried on only a few hundred acres in the mid-1960s (Lessiter 1977:4), by 1981 it was used on nearly 8 million acres (Moldenhauer et al. 1983:144). Most no-till production, however, has taken place in a rather narrow latitudinal band from Maryland to western Kentucky. In 1981 only about 2.5 percent of harvested cropland in the Midwest was in no-till (Moldenhauer et al. 1983:144).

## Kirkwood County

Kirkwood County is in the southern part of Iowa along the Missouri border. Agriculture completely dominates the local economy. There are no manufacturing plants or towns of any size, and the roads are so quiet that the county lacks a single traffic light. Corn and soybeans are by far the most important cash crops, but significant amounts of oats and wheat are also grown. The hills in many parts of the county force some farmers to rely on livestock as their primary source of income.

Kirkwood farmers differ considerably in wealth. A few own more than five hundred acres of good flatland, live in modern ranch houses, drive new cars, and take expensive vacations during the winter. Others live in ramshackle houses guarded by tired dogs and eke out a living farming one hundred or so acres of hilly soil and occasionally working at jobs such as carpentry, bus driving, and construction. Most fall somewhere in between, living well during good years, but suffering when drought strikes or prices fall.

Although households ordinarily consist of nuclear families, most Kirkwood farmers regularly see other relatives living in the area. Many residents are descendants of settlers who came to Iowa during the nineteenth century. The majority are of English or German stock; many also have Dutch, Scandinavian, or other northern European ancestors.

The soils and topography of the southern tier counties such as Kirkwood are somewhat less suited to capital-intensive row crop production than those of most other parts of Iowa. Corn and soybean yields and farmland prices are well below the statewide average. Iowa has some of the richest farmland in the world, however, and these counties would fare well in a nationwide soil comparison.

The rolling topography characteristic of much of Kirkwood County has led to especially serious soil erosion problems. A study carried out by the Soil Conservation Service (1962:3) two decades ago reported that on many sloping fields, less than three inches remained of the original eight to fourteen inches of topsoil and warned that if erosion continued, the capacity of the soil to support plant life would be greatly reduced. In recent years the local Soil Conservation Service has provided considerable technical aid to farmers, and government cost-sharing programs have provided incentives for farmers wishing to construct terraces. Because soil erosion has continued, government officials have been receptive to new conservation methods.

No-till was first tried in Kirkwood County on a small scale in the early 1970s by two men. One retired from farming soon after trying the technique, but the other, a soil conservation official named Lyle Douglas, became an active practitioner and advocate of no-till. Douglas first heard about no-till from a chemical salesman. After reading extensively about the practice and making a trip to Kentucky to talk to no-till farmers, he planted some successful plots of ten to twenty acres of no-till corn and soybeans on his own land. Douglas's job enabled him to discuss the results of his experiments with most of the farmers in the county.

In the years from 1976 to 1979 Douglas was able to provide useful information to the approximately half dozen Kirkwood farmers who decided to try no-till on a large scale. Most of these innovators had a reputation within the community for willingness to try novel agricultural practices. These men purchased no-till planters, which they sometimes used to plant (for a fee) small plots on the land of interested neighbors.

In 1979 the state of Iowa began providing a small financial incentive for farmers wishing to try no-till. The exact amount of money paid and acreage limitations are determined locally. From 1980 to 1984, Kirkwood County farmers could obtain, one time only, ten dollars per acre for up to twenty acres of no-till. This program enabled farmers to try no-till cheaply by hiring neighbors to "custom plant" a small experimental plot.

Since 1980 no-till farming has received extensive publicity in Iowa.

[95]

The *Des Moines Register,* an influential newspaper read statewide, and magazines such as *Wallaces Farmer* and *Successful Farming* have carried articles on no-till, and no-till yield contests have become regular features of county and state fairs. This publicity has made farmers increasingly interested in trying the technique. While there were no more than a dozen no-tillers in Kirkwood County in 1978, by 1982 the local Soil Conservation Service estimated that 20 to 30 percent of the county's 1,100 farmers were doing some no-till. Kirkwood County was one of the most active no-till areas in the state, and articles on several of the more successful no-tillers appeared in *Wallaces Farmer.*

## The Costs and Benefits of No-Till in Kirkwood County

Although farmers in Kirkwood County would like to be able to control erosion without reducing their income from corn and soybeans, they recognize that trade-offs between short-term profits and soil saving sometimes must be made. Farmers considering a particular conservation measure therefore weigh potential benefits from soil saving against the chances of decreased yields and increased costs. They also examine the extent to which the measure can be substituted for or combined with other conservation methods. Decisions about no-till are especially complex because of the many costs and benefits associated with the technique. No-till saves labor as well as time, but involves the use of dangerous chemicals, is hard to learn, and is generally regarded as "risky."

The information presented here on the costs and benefits of no-till comes from two quite different sources: (1) the writings of rural sociologists, agronomists, and economists and (2) a survey of eighty-three Kirkwood farmers conducted in the summer of 1982.[4] As will be seen, there is considerable disagreement about the various costs and

4. The eighty-three farmers were evenly divided among two hilly and two flat townships of Kirkwood County. In each township ten farmers were interviewed from a list of known no-tillers provided by the Soil Conservation Service. These represented about 75 percent of the known no-tillers in the four townships. Of the remaining farmers interviewed, several turned out to have tried the practice. About half the farmers in the four townships were interviewed. Although time constraints prevented me from interviewing statistically random samples of known no-tillers and others, socioeconomic data on age, row crop acreage, land tenure, and education of the farmers interviewed suggest that they did not differ in important ways from their neighbors.

*Table 3-1.* Perceptions of advantages associated with no-till, among experimenters and nonexperimenters, 1982

| Advantage | Percent listing the characteristic as the "biggest advantage"[a] | | Percent listing the characteristic as "an advantage"[b] | |
|---|---|---|---|---|
| | Experimenters (N = 44) | Non-experimenters (N = 39) | Experimenters (N = 44) | Non-experimenters (N = 39) |
| Soil conservation | 59% | 67% | 75% | 70% |
| Time saving | 25 | 13 | 64 | 36 |
| Overall cost saving | 9 | 5 | 25 | 16 |
| Fuel saving | 0 | 3 | 27 | 21 |
| Equipment saving | 0 | 0 | 7 | 10 |
| Other | 3 | 5 | 16 | 26 |
| None | 5 | 8 | 5 | 8 |

[a]Percents do not add up to 100 because of rounding.
[b]Survey respondents were asked to list all of the advantages associated with no-till. These figures included farmers who listed the characteristic as the "biggest advantage."

benefits among both the agricultural specialists and the Kirkwood farmers.

## Soil Saving

The most effective tillage methods for controlling erosion caused by wind and water are those that leave large amounts of crop residue covering the field (Moldenhauer et al. 1983:144). No-till leaves more residue than other reduced tillage systems and is reported to keep erosion at tolerable levels for corn/soybean rotations on fields with slopes of less than 4 percent. On fields planted in corn every year, no-till can protect slopes of less than 6 percent (Moldenhauer et al. 1983:147). Nevertheless, no-till by itself is not a complete solution to problems of soil degradation on the hilly land characteristic of much of Kirkwood County. Except on very gently sloping land, most agronomists recommend that no-till be combined with other conservation measures.

Most Kirkwood farmers readily agree that no-till saves soil (see Table 3-1). A few, however, think that the chemicals associated with no-till will in the long run *increase* erosion by "sealing the soil" and lessening the amount of water that can be absorbed.

Table 3-2. Perceptions of disadvantages associated with no-till, among experimenters and nonexperimenters, 1982[a]

| Disadvantages | Percent listing the characteristic as the "biggest disadvantage"[b] | | Percent listing the characteristic as "a disadvantage"[c] | |
|---|---|---|---|---|
| | Experimenters (N = 42) | Non-experimenters (N = 37) | Experimenters (N = 42) | Non-experimenter (N = 37) |
| Weed problems | 26% | 30% | 39% | 49% |
| Poor yields | 10 | 5 | 14 | 15 |
| Herbicide and pesticide cost | 10 | 11 | 14 | 18 |
| Fertilizer placement | 7 | 8 | 21 | 10 |
| "Unsafe" | 2 | 8 | 9 | 13 |
| Emergence problems | 5 | 0 | 11 | 10 |
| Difficulty getting seed in properly | 2 | 3 | 2 | 10 |
| Unsuitability of farmer's land | 5 | 0 | 9 | 8 |
| Insect problems | 5 | 0 | 9 | 8 |
| Soil compaction | 0 | 2 | 5 | 10 |
| "No good in dry year" | 5 | 0 | 5 | 13 |
| "No good in wet year" | 0 | 3 | 0 | 5 |
| Difficulty obtaining planter | 2 | 5 | 2 | 5 |
| Other | 12 | 19 | 30 | 23 |
| None | 9 | 5 | 9 | 5 |

[a]Information is missing on perceived disadvantages of no-till in four cases.

[b]Percents do not always add up to 100 because of rounding.

[c]Survey respondents were asked to list all the disadvantages associated with no-till. These figures include the farmers who listed the characteristic as the "biggest disadvantage."

## Yields

When discussing the advantages of no-till, Kirkwood farmers most often mention problems related to chemical methods of weed control (see Table 3-2). Many farmers think that incomplete weed killing leads to low yields of no-till corn and, especially, beans. Weeds are a problem when farmers or hired sprayers have inadequate knowledge of proper methods of chemical application. They are also troublesome under certain climatic conditions. When spring weather is cold, no-till crops emerge later than those planted conventionally and are not as able to compete successfully with fast-growing weeds. Because most herbicides require water to be activated, in dry years no-till farmers run risks of incomplete weed killing and herbicide carryover (Gersmehl 1978).

A substantial number of Kirkwood farmers also report that problems with fertilizer placement have lowered their yields of corn and soybeans. They feel that the ability of a plant to use applied fertilizer materials, especially phosphates, depends on the incorporation of fertilizer well into the soil. Whether this is true is currently a matter of some dispute. While advocates of no-till farming have argued that fertilizer placement for no-till crops is not critical (Phillips and Young 1973:151), others think that injecting fertilizer may be preferable to the more common no-till practice of surface application (Fee 1983:258).

Although only a small percentage of Kirkwood farmers regard increased pests as a disadvantage of no-till (see Table 3-2), there is some evidence that pests can lower no-till yields. No-till in Iowa increases the number of wireworms, armyworms, cutworms, corn rootworms, corn borers, seed corn maggots, and stalk borers (Hinkle 1983:202).

*Expenses*

The energy cost per acre of no-till corn in Kirkwood County is not very different from that for corn grown conventionally. No-till requires considerably lower expenditures on fuel because fewer passes over a field are required and smaller tractors can be used. These energy savings, however, are usually counterbalanced by increases in the cost of purchasing and applying chemical herbicides and pesticides. Because no-till beans ordinarily require a greater application of herbicides than no-till corn, the cost per acre of no-till beans is usually somewhat higher than that of conventionally grown beans.

A Kirkwood farmer contemplating no-till must also consider equipment costs. Although government aid will cover the cost of hiring a neighbor to custom plant a few acres, extensive experimentation requires some cash outlay. Farmers must either buy a no-till planter (about $12,000 for six rows) or no-till attachments for a conventional planter (about $3,000 for six rows) or pay a neighbor to custom plant. Farmers switching entirely to no-till may eventually save on equipment by selling machinery used for conventional farming and by using smaller tractors. Few Kirkwood farmers, however, are now planning to abandon conventional farming entirely.

### Labor Saving

Because no-till eliminates plowing and cultivation, farmers switching partially or entirely to the technique can save considerably on labor costs. Gersmehl (1978:76–77) points out that this saving is more beneficial to some farmers than to others. He notes that the time saving is useful to, among others, part-time operators and dairy and feedlot operators who do fieldwork only as a sideline to their main enterprise of raising animals.

### Environmental Consequences of Chemical Use

No-till systems have several environmental disadvantages, although these are mentioned only occasionally in the soil conservation literature or by Kirkwood farmers (listed as "unsafe" in Table 3-2). The extensive use of herbicides in no-till may endanger the health of farmers and lead to increased chemical pollution of the water table and waterways. Chemicals may also change the physiology and development of crop plants so that the plants become more susceptible to pathogens present in low levels in the field. Furthermore, chemical-resistant weeds have evolved (Swanson 1981; Hinkle 1983).

### Managerial Complexity

Rural sociologists (Swanson 1981:2; Choi and Coughenour 1979:13–14), experts on agricultural chemicals (Weed Control 1983:197), and many Kirkwood County farmers agree that no-till requires more complex managerial skills than conventional farming. The reduction in the number of passes over a field gives a farmer fewer opportunities to correct mistakes. No-till is said to require a greater knowledge of soil characteristics and of the proper application of various chemicals than conventional planting.

Table 3-3. Acres devoted to conventional and no-till corn, 1981 and 1982

|  | Conventional | | No-till | |
|---|---|---|---|---|
|  | Mean | Median | Mean | Median |
| Acres planted by farmers using no-till in 1981 and 1982 (N = 19) | | | | |
| 1981 | 155 | 102 | 53 | 31 |
| 1982 | 169 | 125 | 60 | 50 |
| Acres planted by farmers using no-till in 1982 (N = 44) | 168 | 108 | 62 | 40 |

Some Kirkwood farmers think no-till is no more difficult than conventional farming, but still refuse to try the practice because it is so "different." Several farmers told me that they were "too old to change." These farmers knew how to farm conventionally and did not feel it was worth the effort to learn about another method which, while not necessarily difficult, might not be any better than the one they were familiar with.

## Risk

No-till farming in Kirkwood County in 1980 was quite risky. Because farmers could not really predict the financial costs or crop yields for no-till corn and soybeans, they were willing to make only small-scale experiments. As the decade progressed, however, the likely consequences of no-till corn planting became better known and some farmers were able to justify large-scale experimentation. Few Kirkwood farmers have tried no-till beans (mostly because of worries about the expense and adequacy of weed control), and the outcome of no-till trials with this crop remains quite uncertain.

In 1982 the risk associated with no-till corn was still sufficiently high that most Kirkwood farmers using the practice continued to plant the majority of their corn conventionally (see Table 3-3). A few farmers, however, planted over a hundred acres of no-till corn, and many said they were considering greatly expanding their no-till acreage. Only nine farmers surveyed planted no-till soybeans in 1982, none with more than thirty-five acres.

Michael Chibnik

*Table 3-4.* Percentage of farmers using conservation measures other than no-till, 1981 and 1982

| Conservation measure | Percentage of no-tillers using each conservation measure (N = 44) | Percentage of nonexperimenters using each conservation measure (N = 39) |
|---|---|---|
| Reduced tillage (other than no-till) in 1982 | 83 | 69 |
| Terracing in 1982 | 73 | 64 |
| No fall plowing in 1981[a,b] | 64 | 67 |
| Contour plowing in 1982 | 32 | 35 |
| Cultivating conventional corn once or less in 1981[b] | 61 | 26 |
| Cultivating conventional beans once or less in 1981[b] | 36 | 11 |

[a]"Fall plowing" refers to the practice of turning the soil after crops are harvested. This practice can result in much soil being blown away by wind.

[b]Farmers were surveyed in June and July of 1982. At that time they did not know how often they would cultivate their conventional corn and beans or whether they would fall plow. I therefore used 1981 data on these measures of conservation.

## Other Conservation Measures

Farmers weighing the costs and benefits of no-till compare the practice with other conservation measures such as terracing, contour plowing, and less drastic reduced tillage methods. No-till is sometimes used to replace other conservation methods (especially terracing) and does not necessarily save more soil than the methods it replaces. Table 3-4, however, shows that survey respondents experimenting with no-till differed little from nonexperimenters in their use of many conservation practices. Inasmuch as most experimenters were raising only a few acres of no-till corn, few farmers in 1982 were choosing *between* no-till and other conservation measures.

There is one striking way in which the conservation behavior of no-tillers differs from that of nonexperimenters: experimenters with no-till cultivate conventionally planted corn and soybeans considerably less than nonexperimenters (see Table 3-4). "Cultivation" is the loosening up of soil about conventionally grown crops to kill weeds or modify moisture retention of the soil. Frequent cultivation of a field makes it more susceptible to soil erosion. This difference suggests that the extent to which farmers think turning the soil is an important agricultural practice has considerable influence on their decision whether to no-till.

## Characteristics of Family Farms That Affect No-Till Decisions

The extent to which a particular cost or benefit of no-till influences the decision making of farm household depends on characteristics of both the household and the farm. Statistical analyses show that while several of these characteristics have significant effects on no-till decisions, no single one is of overwhelming importance.[5] In this section I describe pertinent socioeconomic and environmental variables and present survey data showing some of their effects on conservation decisions.

### Characteristics of Households

Because very few Kirkwood farmers live and work alone, agricultural decisions ordinarily affect several household members. For this reason decisions about no-till are often discussed by several people. Although one "principal farmer" (usually the male "head of household") may ultimately make most no-till decisions, the opinion of a spouse, parents, in-laws, and adult children can greatly influence choices. In examining how socioeconomic variables affect no-till decisions, therefore, characteristics of both the principal farmer and his household must be considered.

---

5. A stepwise multiple regression analysis was made of the effects of five seemingly relevant variables on a farmer's no-till acreage. The variables were age, education, total row crop acreage, presence or absence of off-farm work, and number of times conventionally grown corn was "usually" cultivated per year. There were weak, but statistically significant (at the .05 level) positive relationships between amount of education and no-till acreage and between total row crop acreage and no-till acreage. There was also a weak, but statistically significant (at the .05 level) negative relationship between the number of times a farmer usually cultivated conventional corn and no-till acreage. With the other three variables controlled for, neither age nor presence or absence of off-farm work had an effect on no-till acreage. These results must be regarded as suggestive rather than definitive because of the nonrandom sample.

Michael Chibnik

*Table* 3-5. Relationship between postsecondary education and no-till experimentation, 1982

| Postsecondary education of "principal farmer" | Number of farmers with some no-till acreage | Number of farmers with only conventional acreage | Total |
|---|---|---|---|
| Some | 22 | 9 | 31 |
| None | 21 | 30 | 51 |
| Total | 43[a] | 39 | 82 |

$\chi^2 = 5.72$, significant at .05 level.
[a]Information on the education of one survey respondent is missing.

*Education.* Principal farmers with postsecondary education were more likely to experiment with no-till in 1982 than those with less schooling (see Table 3-5). Moreover, in some households in which the principal farmer did not have much formal education, other household members (usually adult sons) had some college and were instrumental in a decision to try no-till.

The adoption of no-till requires that farmers drastically alter traditional practices. Nowak (1982:16) and others have argued that education enables farmers to learn new skills such as no-till more easily. Kirkwood residents learn much about no-till from written materials provided by soil conservation officials, agricultural extension agents, and chemical salespeople. While most farmers with postsecondary education are confident they can understand these technical documents, many of their neighbors who have not gone beyond high school find them intimidating.

*Row Crop Acreage.* Farm households devoting many acres to row crops were more likely to use no-till than their neighbors planting corn and soybeans on a smaller scale (see Table 3-6). This relationship holds even when education is controlled for. I am not altogether certain why this is so. Social scientists (e.g., Nowak and Korsching 1983:354) attempting to account for the positive relationships sometimes found between farm size and conservation behavior have argued that wealthier farmers are better able to afford soil conservation practices. This argument, however, seems to have limited application to no-till because the practice is no more costly than conventional farming. Furthermore, row crop acreage probably has only a modest

Table 3-6. Characteristics of experimenters and nonexperimenters, 1982

| | Age | | Total corn acreage | | Total soybean acreage | |
|---|---|---|---|---|---|---|
| | Mean | Median | Mean | Median | Mean | Median |
| Experimenters (N = 44) | 44 | 41 | 236 | 181 | 146 | 101 |
| Nonexperimenters (N = 39) | 48 | 48 | 136 | 100 | 137 | 100 |
| Experimenters with postsecondary education (N = 22) | 37 | 34 | 231 | 190 | 180 | 125 |
| Nonexperimenters with postsecondary education (N = 9) | 45 | 41 | 201 | 81 | 213 | 100 |
| Experimenters without postsecondary education (N = 21) | 49 | 49 | 240 | 180 | 115 | 90 |
| Nonexperimenters without postsecondary education (N = 30) | 50 | 52 | 105 | 99 | 99 | 81 |
| All survey respondents (N = 83) | 46 | 44 | 187 | 130 | 141 | 100 |

positive correlation with wealth in Kirkwood County because many farmers rely on livestock for much of their income.

The managerial complexity of no-till may be more relevant than its cost. Some farmers with only a few acres of corn and beans may not want to make the necessary effort to learn the details of a complicated new conservation measure.

*Land Tenure.* The relationship between land tenure and the use of no-till or other conservation measures is somewhat complicated. Some researchers (e.g., Hauser 1976; Nji 1980) have found that land-owners are more likely than renters to use soil conservation practices. Several writers (e.g., Napier and Foster 1982) explain this relationship by the greater likelihood of owners to reap long-term benefits from such measures. As Rogers (1982) points out, though, this argument is based on the somewhat dubious assumption that the operator rather than the owner is the key decision maker concerning soil use. David Ervin (1982) argues that confusion about who is the primary decision maker in tenancy situations may inhibit renters from trying novel soil conservation practices.

Even if owners are more likely to practice soil conservation than renters (Lee [1980] provides some nationwide data that do not support this claim), the owner-renter dichotomy is too simplified to be of much use in explaining the behavior of many farmers in Kirkwood County and other areas of the Corn Belt. In the Midwest it is quite common for a farmer to own some land and rent other land. More-over, many farmers do some "crop sharing" (splitting yields with a landowner) or "custom farming" (managing land for a salary and some-times a small cut of the profits). Of the farmers surveyed, 43 percent owned all the land they used, 6 percent farmed only rented land, and 2 percent either crop-shared or custom farmed exclusively. The remaining 49 percent farmed some combination of owned, rented, or crop-shared land.

Full-time owners in Kirkwood County are no more likely to try no-till than farmers in other tenure categories. My impression is that this is because Kirkwood renters or crop sharers are not the key decision makers concerning the use of no-till. Perhaps because of the novelty and somewhat revolutionary nature of the practice, many landlords either strongly encourage or forbid no-tilling by tenants.

These conclusions regarding land tenure are quite tentative be-cause information was not collected about the tenure of no-till fields of farmers using land in several tenure categories. These farmers may well be more likely to use no-till on land they own.

*Age of Farmer.* Some social scientists (e.g., Seitz and Swanson 1980) claim that younger farmers are more likely to adopt soil conservation practices because of the greater likelihood that they will be directly affected by the consequences of poor soil management. Others have argued that older farmers are more likely to practice soil conservation because of greater experience with the long-range problems caused by erosion (Pampel and van Es 1977) and a moral commitment to preserving the land for future generations (Buttel et al. 1981:407). Studies of the relationship between soil conservation and farmer's age have reached contradictory conclusions (cf. Buttel et al. 1981; Pampel and van Es 1977; C. Ervin 1981; Hauser 1976).

In Kirkwood County, when education and row crop acreage are controlled for, there is little relationship between a farmer's age and his propensity to experiment with no-till. The explanation for this in my view is the hope by most older farmers that someone in their family will be farming their land in the future. Even though older farmers may not be affected directly by failure to adopt conservation measures, many express the desire to preserve the land for their children or grandchildren. Moreover, many of these younger relatives already exert considerable influence on the soil management decisions of older farmers.

*Off-Farm Work.* Even though many male farmers working at part-time jobs such as carpentry, agricultural sales, and bus driving say that no-till saves them time, survey respondents experimenting with no-till were only slightly more likely to have outside employment (30 percent) than nonexperimenters (23 percent). Furthermore, survey respondents with off-farm jobs were no more likely to list time saving as an advantage of no-till (46 percent) than full-time farmers (52 percent). In Kirkwood County part-time farmers as a group probably have no less spare time than their many full-time farming neighbors who rely on cattle and hogs as a major source of income.

*Beliefs and Attitudes.* A farmer's beliefs about politics, appropriate farming methods, and environmental issues can affect his propensity to use no-till. Ken B., for example, will not take aid for no-till because he dislikes the government program with its requirement that soil

[107]

conservation officials monitor his fields. Richard W. refuses to use no-till because he believes that plowing puts essential nutrients back into the ground, while James P. worries about the effects of chemicals on the local water supply. Duane J., however, feels that the soil-saving aspect of no-till is so important that it outweighs all the disadvantages of the technique.

### Characteristics of Farms

No-till should not be used on all farms. Whether the technique is appropriate in a particular site depends on local crops, soil type, and other environmental factors (Schnepf 1983:134). In Kirkwood County crop specialization has little effect on the decision to use no-till. Although farmers generally agree that no-till is better suited to corn than soybeans, most grow both crops. Soil type and topography, however, have considerable influence on the decision to use no-till.

*Soil Type.* Drainage problems, soil wetness levels, structural stability, water percolation, surface soil texture, and impervious or restrictive layers in the profile are soil characteristics that reduce yields under no-till. A recent report (Cosper 1983) asserts that 43 percent of tillable acres in Iowa have soils not suited to no-till. Quite a few Kirkwood farmers recognize this and refuse to use no-till on some or all of their land because of soil with poor drainage.

*Topography.* Many Kirkwood farmers think that soil erosion is greater in hilly areas and that no-till fields in flatlands tend to be subject to flooding in rainy years. Until recently, therefore, most no-till in Kirkwood County took place in the hillier areas. As flatland farmers have become more familiar with no-till, however, they have begun to adopt the practice in larger numbers.

### Case Studies

Although some farmers in Kirkwood County are enthusiastic about no-till, most are unsure about the practice and are willing to experiment with no-till on only a small scale. There are also some farmers who have been disappointed with no-till after experimentation and a few others who are so suspicious of the technique that they doubt they will try it in the near future. In this section I describe in some detail the opinions about, knowledge of, decisions concerning, and experiences with no-till of three Kirkwood farmers. These case studies illustrate the range in attitudes in the county and the diversity of factors influencing the decision to use no-till.

### Dave L.—No-Till on a Large Scale

Dave L., who briefly attended Iowa State University, owns five hundred acres on which he grows row crops and raises livestock. He also crop-shares an additional five hundred acres owned by various relatives. Dave is about forty years old and is one of the wealthier farmers in the county.

No-till was brought to Dave's attention by a neighbor in 1977. Because of a longstanding interest in conservation, Dave was initially quite receptive to no-till. The time-saving feature of no-till also attracted him. Dave farms on such a large scale that he, his wife, and children work extraordinarily long hours during much of the year. Between 1977 and 1980 Dave read extensively about no-till and discussed the practice with neighbors, chemical salespeople, and soil conservation officials.

In 1980 Dave used government aid to hire a neighbor to plant fifteen acres of no-till corn. The only really difficult decision Dave made in this first year of no-till concerned chemical use. Dave worried about the effectiveness of no-till in controlling weeds and thought that a farmer could not use the technique successfully without proper herbicide application. He therefore learned as much as he could about herbicide use before trying no-till and made the unusual decision to apply all his chemicals himself rather than hiring someone to spray his fields.

Dave was generally satisfied with his first year of no-till and was pleasantly surprised to find fewer weed problems and lower costs with no-till than with his conventionally planted corn. His only disappointment was an increase in pest infestations. He decided to expand his no-till to fifty acres of corn in 1981 and to make certain changes in his use of pesticides. The major decision that Dave made about no-till in his second year of trials was to buy a no-till (slot) planter. In so doing, he decided against continuing to have his neighbor custom plant and modifying his conventional planter.

Dave was again quite pleased with the results of his second year of no-till experimentation and decided to expand no-till production considerably. In 1982 he planted 140 acres of no-till corn and 100 acres using conventional methods. He also planted eight acres of no-till beans, along with his 220 acres of beans grown conventionally. His major decisions in 1982 were which land to use for no-till and whether he should change his rotations as a result of no-till. Some of his neighbors think that soil erosion is not a major problem on no-till fields planted in row crops every year. Dave, however, decided not to decrease or eliminate fallow periods on his no-till fields.

When interviewed in August, 1984 Dave was somewhat less optimistic about no-till. His no-till corn had not done as well as his conventional corn in a drought in 1983, and his experiments with beans had not been successful. Dave had no immediate plans for further experimentation with no-till beans and planned in the future to plant about half of his corn conventionally and half with no-till. He felt that planting no-till corn year after year on the land he had would make the soil "hard as a rock" and so he advocated alternating years of conventional and no-till corn. Dave had also concluded that conventional methods were preferable on land subject to flooding.

Although Dave runs a larger farm than most of his neighbors, the kinds of decisions he has had to make about no-till are not atypical. The choices I have discussed represent only a small fraction of all those he made. Furthermore, I have not described the many important and complicated decisions Dave has made about his farm operations that have been based partially on the results of his no-till experiments.

### Jerry R.—A Cautious Approach to No-Till

Jerry R.'s principal source of income is livestock, but he also earns some money from his 150 acres of corn and soybeans and through the sale of seeds. He is in his late forties, is a high school graduate, and lives with his wife and four teenage children in a hilly part of Kirkwood County. Jerry has known about no-till since 1977, but is not especially well informed about the practice. He has, however, been worried about erosion and learned in the early 1980s about the government aid available for farmers trying no-till. In 1982, Jerry decided to plant twenty acres of no-till corn along with fifty acres of corn and seventy-five acres of beans planted conventionally. He said that he probably would not have tried no-till if the government aid had not been available.

Jerry was skeptical about no-till before using it, and his experiences in the spring and summer of 1982 did nothing to make him more optimistic. When interviewed in July of 1982 he complained about wireworm infestations, insufficient herbicide kill, and problems with fertilizer applications. His future plans concerning no-till were uncertain. There is considerable soil erosion on Jerry's land, and he recognized that his conservation practices of contour plowing, chisel plowing, and terracing had not been adequate. While Jerry thought he could control erosion by building new terraces, he preferred to use a less costly alternative such as no-till. However, Jerry said that if no-till yields turned out to be much lower than for conventional tillage, he would abandon his experiment.

In 1982 Jerry's yields from no-till were only about 60 bushels per acre, compared to about 120 bushels per acre for corn planted conventionally. He abandoned no-till after his one year of experimentation and began attempting to control erosion problems by constructing outlet terraces and using strip farming and various reduced tillage methods. However, when interviewed in the summer of 1984, Jerry was actually considerably more positive about no-till than he had been in 1982. He said it was a proven method and that his 1982 trial had not been a fair test because he had planted no-till considerably later than his conventional corn. According to Jerry, the major reason he was not no-tilling was that he did not have a suitable planter. Because Soil Conservation Service funds for no-till experimentation could be used only once, he no longer could use government aid to hire someone to custom plant. When the time came to buy a new planter, he would seriously consider buying one that could be used for no-till so that he could resume experimentation.

In many ways Jerry R. is a fairly typical Kirkwood farmer. He is close to the mean age of local farmers and has about the same income, assets, and education as many of his neighbors. Jerry's wait-and-see attitude toward no-till combined with his willingness to make a small-scale experiment with the practice are also far from unusual. He is, however, somewhat atypical in his fairly casual attitude toward his no-till experiment. Most Kirkwood farmers trying no-till have read a lot about the technique and say that they would have tried it even without government aid. Jerry, in contrast, seemed to have done little reading or talking about no-till prior to experimentation and tried the practice mainly because of the availability of aid. His lack of knowledge and interest may explain in part the problems he had with no-till in 1982.

## Jim B.—A Skeptic

After moving with his wife and four young children to Kirkwood County in 1976, Jim worked in a factory in a nearby county for several years. By doing so, he was able to save enough money to begin buying the 200 acres he now owns. Jim, a high school graduate in his early thirties, must earn most of his annual income from livestock because only half of his land is tillable, and all of it is hilly. In 1982 he planted 45 acres of corn and 40 acres of soybeans using conventional tillage methods. His income and assets are less than those of most of his neighbors.

Jim first heard about no-till at about the same time he moved into the county. Although he had not read much about no-till when interviewed in 1982, he had discussed no-till on several occasions with Soil Conservation Service agents urging him to try the technique on his hilly ground. Jim, however, had been unwilling to try no-till and was unsure if he would in the future.

Although Jim recognizes that no-till can save soil and time, these advantages are outweighed in his mind by numerous disadvantages. Jim has some quite "conservative" beliefs about farming. He thinks, for example, that turning the ground increases yields by "letting air in and returning organic material to the soil." Because of this belief, he cultivates his corn and beans at least twice after planting, which is considerably more than most other Kirkwood farmers. Moreover, unlike most of his neighbors, Jim rarely does any reduced tillage. Because he believes in turning the soil, Jim says he would use a slot (no-till) planter only if he could be sure that he would be able to continue cultivation.

This rather conservative approach to farming is also reflected in Jim's attitudes toward chemicals. He fears adverse environmental consequences from excessive reliance on herbicides and pesticides and is especially worried about chemical pollution of waterways. The increased use of chemicals associated with no-till disturbs Jim.

Jim's other major concern about no-till is the uncertain availability of slot planters. He cannot now afford to buy a no-till planter and worries that one may not be available for custom hiring at the exact time he wants to begin planting.

When Jim was interviewed again in 1984, his views had changed somewhat. He conceded that yields from no-till corn were often satisfactory, but continued to worry about the effects of chemicals. Jim doubted that he would ever use no-till because his need to feed his cattle led him to rotate corn and hay. This rotation, Jim felt, enabled him to control erosion without using dangerous chemicals.

## Recent Developments

The acreage devoted to no-till and the number of no-tillers in Kirkwood County in 1984 were about the same as in 1982. This leveling off can be attributed largely to unusual economic and weather conditions in 1983. Increased knowledge by farmers about the advantages and drawbacks of no-till, however, may also be relevant.

In 1983 the Payment in Kind (PIK) program of the federal government provided corn and soybean farmers with considerable incentives for taking land out of production. Many farmers in Kirkwood County, as elsewhere, stopped farming their least productive land. Because this usually was the rough, hilly land where most no-till experimentation had taken place, no-till acreage plummeted in 1983.

Extremely hot, dry weather in 1983 resulted in miserable yields for both no-till and conventional corn. Kirkwood farmers therefore were unable to learn much from their experimentation with no-till in that year. Furthermore, the financial losses many farmers incurred despite the PIK program may have led some to be reluctant to expand no-till experimentation in 1984.

With the elimination of the PIK program in 1984, the use of no-till increased on the hilly land brought back into production. However, there were several signs that the use of no-till might not continue to increase rapidly. Farmers interviewed in 1984 seemed more in agreement with one another than in 1982; the emerging consensus was that no-till often worked well for corn, but did not work well for beans or for corn under certain conditions. This consensus suggests that farmers may plant some, but not all, of their corn using no-till methods, but that they will continue to plant beans conventionally. While the number of no-tillers may well increase substantially, a large-scale switch to no-till seems unlikely.

The Soil Conservation Service in Kirkwood County no longer offers incentives to farmers trying no-till. Soil conservation officials feel that most farmers now know enough about the technique to make informed decisions. Although this is doubtless the case, the lack of incentives may discourage some farmers without slot planters from trying no-till.

[113]

Michael Chibnik

## Practical Implications

Despite the extensive publicity surrounding the introduction of no-till to the Midwest, the technique seems likely to have only a modest effect on the conservation practices of no-till farmers. In Kirkwood County the initial excitement concerning no-till is gone, and farmers now regard the practice as only one of several fairly good ways to reduce erosion. No-till has certain advantages that make it attractive to particular farmers using particular pieces of land, but also has disadvantages that make practices such as terracing or rotation preferable for other farmers on other pieces of land. Because no-till is often used instead of other equally effective conservation measures, its overall effect on erosion may not be too great.

Climatic and topographic conditions in Kirkwood County are probably more favorable to no-till than those in most other parts of the Corn Belt. No-till does not work as well in colder or drier areas (Gersmehl 1978) and is not as attractive in less hilly places. Thus over time use of no-till in the Midwest may be no more extensive than its limited, although significant, use in Kirkwood County.

The detailed examination of the use of no-till in Kirkwood County presented here shows why decisions concerning soil conservation are difficult to analyze. It is impossible to isolate one or two major factors having the greatest impact on farmers' decisions about whether to try no-till. Instead, a multitude of factors may affect a particular farmer's decisions about conservation. The holistic methods of sociocultural anthropology are well suited to describing these complications.

Some policymakers are pushing legislation making soil conservation a prerequisite to participation in state and federal farm programs. Framers of these and other laws designed to control erosion should consider the socioeconomic and ecological conditions that make soil conservation especially difficult for some groups of farmers. Without such an ethnographic understanding by policymakers, proposed laws may be inequitable and environmentally ineffective.

## Acknowledgments

Old Gold Summer Fellowships from the University of Iowa supported my research and writing in 1982 and 1984. I thank Michelle Ducharme, LuAnn Hudson, and Mark Swanson for conducting many

interviews with farmers in Kirkwood County and my class in anthropological data analysis for transforming field notes into a form
suitable for computer processing. Members of the Soil Conservation
Service of Kirkwood County provided much useful information about
local agricultural conditions, Peter Nowak and Marjorie Remacle-Tay-
lor helped greatly in my search of the soil conservation literature, and
Ralph Altmaier, Roger Sanjek, and Mark Swanson gave insightful
comments on an earlier version of this paper. My greatest debt is to
the farmers of Kirkwood County who took the time to answer my
many questions.

## References Cited

Berg, Norman. 1982. Discussion. In *The Cropland Crisis: Myth or Reality?* ed.
    Pierre Crosson, pp. 220–224. Baltimore: Johns Hopkins Univ. Press.
Brown, Lester. 1981. World Population Growth, Soil Erosion, and Food Se-
    curity. *Science* 214:995–1002.
Buttel, Frederick H., et al. 1981. The Social Basis of Agrarian Environmentalism:
    A Comparative Analysis of New York and Michigan Farm Operators. *Rural
    Sociology* 46:391–410.
Choi, Hyup, and C. Milton Coughenour. 1979. *Socioeconomic Aspects of No-
    tillage Agriculture: A Case Study of Farmers in Christian County, Kentucky.*
    Lexington, Ky.: Agricultural Experiment Station.
Cosper, Harold. 1983. Soil Suitability for Conservation Tillage. *Journal of Soil
    and Water Conservation* 38:152–155.
Crosson, Pierre. 1982. Future Economic and Environmental Costs of Agricultural
    Land. In *The Cropland Crisis: Myth or Reality?* ed. Pierre Crosson, pp. 165–
    191. Baltimore: Johns Hopkins Univ. Press.
Dallavalle, Rita, and Leo Mayer. 1980. *Soil Conservation in the United States:
    The Federal Role.* Report no. 80-144S. Washington, D.C.: Congressional Re-
    search Service, Library of Congress.
Ervin, Christine. 1981. Factors Affecting the Use of Soil Conservation Practices:
    An Analysis of Farmers in Monroe County, Mo. M.S. paper. Dept. of Geogra-
    phy, Oregon State Univ.
Ervin, David. 1981. Soil Erosion on Owned and Rented Cropland: Economic
    Models and Evidence. Paper presented at meeting of the Southern Agricultural
    Economics Association, Atlanta, Ga.
Ervin, David, and Robert Washburn. 1981. Profitability of Soil Conservation
    Practices in Missouri. *Journal of Soil and Water Conservation* 36:107–111.
Faulkner, Edward. 1943. *Plowman's Folly.* Norman: Univ. of Oklahoma Press.
Fee, Rich. 1983. Fertilizing: Is Injecting the Answer? *Journal of Soil and Water
    Conservation* 38:258.

[115]

Gersmehl, Philip. 1978. No-Till Farming: The Regional Applicability of a Revolutionary Agricultural Technology. *Geographical Review* 68:66–79.

Hauser, W. 1976. Soil Erosion Control in Western Iowa. M.S. thesis. Iowa State Univ.

Hightower, Jim. 1978. *Hard Tomatoes, Hard Times.* Cambridge, Mass.: Schenkman.

Hinkle, Maureen. 1983. Problems with Conservation Tillage. *Journal of Soil and Water Conservation* 38:201–206.

Hudson, Norman. 1971. *Soil Conservation.* Ithaca, N.Y.: Cornell Univ. Press.

Jolly, Robert, William Edwards, and Donald Erbach. 1983. Economics of Conservation Tillage in Iowa. *Journal of Soil and Water Conservation* 38:291–294.

Lee, Linda. 1980. The Impact of Land Ownership Factors on Soil Conservation. *American Journal of Agricultural Economics* 62:1070–1076.

Lessiter, Frank. 1977. No-Till Still Moving Ahead. *No-Till Farmer* 6:4.

Moldenhauer, W., et al. 1983. Conservation Tillage for Erosion Control. *Journal of Soil and Water Conservation* 38:144–151.

Napier, Ted, and D. Lynn Foster. 1982. Farmer Attitudes and Behavior Associated with Soil Erosion Control. In *Soil Conservation Policies, Institutions, and Incentives,* ed. H. Halcrow, E. Heady, and M. Cotner, pp. 137–150. Ankeny, Iowa: Soil Conservation Society of America.

Nji, Ajaga. 1980. The Application of a Conventional Adoption-Diffusion Model to the Adoption of Soil Conservation Practices by Iowa Farmers. Ph.D. thesis. Iowa State Univ.

Nowak, Peter. 1982. Adoption and Diffusion of Soil and Water Conservation Practices. Paper presented at an RCA symposium entitled Future Agricultural Technology and Resource Conservation, Washington, D.C.

––––––. 1983. Obstacles to Adoption of Conservation Tillage. *Journal of Soil and Water Conservation* 38:162–165.

Nowak, Peter, and Peter Korsching. 1983. Social and Institutional Factors Affecting the Adoption and Maintenance of Agricultural BMPs. In *Agricultural Management and Water Quality,* ed. Frank Schaller and George Bailey. Ames: Iowa State Univ. Press.

Pampel, Fred, and J. van Es. 1977. Environmental Quality and Issues of Adoption Research. *Rural Sociology* 42:57–71.

Phillips, Shirley, and Harry Young. 1973. *No-Tillage Farming.* Milwaukee: Reiman Associates.

Rasmussen, Wayne. 1982. History of Soil Conservation, Institutions, and Incentives. In *Soil Conservation Policies, Institutions, and Incentives,* ed. H. Halcrow, E. Heady, and M. Cotner, pp. 3–18. Ankeny, Iowa: Soil Conservation Society of America.

Rogers, Susan. 1982. Allocation and Use of U.S. Farmland: Ownership Categories and Soil Conservation. Unpublished paper.

Schnepf, Max. 1983. Why a Special Issue? *Journal of Soil and Water Conservation* 38:134.

Seitz, Wesley, and Earl Swanson. 1980. Economics of Soil Conservation from the Farmer's Perspective. *American Journal of Agricultural Economics* 62:1084–1088.

Simms, D. Harper. 1970. *The Soil Conservation Service.* New York: Praeger.

Soil Conservation Service. 1962. *Soil Survey, Kirkwood County* [pseudonym], *Iowa.* Washington, D.C.: U.S. Dept. of Agriculture.

———. 1977. *Soil: Iowa's Underrated Resource.* Des Moines: U.S. Dept. of Agriculture.

Swanson, Lou. 1981. Reduced Tillage Technology and Kentucky Farmers. *Culture and Agriculture* 12:1–5.

Taylor, David, and William Miller. 1978. The Adoption Process and Environmental Innovations: A Case Study. *Rural Sociology* 43:634–648.

Timmons, John. 1980. Protecting Agriculture's Natural Resource Base. *Journal of Soil and Water Conservation* 35:5–11.

U.S. Department of Agriculture. 1983. *Agricultural Statistics.* Washington, D.C.

Vogeler, Ingolf. 1981. *The Myth of the Family Farm: Agribusiness Dominance of U.S. Agriculture.* Boulder, Colo.: Westview.

Weed Control. 1983. *Journal of Soil and Water Conservation* 38:194–200.

# PART II

# Sexual Division of Labor

The sexual division of labor has long been of interest to anthropologists. Many ethnographic studies include descriptions of the different tasks done by men and women.

Explanations for the sexual division of labor in particular societies vary. Some authors stress biological factors such as the need for women in preindustrial societies to combine work with breast-feeding. Others assert that men have used their greater political power to force women to perform monotonous, unrewarding tasks. Many anthropologists believe that the sexual division of labor is to a certain extent arbitrary. They argue that some division of work is economically useful and that in all societies a sexual division of labor is an obvious way to allocate tasks. The assignment by gender of many tasks is economically unimportant and thus is "cultural" rather than "natural."

The two chapters in this section describe how changing economic conditions have affected the sexual division of labor on Iowa farms. Deborah Fink argues that the role of women has been transformed by increasing agricultural specialization and the expansion of agribusiness. Using archival and ethnographic materials, Fink shows that prior to World War II the diversified nature of farms allowed a production system in which men and women had complementary work roles. Women had responsibility for poultry, eggs, dairy cattle, and growing food for home consumption; men focused on cash grain crops. The expansion of agribusiness into poultry and the increasing specialization in cash crops, Fink points out, eliminated many tasks traditionally performed by women. Nowadays many women take off-farm jobs and "help men" in their farm operations.

[119]

Despite her agreement with Fink that "American women are not raised to be more than farmer's helpers," Tracy Ehlers notes that some farms are owned and operated by women. She reports the results of her research among Iowa farm women who are the primary decision makers in a family-based agricultural operation. Ehlers shows that most such women have been thrust into this position by forces beyond their control and describes the problems they face. Some of these problems arise from the attitudes and behavior of neighboring farmers; others are a consequence of the women's lack of preparation for certain farm responsibilities. Ehlers also speculates about sexual differences in management styles.

Neither Fink nor Ehlers attempts to explain the traditional sexual division of labor on midwestern farms. Their focus, instead, is on how and why work allocation patterns have changed. Both Fink and Ehlers see no improvement in the economic position of rural women and deplore the lack of recognition given women's agricultural work.

# [4]

# Farming in Open Country, Iowa: Women and the Changing Farm Economy

**Deborah Fink**
*Women's Studies Program*
*University of Iowa*

An eighty-two-year-old farmer told me, with the closest thing to overtly expressed anger that I saw during a year of fieldwork in rural Iowa, that his wife had never worked. He would be ashamed if she had had to work; he would be ashamed if he could not have supported her. He said that rather than working, his wife had helped with the milking, washed the cream separator, done the housekeeping, taken care of the chickens, gardened, and raised four children. As his account indicates, a good farm woman of this farmer's era "helped" her husband. She remained embedded in the family and did not seek recognition or money for what she did. Hence she did not work. Work was what men did. Yet women's work was an invisible presence on Iowa farms of the early twentieth century.

In contrast, the farm woman of the 1980s does few of the tasks her predecessors did. With the disappearance of the small dairy enterprise, women no longer have milking or separating chores. With the steep drop in the number of chicken and egg enterprises, women lost their poultry chores and their customary "egg money." With the demise of labor-intensive farming, farm women's cooking and cleaning chores have diminished to match more nearly those of city women. As a result of these changes, increasing numbers of farm women have taken jobs away from the farm.

*Deborah Fink*

Farm women, shifting from small-scale, household industry to wage labor, capital-intensive farming, or full-time housework, were part of a thoroughgoing economic transformation in rural Iowa. Because the traditional family farms had provided a work setting for the farm women, the change constituted a fundamental re-structuring of the farm economy. Yet because no one, either locally or nationally, female or male, evaluated women's work as being an integral part of the farm system, no one analyzed the effects of these changes in women's work.

In this chapter I analyze women's work and some basic changes in Iowa farming since World War II. Focusing on a rural Iowa area I call Open County, I present results of my research carried out during a year's residence on an Open Country farm in 1982.[1] From a feminist perspective, I consider the change in farm structure as it relates to women. This perspective can add to a general analysis of farming by correcting the tendency to ignore women's input. Although many researchers who have examined American farming focus on men as the farmers, those who disregard the contribution of women to the farm production system miss a dynamic aspect of Iowa farming. Talking to women was an essential first step in my fieldwork.[2] By including women's production for home consumption, their small egg enter-

1. Open Country and most other proper names are pseudonyms. The book *Open Country, Iowa: Rural Women, Tradition, and Change* (Fink, forthcoming) presents a broader analysis of the change in the economic and social patterns of Open Country women.
2. I interviewed forty-three women and five men. The interview sample was chosen to include a range of ages (twenty-six to ninety-nine), ethnic backgrounds, and farm and nonfarm occupations within the rural economy. Rather than use a random selection process, I contacted the interview subjects through personal networks. Some people refused to be interviewed, even when approached through friends and relatives; but I have no reason to believe that my findings were distorted in any systematic manner as a result. These interviews provide the backbone of my data and the source of the quotes in this chapter.

I also lived in the community and participated in the social life as I was observing it. As a participant observer I lived on a farm, worked with farm women on a variety of tasks, including housework, poultry work, and weeding soybeans. I relaxed and chatted with women in a bar and attended religious services. I attended a variety of meetings, including church women's groups, Farm Bureau Women, community betterment councils, Jaycee Women, and women's social clubs; I co-chaired an ethnic study committee for a local centennial celebration. In short, although I remained an outsider, I became well acquainted with a number of rural women and their day-to-day activities; this chapter is based in part on the insights from this interaction.

In addition, I had access to local sources on Open Country history, including records in newspapers; personal diaries, letters, scrapbooks, and household records; county extension files; and church records.

prises, and their nonfarm labor in an examination of a farm economy, we gain a more realistic picture of farm production than we do by examining only farm commodity production.

I begin with a brief orientation on the social structure and geography of Open Country. I then present the concept of a family farm economy, describing both subsistence and commodity components. I assess what the shift in this economy has meant for women's farming roles. I proceed to narrow the focus to women and the loss of their egg enterprises in order to provide a more detailed picture of one small part of the many-faceted change in Iowa farm production. Finally, I examine some of the new ways in which women have come to contribute to farm households. I contend that the change in women's roles has entailed a fundamental change in Iowa farming systems.

## Open Country

Open Country is the central part of a county in northwest Iowa. It is not a political unit, but was simply my sphere of interaction during my year of fieldwork. Lacking natural boundaries, the counties and townships of northern Iowa are laid out in blocks. A county has sixteen townships; each township has thirty-six sections of one square mile each. Open Country covers twelve of these townships. Within a township each section is delineated by a road, so that there is a neat, straight checkerboard of roads overlying the farmland. Open Country includes two small incorporated towns ten miles apart, a number of other unincorporated population clusters, and several hundred farms. The towns have farm service and supply centers, some retail establishments, schools through grade twelve, and medical and governmental services for the rural population. Major purchases of groceries, furniture, and clothing are made in small cities approximately twenty-five miles from Open Country. There are some small factories located in these cities, but the closest substantial industrial center is sixty miles away. Each of the two incorporated towns in Open Country has a population of approximately 1,000. Following the U.S. census definition, Open Country, including the two towns, is rural in that there are no population aggregates of more than 2,500.

Open Country was settled after 1880 by immigrants or first-generation Americans of Northern European descent. The population peak for the entire rural area was reached in 1940, although the farm population had reached its maximum five years earlier, in 1935. Since that time the two small towns have maintained their populations while the farm population has dwindled. Social interaction was made easier as cars became commonplace and country roads were improved to enable rapid, year-round travel. But social boundaries, like those for counties and townships, were always somewhat arbitrary as one national group blended into the next and social networks crossed county lines.

The natural tree cover in Iowa diminishes from east to west and from south to north. The few original trees in Open Country were close to the creeks; all other trees in the uplands were planted as windbreaks around farmhouses and in towns. Average annual precipitation is twenty-five inches. The land rises to the state's highest point near Open Country. The gently rolling land is composed of glacial drift and loess, making it well suited for growing grain, grass, and soybeans. None of the land is irrigated. The erosion-prone areas around creeks are usually left in pasture. Driving the roads, one sees clumps of trees around farm buildings. Grain elevators and water towers reach out of larger clumps of trees to mark the towns.

## The Family Farm Economy

Until recently most midwestern farms have operated under what Julie Matthaei (1982:30) calls a family economy: "In general, husbands took up commodity production, while wives centered in self-sufficient production, given that the former was production of wealth, oriented toward the market, while the latter was production to directly fill the needs of the family." On Open Country farms men were responsible for the production of livestock and crops, which were the wealth of the family; women tended and nurtured the people of the farm households. The traditional family farm is defined here as one on which most of the labor is supplied by the family of the person who owns and operates the farm (Goss et al. 1980:113). The family farm supplied the family members with their food and fuel, and the family members in turn constituted the workers for the farm. Women's part of the family farm economy was production to meet the needs of the family members, who constituted the major part of the farm labor force. In meeting these needs, women produced both for consumption within the household and for sale outside the household.

Women produced and/or processed most of the food for the household table, including vegetables, potatoes, sausage, poultry products, eggs, fruit, dairy products, lard, and baked goods. They constructed, laundered, and mended clothing for the members of the household. They also did a significant amount of work in coordinating the household, watching and tending the various animals and machines and making sure that people were doing what they were supposed to be doing. The presence of hired help in some farm households increased women's work. In fact, in the 1930s some hired men received only room and board in return for their work, and the farm women were responsible for cooking their meals, doing their laundry, patching their clothes, cleaning their rooms, and making their beds. The massive unemployment of the thirties had inflated the amount of labor available for farm production. Because farming remained a family operation, there was a certain obligation to maintain and adjust production to employ nonfarming relatives. Willard Cochrane (1979:123) refers to "a large, redundant, or underemployed labor force in the farm sector which did not appear unemployed because the individuals involved shared the forced leisure and the low returns from farming with other members of the immediate families with which they lived." Women bore major responsibility for the daily provisioning and nurturing of this swollen farm labor force. One woman, having read Cochrane's analysis, replied, "Forced leisure is a laugh!" While there was always more work to be done than people to do it, the low returns were very real.

There was considerable variation in the extent of reliance on women's home production, but there are indications that women's work was a substantial part of the household economy of the 1930s. Since women were considered nonworkers, no one was inclined to appraise women's production in monetary terms. During the depression, however, the Farm Securities Administration acknowledged the importance of home production for consumption and attempted to promote home production and processing of foods as a means of improving the economic status of low-income farm families. To this end studies were done and records kept for the first time, both to demonstrate to the farm families the importance of producing their own food and to demonstrate to the relief administrators that those farm people being helped were the industrious poor and not the improvident or shiftless. The data recorded were the basis for a number of articles and reports. One of the national surveys of home production undertaken in the

[125]

1935–36 year indicated that among farmers of "moderate means" (yearly income in the $1,000 to $1,250 bracket, somewhat above the median) the value of home-produced goods constituted an average of 45 percent of the net income (Monroe 1940:850). Stenswick (1939: 30,38), an Iowa State College researcher, found that in one Iowa county in 1938 the value of home production in farm households assisted by the Farm Securities Administration averaged $352.63, while they spent an average of $324.67 in cash.

But the precision implied in these figures is misleading. Even assuming that everything produced in a home can be enumerated, the criteria for assigning values to these products are ambiguous. The national survey done in 1935–36 did not specify what means were used to assign values (Monroe 1940). While the people who recorded the numbers must have chosen some criterion, it is doubtful that the farm people themselves evaluated their production in a similar way or even in any uniform or systematic way. Chibnik (1978:573) points out that there is a difference between market value and retail value of home production. One Iowa State home economist who worked on the studies in the 1930s acknowledges that the failure to grapple with this difference was indeed a weakness of the studies.[3] Stenswick (1939:18) noted the difficulties of even establishing valid market or retail prices in the 1930s in the face of the great variation according to season and geographical area. She utilized a very low retail price.

As Chibnik points out, there would be choices to be made between subsistence and commodity production even if the farmers themselves did not make the exact calculations the government agencies were attempting. However, the fact that women were the major subsistence producers and the insistence that women, unlike men, did not work buttressed the resistance among farm people to reckoning the value of women's production in the same units as men's. Women's work and men's work may not have been explicitly weighed off against each other because they were not the same order of thing. Families needed to eat, and they needed to get their bank books straight; but they may not have perceived these as competing goals, particularly because women were concerned with one and men with the other. The problem of this balancing will be taken up later in the chapter in the discussion of the poultry enterprises of farm women.

Women's concern for everyday maintenance of the house and fami-

3. Margaret Liston, personal communication.

ly did not preclude their involvement in production for exchange outside the household. Their traditional products were eggs, butter, and poultry, which were taken into nearby towns on Saturdays and exchanged at stores for groceries and dry goods. This bartering was a very common means of exchange before 1940. Typically no money changed hands. A woman would simply take her egg money in trade at a grocery or general store. She could also accumulate credit at the store if her egg trade surpassed her weekly needs. Charles, whose family had run a general store in Open Country, said: "Well, of course, everyone figured their butter and eggs had to buy groceries. Nobody paid cash. I can't remember anyone coming into the store and giving you a bill of goods and paying for it. If they brought cream and eggs, they'd apply the cream and eggs on the bill. Maybe there was a little too much. They'd just get credit for it." Other sources of income for Open Country farm women included cash from keeping boarders, from doing domestic work for pay, and for sales of baked goods, ice cream, and garden produce.

A farm journal article described letters written by farm women of the 1930s telling of many extra things they did to earn money during the hard times. These included custom processing of dairy and poultry products, catering meals, and selling a variety of homemade items (Swelling Farm Incomes 1933:220). Nor was the phenomenon limited to the depression years. Although women intensified their efforts to earn cash during the depression, most farm people seem to have taken it for granted that women were income producers in farm homes. My interviews yielded many descriptions of earlier farm women running such small enterprises as an egg-hatching service, boarding guests, and selling food and other homemade products. In 1914, before setting up the county extension service, the U.S. Department of Agriculture put out a request to hear from farm women on how the department could help them. In the report on these responses entitled "Economic Needs of Farm Women," women described the need for more ways to make cash in their homes, such as addressing envelopes during the winter. They wanted to know how to improve profits from home gardens, poultry, and butter making, and other "pin-money" occupations (USDA 1915:20). By 1940 7.8 percent of Iowa's farm women had jobs outside their homes (U.S. Bureau of the Census 1943:867). Yet the money made by women was (with some exceptions) kept separate from men's income, which was treated as capital for reinvesting in the farm enterprises or was applied to farm debts.

The money from poultry and eggs alone was a sufficient supplement to home-produced items to constitute an adequate budget for domestic needs in many homes. The poultry specialist at Iowa State College (later Iowa State University) in Ames kept yearly records on twenty-five to sixty individual poultry flocks across the state from the 1930s through the 1960s. Poultry producers signed up to participate in the program through county extension agents and received printed postcard forms on which to record such things as flock size, death loss, and egg production and to itemize their monthly expenses and receipts. They mailed these postcards to Ames each month and in turn received individual advice on upgrading their enterprises. The producers accepted into the program probably represented more prosperous than average farm people, but their accounts suggest the kind of money a well-run egg operation could yield. The records of the state extension service show average egg operations netting several hundred dollars yearly throughout the depression. In 1940, for example, the flocks recorded by the service yielded average profits of $456.48 for eggs.[4] Interviews consistently confirmed that groceries, clothing, and routine household items were purchased with poultry income, whether through barter or sale. What distinguished women's trading from men's was the use of the income for household sustenance rather than directly for the expansion of the farm operations.

Women's work was demonstrably central to the maintenance of the pre-1940 farm economy, but men's work on the farm was that which is more typically considered to be farming. Farming as an expanding, commodity-oriented operation was the impetus for settling Open Country as settlers followed the railroad and purchased the untilled prairie land in the 1880s. Women followed reluctantly. An early history celebrated "the man that scours the plow, that kills the weed, that saves the corn, that feeds the hog, *that buys more land*" (Peck et al. 1914:182, emphasis added). A successful farmer used his assets to increase his landholdings.

In 1940 Iowa farms were diversified, with income coming from corn and other grains, dairying, hogs, and beef cattle. Growth of the farm operation hinged on the profits received from sales of these commodities. Hogs, a major enterprise of farm men, were known as

4. Information from the State Extension Poultry Service, Iowa State University, Ames.

*Table 4-1.* Characteristics of a county of
northwest Iowa, 1940 and 1980[a]

|  | 1940 | 1980 |
| --- | --- | --- |
| Farm population | 8,883 | 4,331 |
| Number of farms | 1,986 | 1,390 |
| Average farm acreage | 180.6 | 264 |

[a]Data are for the county in which Open
Country is located. Data are fromth U.S ag-
ricultural and population censuses and the
Iowa Crop and Livestock Reporting Service.

"mortgage burners" because of their income-producing potential. Although many women, as a help to their husbands or other male kin,
did virtually any kind of farm work, they clearly distinguished capital
growth enterprises as men's work. As implied in the sentiments of the
farmer cited at the start of this paper, there was a stigma attached to
those families that required too much "men's work" of the women.

World War II provided opportunities for surplus farm laborers to
join the military or to find nonfarm work in the booming wartime
economy. The war gave impetus to a movement off the farm that
decreased Open Country's population by more than 50 percent between 1940 and 1980. In these same years the number of farms decreased by one-third while the average farm size increased according-
ly (See Table 4-1). What these figures indicate is that a number of
farmers acquired more land, while others found other employment
and sold their major farm holdings to the more successful competitors.

With this outflow of farm population, the farm production system
became less labor-intensive and more capital-intensive. Cochrane
(1979:325) provides a table indicating that nationally between 1940
and 1975 labor inputs into farming decreased by more than 50 percent
while capital inputs more than doubled. In Open Country this process
entailed a simplification of the diversified farming system and a drastic
decline in the number of farms with livestock and poultry. Rather than
the complex, diversified small grain, hay, corn and soybean rotations
of the earlier farming systems, 96 percent of the land harvested in
Open Country in 1982 was planted in corn or soybeans (ICLRS
1983:19, 31, 41). Dairying and egg production have nearly disap-

*Table 4-2.* Percentage of Open Country
farms with selected enterprises, 1940–1982[a]

| Year | Dairy cows | Hogs | Hens |
|------|------|------|------|
| 1940 | 94 | 90 | 94 |
| 1945 | 92 | 86 | 92 |
| 1950 | 84 | 87 | 88 |
| 1959 | 52 | 78 | 75 |
| 1964 | 39 | 72 | 51 |
| 1969 | 22 | 61 | 24 |
| 1974 | 13 | 47 | 11 |
| 1978 | 7 | 53 | 6 |
| 1982 | 7 | 45 | 4 |

[a]Data are for the county in which Open
Country is located. Data are from U.S. agricultural censuses and the Iowa Crop and Livestock Reporting Service.

peared, and far fewer farms were producing hogs in 1982 than in 1940
(See Table 4-2). A side effect of specialization was increased dependence on purchased inputs for weed control, soil maintenance, and
livestock feed, as the crop rotations and the complex interface of
different farm enterprises disappeared. The farmers of 1980 owned
more land and used more machinery and purchased goods and less
human labor to work this land than the farmers of 1940. The single
greatest increase in expenditures has been in the area of agricultural
chemicals, the consumption of which tripled in the Midwest after
1950 (Schertz 1979:285). There are also substantial outlays for fuel and
oil connected with increasing mechanization. The percentage of the
agricultural dollar going to farmers has decreased as nonfarm inputs
and product-marketing components have increased their shares (Goss
et al. 1980:97–98).

Women's work in providing food and other necessities for the farm
labor force diminished as the farm population decreased. Modern
conveniences such as electricity, running water, and processed foods
also simplified their work (Fink and Schwieder 1984:2). Men's farm
production, that oriented toward capital growth, expanded. To assess
the meaning of this shift in emphasis I turn now to a closer examination of women's work in egg and poultry production.

## Women and Eggs

An Iowa State Extension pamphlet of 1929 began its information on egg production with the following comment:

> Practically all the eggs produced in Iowa come from farm flocks. The farm flock is cared for and managed by farm women. The poultry industry of Iowa is a farm woman's enterprise. The farm woman is not only interested in eggs as food for her family, but also as a salable surplus product. With the money received from the sale of poultry products, she buys food and clothing, educates her children, and buys other essentials and meets debts. [ISES 1929:1]

Advice on egg production was directed toward women, and women were assumed to control the earnings. So closely was poultry work tied to women that older Open Country persons sometimes lumped it with housework and, as such, it was not considered real work.

As women's nonwork, poultry raising was not something Open Country people thought of as being comparable to men's cattle or hog operations. This was true notwithstanding its earning potential. Insofar as poultry raising provided income for the home, it was not like men's enterprises. But poultry required at least some capital outlay for buildings, and most successful producers used purchased chicks and feed. Even if poultry work was not really work, it represented some competition to men's enterprises. While I heard no stories of household squabbles over farm operation decisions, I heard a number of joking reports of how much men detested poultry. As early as 1894, two farm experts at the local Farm Institute (the forerunner of the county extension program) addressed "The Poultry Question" as follows: "They [the Institute planners] could not have made a worse selection for this subject; it is one that I am not at all interested in: I have not read up on the subject at all; not even read the poultry departments to the agricultural papers that I take" (*Open Country Bulletin* 1894). Another farmer added: "I presume you would not think a cattle man would have anything to do with ducks, [but] my wife got it into her head one time that she would like to keep a few ducks. I finally consented and she got her ducks. The result was the ducks began to raise Cain and I began to raise Cain and my wife being of a kind disposition sold the ducks" (*Open Country Bulletin* 1894).

Although poultry were raised on nearly every farm in Iowa before 1940, they were never considered worthy of the time of a real (male) farmer.

As poultry production became more scientific, one of the obstacles that the agricultural extension agents recognized as impeding the modernization of poultry operations was the reluctance of men to become involved. The 1931 *Annual Poultry Record Report* of the poultry extension specialist at Iowa State featured a split-frame cartoon. On one side was a truck with "New Era Poultry Farm, B. Bright, owner" painted on the side. The caption read, "Farm Man and Wife Operating a Good Poultry Unit." On the other side of the cartoon was a car with "Sideline Poultry Farm, J. Gloom, owner" painted on the side. This caption read, "A Little Help from the Husband Needed Here" (ISES 1931).

Despite the efforts of the farm experts, women continued to be the major poultry producers, as several surveys of farm task allocation during the 1940s revealed (Should Egg Money Be Mary's Share? 1942:140; Gough 1943:5; "Chickens?—That's Woman's Job" 1948:305). Sally, an Open Country farm woman born in 1937, gave a description that was typical of accounts of other women who lived on farms in the 1940s:

> [Mother] had 500 chickens. . . . Saturday afternoon you took the eggs to town and sold them and you bought groceries. . . . Later on I can remember that there was an egg truck that would haul them in. . . . She always made sure the egg money bought the groceries. If there was any money left over, we could get something else, but the egg money pretty well was grocery money. . . . Everybody had chickens then.

Farm women expected to make enough money to cover everyday household needs.

During World War II profits from eggs and cream rose. Through wartime farm programs the government urged farm people to produce the maximum amount of food for the war effort. Egg production was projected to be increased by 13 percent nationally (Thompson 1942: 61). The government provided price supports and agricultural extension advice on how to restructure production for war needs. Between 1940 and 1943 egg prices increased by 140 percent (USDA 1965:130).

In those years Iowa State extension records show that on average, income produced per hen increased from $1.36 to $3.56.[5]

The push to increase production occurred as farmers and hired men were enlisting and being drafted into military service. Farm labor became scarce. The combination of the labor scarcity and higher prices eroded some of the traditional distinctions between men's and women's farm work. In Open Country a farm labor advisory board placed women and children, as well as men, in farm jobs. On the other side, an article in the popular farm journal *Wallaces' Farmer* advised women to try to get their husbands to help them with their poultry work, even though this had previously been anathema to most men. The journal suggested that women show their husbands the cost accounts on laying flocks. These, the article assured, would "look pretty good alongside his ups-and-downs in cattle feeding" (Thompson 1942:61). Thus, even with the shortage of male labor, men were being encouraged to produce chickens and eggs, the appeal being that eggs were profitable. Still, the major share of the labor for poultry raising seems to have been provided by women and children throughout the war (More Chicks This Year 1943:118).

Before World War II most women's earnings were immediately consumed in the support of the farm households. Egg credit accounts were kept at stores, but there were few detailed records in farm homes. During the war, with greater profits, more women kept accounts. Rose, a farm woman, left a relatively complete account of her wartime egg and cream income and her expenditures. Part of her expenditures went for maintenance of her enterprise: these included wages for hired "girls" and payments for a brooder stove, chicks, fencing, and chicken feed. Other money went for the household: food, clothing, doctor bills, medicine, and home furnishings. Besides these items there were expenditures related to maintaining social ties within the kin group: paying for a daughter's wedding, buying gifts for family members, and paying the telephone bill. She also bought $633.75 in government bonds for her children. After these expenditures there was still a surplus of several hundred dollars, and the records do not make clear what happened to this money. Significantly, rather than greatly expanding or mechanizing her production opera-

5. Information from the State Extension Poultry Service, Iowa State University, Ames.

tion with the realized profits, she chose to invest in her children, buying them gifts, government bonds, and a wedding. As had traditionally been the case, women's money was spent on people rather than used directly as farm capital.

While World War II gave this boost to women's egg production, it also laid the seeds for its destruction. The need for large quantities of eggs for military uses provided the impetus for the development of the first factory-type production in eggs and poultry. Sawyer (1971:80) cited a report of 1943, which stated, "A decade ago the broiler factory was just a crazy idea of a few poultrymen. Today egg and broiler factories are classified [as] essential war industries." These new "egg factories" proved to be formidable competition for Iowa farm women, who were set up for shock and disbelief in the following years of sharp decline in profits. Even the laying flocks about which records were kept by the State Extension Service in Ames started to show losses in the 1950s. By 1955 the average net income on these flocks was minus 52 cents per hen.

The small egg enterprises of individual farm women added up to big business: Between the turn of the century and World War II, Iowa was the nation's leading producer of eggs (Baker 1945:570). This production shifted after World War II, and in 1959 California replaced Iowa for the first time as the leading producer of eggs.[6] Increasingly, egg production has shifted to the more densely populated regions, with fewer eggs being shipped long distances from the points of production (Schrader et al. 1978:14). The 1950s saw the beginning of vertical integration, which has now come to dominate the egg production industry. Vertical integration means that contract growers or large-scale, company-owned facilities may be served by a company hatchery and feed mill and that the same company may handle packing, trucking, and distribution. Horizontal integration has recently become more common as well, with one company owning several vertically integrated units (Rogers 1979:155–156). During the 1950s and 1960s much of the government-sponsored research on egg production centered on documenting potential economies of scale (Rogers 1979:164). The few truly commercial egg enterprises in Iowa had thousands of hens (U.S. Bureau of the Census 1981:159). The

6. Information from annual *Agricultural Statistics* (1945–65), published by the U.S. Department of Agriculture.

declining egg production in Iowa has thus been concentrated into fewer and larger enterprises.

The poultry record bulletin put out by the State Extension Service at the end of 1945 reflects some of the changes that occurred at the end of the war. Although there was no explicit mention of women being put out of the poultry business, most of the state poultry flock records were submitted to the extension research station in men's names after the War. At that time the extension required as a basis for selection for the record flock program that "both man and wife [be] interested in improving the income from poultry sufficiently to make changes in practices, housing or equipment" (ISES 1949/50). An enterprise run solely by a woman would likely be disqualified from participation. Before and during the war approximately half of the poultry records were submitted in women's names, but starting in 1945 only one of the fifty-five recorded poultry flocks was in a name which I could identify as that of a woman (ISES 1945). I have found no evidence that women were encouraged to upgrade their own egg enterprises at this time. Rose, who kept detailed records of her egg profits during the war, made fewer and less orderly entries after the war. Her last entry was made in 1946, although she kept her laying flock for years after that. I assume that her income was no longer substantial enough to require written accounting. In fact, the restructuring of the industry depended on the majority of producers eventually going out of business rather than upgrading their enterprises.

In 1955 a new law on candling and grading eggs effectively abolished the longstanding practice of selling ungraded eggs to small grocers for resale (*Des Moines Register* 1955:12). In 1962 a two-tier pricing system was established for Iowa eggs. Grade A large eggs produced under "quality and volume incentive programs" brought one price; Grade A large eggs labeled "other production" brought a lesser price independently of any difference in the eggs. In 1962 the price difference was only 3.2 cents per dozen, but by 1975 the difference between the two prices was 11.8 cents, a factor of approximately 30 percent of the lower price (Schrader et al. 1978:71).

The forces of modernization and progress had apparently gripped the egg industry, and the inevitable losers would be the many women who had been small producers and who lacked the necessary capital or access to financial institutions to develop their small businesses into large ones. Egg factories came to dominate the industry, the consensus being that large, coordinated, and mechanized production plants

[135]

could make efficient use of full-time hired labor and that this system would be superior to using the labor of individual farm women. One of the drawbacks to the continuing corporate takeover of farming has been the difference between production time and labor time. Because farm production is subject to the laws of nature, it has not often been possible to use labor efficiently on a year-round basis in farming (although migrant labor is used successfully in some areas). Through advances in genetics, disease control, and other technology, these factors have been largely overcome in egg and poultry production, thus making these enterprises more amenable to direct control by corporate capitalism.[7] Yet by the 1970s these large egg producers were running into trouble. Ralston-Purina was among the large companies leaving the business (U.S. Congress 1972:85). In the summer of 1983 the few remaining egg producers, some with operations as large as a million layers, appealed to Congress for protection from the brutality of the free market (U.S. Congress 1983:23). Congress then approved a measure that would allow for an egg board to establish egg marketing orders (or permits to sell). Through this system, if it is approved by vote of the existing commercial egg producers, the egg board would regulate the supply of eggs and thus even out the price. With marketing orders, producers would trade their freedom to expand at will for the security of a more reliable income. Ironically, the earlier farm woman might have been even more receptive to such a system than the larger producers of today, had Congress been concerned with stabilizing their industry earlier.

The larger picture was obscured in the information reaching Open Country during the 1950s. A Farm Home Supplement of the local weekly newspaper ran regular illustrated features on poultry production during this time, and these articles suggested that volume and mechanization were reasonable goals for farm producers. A typical article stressed that the man with the most efficient equipment would make the most profit (*Open Country Bulletin* 1952). For a time there was a hatchery forty miles from Open Country which sold caged layer units and feeding systems for hen flocks of 5,000, a number that proved much too small to compete in the reorganized egg industry (*Des Moines Register* 1966:1). The Extension Service did not give the people of Open Country a broad economic analysis of the factors of production and their place in the egg and poultry industry, even as it became increasingly clear that most egg producers would not share in

7. Susan Mann and James Dickinson (1980:301–308) discuss this process.

the big profits to be made by a few. The 1954 annual report of the Iowa State Extension's poultry service stated:

> Your success with chickens both now and in the future depends largely upon your attitude. If you like chickens and enjoy working with them you have the first essential to success. One of the weaknesses of Iowa farm producers is the attitude that chickens are not a satisfactory source of income. . . . Another factor underlies success. It's called integrity. Integrity of a person is his honesty to himself and to his fellows. The lack of integrity among farm producers or others within the poultry industry produces a lack of confidence in the industry. [ISES 1954:1]

Table 4-2 shows the eventual decline in the number of egg enterprises in Open Country. Because of the self-sufficiency and hence the sense of security women gained from their egg-producing enterprises, many kept them up, even after it was obvious that no money was being made. In 1964 more than half of the farms in Open Country were still producing eggs. Sally, whom I quoted previously about her mother's egg operation of the forties and fifties, told of convincing her mother to stop her egg production in the early sixties:

> I can remember when we finally got Mom talked into getting rid of her chickens. It just wasn't paying. She was paying more for feed than what she got for eggs and chickens and everything combined. . . . We just kept laughing, saying, "Mom, it's a losing proposition." But she always said, "What am I going to have for spending?" Of course, by this time it wasn't buying the groceries anymore. It was just a matter of some spending money for her. She said, "Where am I going to get my money from if I don't have my eggs?" And we said, "Well, Mom, this is so funny because it's a losing proposition. It's coming out of the farm income. You're going in the hole. You're not making any money."

Open Country women quit their egg enterprises only after going for years without making money. There is no evidence that they found it comfortable or "traditional" to be without their own sources of income.

## Open Country Farm Women and the Household Economy in the Eighties

One of the casualties of the increasing specialization in farm production has been the measure of self-sufficiency of farm households. Because most of the items such as eggs, milk, and poultry are no longer

*Table 4-3.* Percentage of farm women in the
labor force, 1940–1980[a]

| Year | Iowa | "Open Country"[b] |
|------|------|-------------------|
| 1940 | 8.3  | 7.5  |
| 1950 | 13.1 | 7.0  |
| 1960 | 19.3 | 12.1 |
| 1970 | 26.5 | 21.5 |
| 1980 | 39.4 | 26.4 |

[a]Data are from U.S. population censuses.
[b]Data in this column are for the county in
which Open Country is located.

produced on the farm, households have drastically reduced their consumption of home-produced items. Modern comforts and conveniences such as central heating, packaged baked goods, and micro-
wave ovens are now as commonplace in rural as in urban homes. All of
these have reduced women's work in providing the basic needs for
their households. Many Open Country farm women raise vegetable
gardens and sew some clothes, but no longer to a significantly greater
degree than do nonfarm women. The role of farm women in production for consumption needs of the farm labor force has now largely
merged with that of other women whose housework contributes to
care and feeding of the nonfarm labor force (Glazer-Malbin 1976:919).

With the demise of women's egg enterprises and their home production for consumption, some Open Country farm women have
sought nonfarm jobs (Table 4-3). Although the percentage of Open
Country farm women who have joined the labor force is not as great as
that of other Iowa farm women (a fact which I attribute to their distance from an industrial center and the consequent lack of job opportunities), they have certainly increased their participation considerably over the years. My interview sample included eighteen working-
age women who lived on farms and who discussed their past and
present work in depth. Six of these who were unemployed indicated
that they would have liked nonfarm work, given suitable pay and
transportation arrangements. Seven women had had nonfarm jobs in
the past but had not been able to continue, usually because their labor
was needed at home. Only three of them had reasonably permanent
jobs outside the farms at the time of my research, but seven of the
others habitually took part-time, temporary jobs such as bartending,
teaching swimming, and babysitting. It is difficult to categorize farm

women as in or out of the labor force because of their often uncounted work on the farm and because of their sporadic employment off the farm.

Farm women seeking nonfarm employment had difficulty finding it, even when they had college educations. The few available teaching jobs were widely sought, and the geographic limitations of a farm made finding teaching positions harder. Some schools were able to require informally that teachers live in the town where the school was located, an impossibility for farm women. One farm woman, a college graduate who was qualified as a recreation director, had worked in a retirement home for minimum wage. A few women were nurses, who could usually find employment, albeit at low pay. Within commuting distance there were also several factories that hired rural women as nonunion labor, but most women who worked there had left the farms. Other women worked for less than minimum wage. Because businesses doing less than $362,500 in yearly sales (and a few others such as restaurants and newspapers) were not required to pay minimum wages, there were women working in small-town variety stores and other businesses for less than minimum wage. In 1982 Open Country was saturated with women selling such things as cosmetics, vitamins, and home decorations from their homes.

In 1979 the average white Iowa farm woman with an income earned $3,926, compared to $11,494 for a white farm man, $5,089 for a white urban woman, and $13,104 for a white urban man (U.S. Bureau of the Census 1983:76). The low incomes translate to a high incidence of poverty. In 1979 15.6 percent of the white people on Iowa farms were living in poverty (U.S. Bureau of the Census 1983:78). This level of poverty is significantly higher than that of urban areas, where 8.5 percent of Iowa's whites were living in poverty (U.S. Bureau of the Census 1983:78), but even this comparison understates the difference. Based on the assumption that farms were to some degree self-sufficient, the farm poverty threshold was set at 85 percent of the nonfarm figure. Beginning in March, 1982, this distinction was eliminated because most farms no longer provide significantly greater amounts of home-grown food or fuel than do nonfarm households (U.S. Bureau of the Census 1982:5). Future computations of poverty among the Iowa farm population will probably show a higher incidence of poverty.[8] We can

8. Ironically, the "farm crisis" of the 1980s may lessen the poverty level on Iowa farms because a number of marginally profitable farm operations may be lost. Hence these people, while still poor, would no longer be counted among the farm population.

assume that the nonfarm income of farm women, although inadequate by most standards, has become a necessity in most farm households in which women have such income.

Most of the farm women in Open Country occasionally do some farm work. They haul corn and soybeans from the fields during harvest, weed soybeans, run errands, and do bookkeeping. Agricultural agents have been encouraging farm women to learn to use computers as computer programs for farm decision making are being developed. Six of the eighteen working-age farm women I interviewed do substantial outdoor farm work on a regular basis. Some do tractor work such as disking and cultivating; a few drive combines; others take care of animals; only one does seeding. While a majority of U.S. farm women do some bookkeeping for the farm, only a minority ever do any fieldwork, make major farm purchases, market commodities, or supervise farm labor (Jones and Rosenfeld 1981:18).

Rather than maintaining separate enterprises as did the women with egg businesses, many farm women of the eighties contribute directly to the capital growth of the farms. Articles on farm women today often depict the farm woman as a "full partner" of her husband (Erb 1984). This has different meanings. For some, it means that an increasing share of the farm assets are put in the woman's name. In a few instances it means that women are in the fields doing a large part of the labor of raising crops. In other cases it means that the couple makes decisions jointly. In every instance I have observed of men and women farming jointly there has been a division of labor, expertise, and control. Only if the man was extremely disabled did the woman participate equally in or in fact do most of the work of the farm enterprise. Interestingly, almost all of the women working on farms with their husbands say they are "helping" their husbands or working for them, rather than claiming their own share in the farm operation. Sally, whose mother was forced out of her egg enterprise, said,

Well, you know, the chickens are gone and as far as feeding the hogs or the cattle, the men do that. . . . As far as earning more money, I felt I could save us more money by working for Frank [her husband] than I could earn if I went out and got a job. . . . If Frank would've had to pay someone for all those hours, that would be a lot of money. . . . So really, for a farm wife, if she gets out and helps her husband, I'm sure she can save more than what she can earn.

Women's work options are now expressed in terms of money, not in terms of any particular use value. The emerging sexual division of labor seems to be between manager and laborer rather than between subsistence and commodity production. The husband-wife relationship softens the antagonism that might arise between management and laborer, but it does not eliminate it in most instances.


## Conclusion

The family farm has changed so that women and men no longer work in an interlocking, complementary production system. Women, once an integral part of the system when they provided for the daily needs of the farm labor force through home production and sales of farm produce such as eggs and poultry, now provide for their families through nonfarm jobs and "men's work" on the farms. Thus some women are more directly involved in the men's side of the farm operation than they were previously, but they no longer play a role as producers of a qualitatively different sort from men. Many are, instead, working for their husbands. In many farm households, the concept of a family farm economy no longer applies because a large and growing share of the income comes from nonfarm sources. It is not enlightening to subsume the work of farm women under that of their husbands because their work has been different.

Because of the fundamental changes that have occurred in the organization of what is still called a family farm, I concur with those who doubt that the family farm concept can provide a constructive, nonexploitative model for policy development. These include Goss and coauthors (1980:97), who see the family farm as an "unenlightening conceptual apparatus," Davis (1980:147), who assesses the family farm as an ideology that facilitates agrarian social control; and Hedley (1981:74), who contends that the family farm ideology exploits women and children. Elsewhere I have addressed the ambiguity of the meaning of "family" as applied to the family farm (Fink 1984). Confusing the analysis is the commonly cited contrast between family farming and corporate farming and the resulting polemics. Although a proper discussion of this issue goes beyond the scope of this chapter, I submit that this is casting the debate in terms that are too narrow and misleading.

[141]

Deborah Fink

Because farm people as well as farm planners have not fully understood the importance of women's subsistence production, they have not sought to preserve or reward it. They have not even called it work. Women, still invisible on the farms, continue to contribute, but in new ways. Their interests lie in increasing measure in the nonfarm economy as well as in the farm economy. It is to the benefit first of farm women and second to their families as well as to the society at large that we recognize women's unique history and current status as workers.

## Acknowledgments

I thank Michael Chibnik, Christie Dailey, Walter Goldschmidt, Rebecca Henderson, and Dorothy Schwieder for their critical comments on drafts of this chapter. Leonard Eggleton and William Owings of the Poultry Extension Service at Iowa State University provided access to egg reports and discussed the egg industry in Iowa with me, and I thank them. I am also very grateful for the moral and material support that Horace and Mary Autenrieth and A. M. Fink provided throughout the period of study.

## References Cited

Baker, R. L. 1945. The Growth of Iowa's Poultry Industry. *Iowa Department of Agriculture Year Book* 46:569–574.

Chibnik, Michael. 1978. The Value of Subsistence Production. *Journal of Anthropological Research* 34:561–576.

"Chickens?—That's Woman's Job." 1948. *Wallaces' Farmer* 73:805.

Cochrane, Willard W. 1979. *The Development of American Agriculture: A Historical Analysis*. Minneapolis: Univ. of Minnesota Press.

Davis, John E. 1980. Capitalist Agricultural Development and the Exploitation of the Propertied Laborer. In *The Rural Sociology of the Advanced Societies*, ed. Frederick H. Buttel and Howard Newby, pp. 133–154. Montclair, N.J.: Allanheld, Osmun.

*Des Moines Register*. 1955. July 6, p. 12.

*Des Moines Register*. 1966. Home and Family section, Dec. 18, p. 1.

Erb, Gene. 1984. Experts See Expanding Role for Farm Women. *Des Moines Register*, Sept. 9.

Fink, Deborah. 1984. Rural Women and Family in Iowa. *International Journal of Women's Studies* 7:57–69.

————. Forthcoming. *Open Country, Iowa: Rural Women, Tradition and Change*. Albany: State Univ. of New York Press.

Fink, Deborah, and Dorothy Schwieder. 1984. Iowa Farm Women in the 1930s: A Reassessment. Paper presented at a conference entitled American Farm Women in Historical Perspective, Las Cruces, N. Mex.

Glazer-Malbin, Nona. 1976. Housework. *Signs* 1:905–922.

Goss, Kevin F., Richard D. Rodefeld, and Frederick Buttel. 1980. The Political Economy of Class Structure in U.S. Agriculture: A Theoretical Outline. In *The Rural Sociology of the Advanced Societies*, ed. Frederick H. Buttel and Howard Newby, pp. 83–132. Montclair, N.J.: Allanheld, Osmun.

Gough, Phyllis Elvira. 1943. Tasks Done by 100 Iowa State College Freshmen Women Living on Farms during 1942 in Iowa and Surrounding States. M.S. thesis. Iowa State College, Ames.

Hedley, Max. 1981. Relations of Production of the "Family Farm": Canadian Prairies. *Journal of Peasant Studies* 9:71–85.

Iowa Crop and Livestock Reporting Service (ICLRS). 1981. *Iowa Agricultural Statistics 1980*. Des Moines: Iowa Dept. of Agriculture.

————. 1983. *Iowa Agricultural Statistics*. Des Moines: Iowa Dept. of Agriculture.

Iowa State Extension Service (ISES). 1929. *A Project of Marketing and Nutrition Related to Eggs*. Iowa State College, Ames.

————. 1931. *Poultry Record Report 1931*. Iowa State College, Ames.

————. 1945. *Iowa Demonstration Record Flocks*. Iowa State College, Ames.

————. 1949/50. *Plan of Work*. Iowa State College, Ames.

————. 1954. *Report, Iowa Poultry Demonstration Flocks 1953–54*. Iowa State College, Ames.

Jones, Calvin, and Rachel A. Rosenfeld. 1981. *American Farm Women: Findings from a National Survey*. Report no. 130. Chicago: National Opinion Research Center.

Mann, Susan A., and James A. Dickinson. 1980. State and Agriculture in Two Eras of American Capitalism. In *The Rural Sociology of the Advanced Societies*, ed. Frederick H. Buttel and Howard Newby, pp. 283–325. Montclair, N.J.: Allanheld, Osmun.

Matthaei, Julie A. 1982. *An Economic History of Women in America: Women's Work, the Sexual Division of Labor, and the Development of Capitalism*. New York: Schocken.

Monroe, Day. 1940. Patterns of Living of Farm Families. In *Farmers in a Changing World: The Yearbook of Agriculture 1940*, pp. 848–869. Washington, D.C.: U.S. Dept. of Agriculture.

More Chicks This Year. 1943. *Wallaces' Farmer* 68:118.

*Open Country Bulletin* [pseudonym]. 1894. April 18.

*Open Country Bulletin* [pseudonym]. 1952. Farm and Home Supplement, May 14.

Peck, J. L. E., O. H. Montzheimer, and William J. Miller. 1914. *Past and Present of O'Brien and Osceola Counties, Iowa*. Indianapolis: B.F. Bowen.

Rogers, George B. 1979. Poultry and Eggs. In *Another Revolution in U.S. Farming?* ed. Lyle P. Schertz et al. Agricultural Economic Report no. 441, pp. 148–189. Washington, D.C.: U.S. Dept. of Agriculture.

Sawyer, Gordon. 1971. *The Agribusiness Poultry Industry: A History of Its Development.* New York: Exposition Press.

Schertz, Lyle P. 1979. The North Central. In *Another Revolution in U.S. Farming?* ed. Lyle P. Schertz et al. Agricultural Economic Report no. 441, pp. 277–302. Washington, D.C.: U.S. Dept. of Agriculture.

Schrader, Lee F., et al. 1978. *The Egg Subsector of U.S. Agriculture: A Review of Organization and Performance.* North Central Research Publication no. 258. Purdue Univ. Agricultural Experiment Station, West Lafayette, Ind.

Should Egg Money Be Mary's Share? 1942. *Wallaces' Farmer* 67:140.

Stenswick, Mildred L. 1939. Farm Security Studies. I. Certain Home Management Practices of 73 Families in Union County, Iowa. M.S. thesis. Iowa State College, Ames.

Swelling Family Incomes. 1933. *Wallaces' Farmer* 58:220.

Thompson, Arthur T. 1942. Also Let's Keep 'Em A-Laying. *Wallaces' Farmer* 67:61.

U.S. Bureau of the Census. 1943. *Sixteenth Census of the United States: 1940.* Population. Vol. 3, *The Labor Force.* Pt. 3, Iowa–Montana. Washington, D.C.

———. 1981. *1978 Census of Agriculture.* Vol. 1, *State and County Data.* Pt. 15, Iowa. Washington, D.C.

———. 1982. *Characteristics of the Population below the Poverty Level: 1980.* Current Population Reports, ser. P-60, no. 133. Washington, D.C.

———. 1983. *1980 Census of the Population.* Vol. 1, *Characteristics of the Population.* Ch. C, General Social and Economic Characteristics. Pt. 17, Iowa. Washington, D.C.

U.S. Congress, Senate, Committee on Agriculture. 1972. *Egg Industry Adjustment Act,* hearing before the Subcommittee on Agricultural Production, Marketing and Stabilization of Prices of the Committee on Agriculture, on S. 2895, 92nd Congr., 2d sess.

———. 1983. *Egg Handling Regulations,* hearing before the Subcommittee on Agricultural Production, Marketing and Stabilization of Prices of the Committee on Agriculture, on S. 1368, 94th Cong., 1st sess.

U.S. Department of Agriculture (USDA). 1915. *Economic Needs of Farm Women.* Report no. 106. Washington, D.C.

———. 1946–65. *Agricultural Statistics* (annual publications). Washington, D.C.

———. 1965. *Prices Received by Farmers for Chickens, Turkeys, and Eggs.* Statistical Bulletin no. 357. Crop Reporting Board. Washington, D.C.

# [5]

# The Matrifocal Farm

### Tracy Bachrach Ehlers

*Department of Anthropology*
*University of Colorado*

In recent years, social scientists have shown increasing interest in the role of women in agriculture (Deere and de Leal 1981; Chaney and Schmink 1976; Staudt 1979). Their studies have shown that in many parts of the developing world, women work primarily as subsistence food producers, while men are involved in the production of cash crops for urban and international markets (Boserup 1970). The ramifications of this sexual division of labor have been to severely dichotomize male and female producers. As Boserup has noted: "Unfortunately, it is precisely when only men take the step from family production to specialized production—while women continue to work for the family only—that the problem of women's contribution to the local and national economy becomes acute" (Boserup and Liljencrantz 1975:12). The reasons for this dichotomy are clear. Although women in developing countries do a large share of the agricultural work, they have little access to capital, efficient methods, or modern tools (Tinker 1976). Only men are taught how to apply scientific methods and are given access to credit for machinery, fertilizers, and seed—all for the production of crops to be sold rather than consumed in the home. As men have contributed to and profited from the commercial farm economy, women have remained in the subsistence sector, where in many cases they are no longer able to meet the nutritional needs of their families (or in more and more cases their communities).

Several authors suggest that at the heart of this problem lies the western assumption that agricultural production is, or should be, a strictly male domain. For example, Margaret Mead (1976:10) notes that the American tendency to associate food production with males and food processing with females has had "disastrous" effects. American farm women have been stereotyped as playing only a supportive or secondary role in production, while at the same time a strong emphasis has been placed on their domestic responsibilities. Consequently, they have been excluded from federal and state agricultural programs and often limited to County Extension Service training in home economics. Their agricultural labor has been largely ignored. Sachs's 1983 study shows that although American women have worked for centuries as farmers, laborers, and subsistence producers, their work has seldom been recognized. Ultimately, this western bias has been transferred to developing countries as part of the modernization process. Boserup observes: "The lack of training of women in agriculture in countries where agricultural training is offered to men is derived from the general belief—shared by most agricultural experts—that agriculture with female labour is backward and that female labour should if possible be replaced by male labour when agriculture is modernized" (1975:15). International agencies thus make assumptions about the value of women's work that effectively segregate them from development and from access to resources.

If the precedent for this pattern does indeed originate in an under-assessment of the importance of women in the American farm system, then we are fortunate that work has begun to redress the problem at home. Challenged in part by Frances Hill's call to "recognize, respect and remunerate" America's "invisible farmers" (1981), writers have begun to document the participation of women on farms and ranches in many states (Gladwin 1982; Sachs 1983) and in Canada (Kohl 1976). In this chapter, based on my research in Iowa in 1983, I argue that North American women continue to play a subordinate role in farming, even though, like their Third World counterparts, they participate in a broad range of tasks and responsibilities. I further propose that when the death or injury of a spouse abruptly thrusts the "farmer's wife" into the role of farm manager, the handicaps placed upon her by our economic and social systems become all too evident.

In her 1979 study, Pearson (1979) described four types of farm women:

1. The supportive homemaker who might have an off-farm job
2. The seasonal helper, a one-woman surplus labor supply
3. The "farm partner," part of a new and growing group who work alongside their husbands

4. The farm operator independent of male farmers

My emphasis in this research has been on this last category, women who are primary decision makers in a family-based agricultural operation—the "matrifocal farm."[1]

For many years, the contributions of female farmers have been remarkably hidden in rural culture, unrecognized and discounted by policy makers, administrators, and researchers.[2] The purpose of my study was to illuminate these women's contributions by documenting and analyzing their lives and work. Research began in January 1983 in Iowa, where I gathered the names of 144 female farmers for interviews and surveys and selected a core group of twelve for in-depth questioning and participant observation over the course of the agricultural cycle.[3] Together these two groups make up approximately 5 percent of the more than 3,000 matrifocal farms in Iowa (U.S. Bureau of the Census 1981). I selected Iowa as the research site because it seemed to be the consummate agricultural state, consistently ranking first or second in the country in agricultural exports and production of crops and livestock. The women of the core group were chosen because their farms are typical of the state's agricultural profile. They are involved in feed grain production, raising swine (both feeder pigs and farrow-to-finish), cow-calf and purebred cattle operations, dairying (grades A and B), heifer replacement, and raising sheep.[4] The twelve

1. I am indebted to Michael Whiteford, Department of Sociology and Anthropology, Iowa State University, for coining the term *matrifocal farm*.

2. The United States Department of Agriculture did not ask the gender of farmers until its 1978 agricultural census. According to those figures, 128,170, or 5 percent of all American farmers are women (U.S. Bureau of the Census 1981). Skepticism about the reliability of census data on females abounds in the social scientific literature (Benería 1982:124). Unfortunately, we have no other statistics than those of the Census Bureau. The U.S. Department of Agriculture, however, surveyed 2,509 American women living on farms; 55 percent of these women considered themselves "one of the primary operators" of their farms. Thus there seems to be significant room for scrutiny of so small a national count as 5 percent (Jones and Rosenfeld 1981). Somewhere between those two figures lies an accurate tally of women agriculturalists, who may indeed be hidden behind the customary ascription of "women's work" but who are farming nonetheless.

3. My fieldwork in Iowa lasted approximately ten months so that I could observe as much as possible of the yearly agricultural and livestock activities. The availability sample I used in the study was drawn from data supplied by ninety-nine County Cooperative Extension directors whom I asked for the names and addresses of women in their counties farming on their own.

4. Farmers who specialize in feeder pig operations buy pigs after they are weaned— at about 60 pounds—and then fatten them for sale to meat packers. Farrow-to-finish

women in the core group farm in several regions of Iowa and differ with respect to age, marital status, and affluence.

In the sections that follow, I examine what happens when women become farmers on matrifocal farms. Using case materials, I demonstrate that most farm women are unprepared for what is for some an inevitable responsibility. Names and locations have been changed to insure privacy. My approach is often anecdotal and occasionally speculative. My goal here is to impart some of the flavor of the matrifocal farm.


## Male and Female Farmers

Rural tradition dictates that farms pass from fathers to sons. On farms across North America, young boys sometimes become middle-aged men under the tutelage (and often domination) of their fathers (Kohl 1976). The process of male transference of ownership and control on the farm is well captured in Kramer's (1981:18) description of his interview of an old, ailing ex-farmer in Massachusetts: "'I don't have much left to do but enjoy what I see out the window.' Then he sat me down and fed me tea, and after much discussion of a great many topics, he pointed out the window by the recliner, out into the cornfield where his son Leland still labored and said, 'Any old farmer would like looking out and seeing his son at work.'" Despite the relatively romantic notion of the constancy and tenure of a family's land, father-son farming is often fraught with generational conflict and rivalry, which are exacerbated in difficult economic times. Nonethe-

---

farms include feeder operations, but the farmers also maintain sows and boars for breeding. Once litters are produced (or "farrowed") the farrow-to-finish farmers carry through with fattening the swine to a marketable weight. Farmers with cow-calf operations typically keep herds of breeder beef cows for the production of calves, utilizing either resident bulls or artificial insemination to impregnate the cows. Calves are raised on the farm until they reach 400 to 600 pounds, at which point they are sold to feedlots for fattening. Operators specializing in purebred cattle raise one kind of breed stock (e.g., Angus, Hereford) to sell to cow-calf farmers who wish to replenish their herds. Grade A milk is produced for the fresh consumption market. Farmers who milk for grade A dairies are subject to careful regulation, inspection, and standards. Grade B milk producers have a less rigid inspection system because the milk is used in manufactured dairy products such as cheese and ice cream. (It is also sold at a lower price.) Farmers with heifer replacement operations buy newborn dairy heifers (usually at auction) to raise and sell to replenish dairy herds with mature milk cows.

less, the notion persists that sons will inherit the farm after years of dutiful assistantship, daughters notwithstanding.

Expectations for daughters' roles on the farm have varied widely over time. In this century, women have been expected to handle domestic responsibilities and also to be part of a reserve labor force. Economic exigencies have demanded that girls garden, can fruits and vegetables, milk the cows, collect the eggs, and raise animals for home consumption, and also assist in child care and domestic chores. Many girls trailed along after their fathers, day after day, working with them, mastering the logic of successful farming just as their brothers did, with no possibility of inheriting land.

However familiar girls may be with the farm routine, even today daughters are rarely primed to take over farm management. If a daughter does inherit land, it is usually with the unspoken codicil that she marry a farmer, most likely someone who is not in line to inherit his own farm. In general, rural women who own land rarely farm it (Salamon and Keim 1979). Rather, a woman typically transfers that authority from one male, her father, to another, her husband. Sometimes widows effectuate this transfer by immediately deeding over their property to their married daughters or sons, thus preventing themselves from ever entering the male domain of agricultural ownership or management.

In short, North American women are not raised to be more than farmers' helpers, the assumption being that even if women own the farm, men are the farmers while women raise the children (Salamon and Keim 1979:115). Some women actively seek to break this mold, successfully contesting the male monopoly of the title of "farmer." But they are relatively few. Only 16 percent of the Iowa female farmers sampled have actively *chosen* to farm, whether as heirs to the family farm or as independent homesteaders, starting out on their own. The other 84 percent are farmers "by default" (Kohl 1976:5), women whose jobs as farmers have been thrust upon them by a crisis in the family. Most (63 percent) are widows (see Table 5-1). Others are divorced women whose husbands were farmers, or they are married to farmers who had to find work off the farm or who were incapacitated through injury or illness. In most cases, these women suddenly find themselves with a farm to work through no choice of their own. The problem is that many lack experience in the decision making, field-work, or farm management that are the norm for any male operator.

Because they were not socialized to be farmers and because they

[149]

*Table 5-1.* Marital status of Iowa female farmers participating in the survey

|  | Number | Percent of total |
|---|---|---|
| Widowed | 90 | 63 |
| Divorced | 7 | 5 |
| Married | 19 | 13 |
|    Husband works off the farm | 12 | |
|    Husband incapacitated | 5 | |
|    Husband farms a separate farm | 2 | |
| Single | 28 | 19 |
|    Total | 144 | 100 |

tend to enter farming after a family crisis, female operators are rarely prepared for their new responsibilities. Most quickly develop networks of reliable assistance, advice, and mutual aid. While the helpful efforts of male friends and neighbors sometimes smack of a certain paternalism, many female farmers could not maintain their enterprises without that support. The situation of Sophie F. (age forty-one) is not atypical.

Sophie's husband was severely injured in an automobile accident. Struggling to maintain their dairy business on her own, she found herself with extremely limited funds, unable to buy the quality of heifer she needed to improve her herd. A dealer friend proposed to sell fourteen Holstein heifers to Sophie for $5,000. She said, "Sure I want them, but I don't have the money." His response was, "Who said anything about money? Pay me when you can." Nothing down. No interest. Fourteen new heifers to boost the productive potential of her herd.

Some women make major changes in the nature of their farm operation based on a history of critical observation of the way their spouses managed. Usually women have been excluded from decision making on major operations. While couples confer on many routine issues, the final say most often falls to the husband. Thus the style of farming may be characterized by exclusively male priorities. For years, Sophie's husband, Adam, had juggled the management of two separate dairy herds with custom harvesting (for cash) in three counties. They worked seven days and nights a week to improve their cash flow, but still herd management was slipshod, costing them thousands in lost calves and unproductive cows. And the family never saw Adam. Her husband's accident forced Sophie to make some changes to allow them to stay in business. This she did gladly by refusing all custom jobs, selling weaker cows, concentrating the two herds into one, and rebuilding it. She recruited two of her high school–aged children as full-time hands. The results were impressive. In her initial ten months as a farm operator, Sophie brought their dairy business into the black for the first time in its eighteen-year history.

Being suddenly alone or in charge of a farm also permits women to make changes in management style and operation that are appropriate to their status as novice farmers. Not only do women pare down the scale of their personal responsibilities by renting land or culling their herds; some completely eliminate activities that previously were integral to the farm under male supervision. Such changes usually follow careful evaluation of available labor and capital, as was the case for Rachel B.

Rachel, age thirty-four, an only child, had promised her father she would take care of her mother when he died, never thinking it would mean actually farming their 225 acres. Although she says she is running things "just like Dad," Rachel's first action as farm manager was to sell off all the livestock. She reasoned that to raise cattle properly, she would have to purchase expensive new equipment to upgrade and modernize the operation. Without such equipment, she would need several hired hands. Because she decided that she would manage the operation without going into debt, liquidation was a clean and fast solution. In the three years since, Rachel has never regretted her decision.

It is tempting to speculate about the tendency of female operators to concentrate their resources rather than hungrily expand as male farmers have been wont to do. I have observed many women remodeling diversified, unwieldy, and debt-ridden operations into more manageable size and shape. But I can also point to women, although fewer in number, who are willing to go deeply into debt to buy more land and bigger machinery. It is interesting to note that in almost every instance, female farmers who are expansionist in their outlook and behavior are married to farmers and ex-farmers whose point of view they share. It is premature to draw any conclusions about specific farming styles as representative of male or female farmers. But I suggest that, except for the women whose husbands are working off the farm, female farmers are women who are economically and personally vulnerable. They are novice managers whose inexperience may well drive the operation under. They require patience and assistance from neighbors, suppliers, and bankers. Many of them are supporting families. It seems logical that they might want to be conservative in concentrating their energy and resources, at least for the first few years, rather than commit themselves to major indebtedness and production demands beyond their capabilities.

## Widows

Widowhood has been called the most powerful time in a farm woman's life (Salamon and Keim 1979). After years of domesticity and unpaid farm labor, widows may find themselves with a farm of their own to run. Not all choose to do so. Some sell off their acres and homes to retire to town. Others turn over farm management chores to their children or rent out the barns and fields for cash or a share of the harvest. Many however, elect to remain on the farm.[5] Pearson (1979) and Sachs (1983) have noted that women without child-rearing responsibilities tend to be more involved in farm management than women whose domestic work continues to dominate their lives. While this may be true, factors other than housekeeping and child care enter into the widow's decision whether to farm.

The choices available to widows depend on a myriad of complex and overlapping factors including age, number and age of children, tax and corporate status of the farm, mechanization and specialization, availability of labor, type of operation, and, especially, the role the widow played on the farm before her husband died. If she was an active partner or, as in more than a few cases, the de facto manager of the farm, she may wish to continue managing, even if an eager son is waiting in the wings. While the son (or his wife) may resent her persistence at first, the widow on a matrifocal farm may offer her apprentice children, male or female, a larger role in running things than do fathers in father-son operations, and a correspondingly larger percentage of the financial remuneration.

---

5. I have noted that there is a dearth of national data about female farmers. What we do know is that since 1981, when inheritance tax laws stopped penalizing the surviving female spouse, it has become easier for widows economically to hold onto their farms, and more and more have elected to remain as operators (Sachs 1983).

Whatever the degree to which the widow was involved with the farm before the death of her spouse, she was probably primarily responsible for the feeding and care of livestock. Popular sentiment among Iowa farmers suggests that women are better than men with livestock largely because of their patience and that elusive female quality, the "nurturing instinct." Either for this reason or because animal buildings are usually located in the woman's traditional domain near the house, farm wives often specialize in animal care (although women are not often found in feedlot management). Correspondingly, males have historically dominated in the fields where, in planting and harvesting crops, they use and maintain heavy equipment, work which since the invention of the plow has been deemed too difficult for women (Boserup 1970). Even today, when farm machinery is fast becoming computerized, safer, and more manageable, many women are practically helpless when machinery breaks down in the fields, never having been trained to repair it. Although more and more women who are married to farmers are actively involved in fieldwork (Hill 1981), few are permitted to do the two critical tasks that make or break a crop: planting and combining. When her spouse dies, a widow must rapidly expand her knowledge of farm activities, sometimes a difficult to nearly impossible task, particularly for an older woman. The incorporation of her offspring into the operation is often what makes the task possible. Unless the children are very young, untrained, or living away from home, few widows would venture alone into a heretofore male domain. Instead, most will wisely allocate most of that work to their grown children, those who were being tutored in those areas for years before.

The female connection to the livestock business remains a source of power and revenue for widows largely because of their familiarity with the routine systems involved in breeding and raising. My research suggests that widows who own livestock are more likely to keep their hand in farming than widows with grain-only farms. In fact, if there are no interested children, widows often keep the livestock enterprise for themselves while renting, sharecropping, or selling off their acreage to neighbors or friends. Robbie E. is typical in this respect.

Robbie (age sixty-one) has been widowed for ten years. At her husband's death, her 25-year-old son Milton, who lived with his family in town, had been merely a hired hand on their large dairy farm; "Dad did it all." Between his father's death in November and spring planting, Milton had "caught up" with the literature on high protein

[153]

haylage through long sessions with the county extension agent and by reading scores of farm magazines. Mother and son continued as a team; he took over the fieldwork, and she took charge of milking and breeding decisions, work she had done for years. Eventually, they traded houses so that Milton and his large family could have more room and Robbie could have a social life in town. At first, Milton's wife, Kay, thought Robbie wanted to retire. But Robbie surprised the family when she solidified her position by incorporating with Milton. She is president and secretary; he is vice-president and treasurer. When I interviewed her, Robbie suggested that Kay, who was raised in a city, had no idea what milking 100 cows twice a day meant in terms of labor and that she failed to see that without Milton in the field, Robbie in the milking parlor, and Kay helping out where needed, their production efficiency would drop precipitously. As a team, they thrive. Milton has regularly won awards for his top quality haylage, and recently Robbie won a prestigious dairying award, never before awarded to a woman.

### Divorced Women

Seven women (5 percent) in the sample are divorced. Some of them are so devoted to farming that when their marriages ended, they fought tradition to stay on the farm. Others found themselves stranded because they lacked good alternatives for employment or income off the farm. Still others are women whose husbands either did not farm or were not interested in continuing to farm. Some women in each group had clear title to the land and equipment through inheritance from their own families. Rural lawyers stress that there is no real norm in farm divorces because property ownership varies so greatly. Nonetheless, they agree that it is rare for a woman to retain title to a working farm, especially because in most cases they must pay alimony in lieu of dissolving the farm and dividing the profits. Divorced women consequently start out with a dual financial burden: previously incurred debts and the new payments they must make to their husbands.

As one might expect, divorced women are quick to criticize their husbands as farmers and to make changes that represent their own priorities and management styles. Helen D.'s case is typical.

Helen (age forty-three) divorced her husband, Harvey, after twenty-three years of marriage, the first seventeen having been spent on his parents' farm where, according to Helen, Harvey, "in the prime of his life," worked for his parents, not for himself and his family. Helen, meanwhile, started a small feeder pig operation on her father's farm which she worked with her children. When they finally moved to their own place, Helen continued her business while Harvey did the fieldwork. They also had a few hired hands. Helen now characterizes Harvey as a man who loved coffee breaks and regularly made his first appearance in the barn at 8:00 A.M., hours after such work normally begins. He apparently kept few records and did not keep their equipment in good repair so that Helen was forced to sell it cheaply when Harvey left her (to open a business in a nearby city). Since the divorce, Helen and her hired men are farrowing twice as many sows (approximately thirty every six weeks). A long and costly court battle ($11,000 in attorney's fees) ended with an equal split of the land and its accompanying debts (her share of indebtedness is $75,000). Expert testimony convinced the judge that Helen was indeed a serious full-time farmer, and she was awarded the entire hog operation, for which she paid Harvey $32,000.

Because divorced women tend to be younger than widows, the care of children may play a significant role in their lives. The amount of time they are forced to spend away from their children is a source of guilt and confusion, and many women are embarrassed at how haphazard their housekeeping has become. But under the strain of farm debts and alimony, many women feel that full-time and overtime farming is their only option. Every pig saved at birth is money to pay debts, repair machinery, and feed children, which is why most nights, Helen can be found in the farrowing barn until well after midnight.

Divorce would seem to give women a clearer chance for a life off the farm than widowhood does. Divorced women are younger and seemingly more flexible than widowed women. They have better opportunity to liquidate and invest elsewhere. Important ties are broken, and the time is ripe for starting over. Yet after years of living and working on a farm, many divorced women, when asked why they did not go elsewhere after the divorce, respond, "Where would I go?," "Where could you get a job?," or "I don't know anything else." Admittedly, the love of the outdoors and the independence are part of the appeal of the farming lifestyle for either sex. But it would be naive to overlook the realities of the rural labor market and what farm women have to offer and to gain as workers off the farm.[6]

6. For information on rural women in the labor force see Semyanov 1983.

## Married Women

Nineteen women in my sample of female farmers are married. Eleven have husbands who, owing to poor crops or rising debts, were forced to give up farming to earn a salary off the farm. In some families, the woman had worked briefly in town or had considered looking for work, but it was usually more advantageous for the man to take a job because the rural economy offered men better jobs and higher salaries. The husbands of two farming women are farmers who work entirely separate operations near the matrifocal farm, and one is married to a nonfarmer. Five women are married to men who are unable to farm owing to injury or illness.

Many married female farmers are able to farm only because of their husbands' paychecks. Without that income, the farm would probably be liquidated or parceled up. All but one of the couples in which the husband works off the farm had farmed together (with varying degrees of cooperation) until an economic crisis forced the husband to find a more secure income in a nearby town, leaving the wife to manage the farm on her own. None of the farmers' husbands makes more than $16,000 at his job, but a percentage of this money is normally earmarked for farm expenses. Off-farm income often raises a family's standard of living, but all of these couples put some of the husband's paycheck straight into the farm account or use it to pay farm bills when emergencies arise.

As is true with other female farmers, women with working husbands farm with varying degrees of success. But unlike many others, they have a secure backup income that provides some degree of insurance. These women are unusual in that their "hired hands" are their husbands, who help after work, on weekends, or during vacations. This situation is just the reverse of the more common one in which the husband devotes full time to the farm and the wife has off-farm, income-producing employment. Among the group, decision making varies greatly. At one extreme are the women who depend on their husband's opinion on all but the most routine chores. While not merely menial laborers, they also do not operate truly independently. Although they do the lion's share of the work and may be quite knowledgeable, they make few management decisions entirely on their own.

At the other extreme are women such as Elinore H., who eschews any assistance from her husband, Ward, preferring to do everything on the farm herself. Since 1977, Ward has worked off the farm while Elinore works 425 acres and raises hogs. Ward hates his job and longs to return to the farm where he grew up, but Elinore has persuaded him to keep his job. She says that he earns good money and that if Ward were on the farm, "he would only get in my way." Ward seems particularly handicapped when it comes to raising hogs. Elinore boasts, "I put my arm up a sow. He won't. I milk runts. He won't. I give shots. He won't. I go over to check the pigs at night. He's asleep." All Elinore's hog income goes right back into the farm. Ward's wages are used for clothes, leisure activities, and paying farm bills when necessary. Elinore spent $1,000 on gifts last Christmas. And she wants a new house just behind the old one they live in now.

Between these two extremes are the couples who confer on management issues and make some decisions as a team, although they recognize the wife as the primary farm operator. Because so many of the men who are married to farmers have been farmers themselves, the power shift from husband to wife is never easy. Insecure about abandoning the farmer status they had practically been born to, many men are resentful of their wives working the farm. In addition, going to work off the farm is, for some, publicly admitting that they failed as farmers. One husband complained that when the farm revived, the community gave "her" all the credit and thought him lazy, forgetting the critical impact his wages have on family farm survival.

Five of the married women in the sample work alone, though their husbands are at home. Each of them cares for an incapacitated spouse who through accident or illness is no longer able to farm. In every case, children living at home make the care of their father and continued farm operation possible by assuming responsibilities both within and outside of the home. Some of the husbands receive small disability pensions, but often a sizable medical bill encumbers the farm beyond its normal operational indebtedness. This situation often engenders bitterness and guilt in the family. At the same time, family members seem to rally together, developing new routines and carrying on. And while having a helpless spouse around may be a burden, it also affords some women the opportunity to take over in a gradual way because their husbands can answer questions and give advice.

Several women married to handicapped husbands were eager to have the opportunity to farm on their own. These women are glad to be able to use their long quiescent agricultural abilities and, in some cases, to "show up" their husbands. Sophie, whose husband is no longer able to farm, told me that she wakes up each day "with a song in my heart" just to be working her land and milking her cows. She said that before Adam's accident, "he spoke for both of us." She hauled grain and helped with the milking, but he rarely permitted her to make decisions, never let her use the important equipment, and did all the home doctoring himself. Recently, she wrote "farmer" as her occupation after more than twenty years as "housewife."

## Single Women

The twenty-eight single women (19 percent of the sample) are the most varied group on matrifocal farms. Most are what extension agents call "maiden ladies," those women over forty or fifty who never married and usually live with their siblings or elderly parents. Middle-aged unmarried women (or men for that matter) still living at home are not uncommon in rural areas. Farm life seems to provide a safe alternative to marriage and children for single people who choose to live out their lives with their natal families. I encountered several brother/sister, sister/sister, father/daughter, and mother/daughter farms throughout Iowa, in all of which the farmers were over fifty years of age.[7] The following case is typical.

Betty (age sixty) and Dinah T. (age fifty-two) are sisters who live on the 160-acre grain farm where they grew up in northern Iowa. They have been farming alone since their father's death thirty-two years ago and have never been married. Until 1977 they lived with their two older brothers, who have since died. During their brothers' lives, Betty and Dinah were responsible for the home farm while the "boys" did custom work for farms around the county. Betty and Dinah know how to fix " 'bout anything that runs." They learned as children from their brothers, and when the boys went into service, their father relied on Betty and Dinah, and so they were able to apply what they had learned with great satisfaction. For example, in 1929 their pig herd died from cholera, the cows aborted, the family had whooping cough, and the crops were hailed out. Despite all of that, they made it through the depression and have since been mindful of what their father told them during that disastrous year: "Don't ever buy anything

---

7. Inheritance taxes are particularly high among sibling farmers, and I am always surprised that such partnerships persist nonetheless.

until you can pay for it." They never do. In their tenure as farmers, they have never borrowed once. There is seemingly no conflict between them. Labor is evenly and routinely divided. And now that they are "gettin' on," as Betty says, they minimize their efforts as much as possible. For example, much of their planting and combining is done by a hired hand. They have five tractors of their own which they have accumulated so that they do not have to hook and unhook equipment as much as they would with fewer tractors. They sold their cow-calf herd so that instead of doing chores in winter snowstorms, they can sit in the house "with our feet up" and reminisce.

A growing number of single farmers are women who work with their fathers or, in some cases, their mothers. This group has grown as more women have recognized farming as a legitimate occupation for females, a fact evidenced by the dramatic rise in the number of undergraduate women enrolled in agriculture courses at land-grant universities (Lyson 1979). There has also been a growing acceptance by parents, specifically fathers, of the role a daughter can play in perpetuating the family farm. Father-daughter teams, however, may last only until the daughter marries and her husband assumes control. For example, Missy's widowed father asked her to leave her job in Chicago to assist him on the farm when none of her brothers could. She decided to give it a try. The farm produces livestock (her father's responsibility) and crops (her area). Missy's father is a thoughtful, progressive farmer whose ideas on conservation tillage have been carefully passed on to her. She is not really a novice farmer, having grown up working acreage with her siblings. But she knows little of financial management or planning. Nor will she bother to learn because she expects leadership to be the province of her fiancé, who farms nearby. For Missy, the responsibility for the crops is but an interlude until another man enters her life to take over.

A separate issue in matrifocal farming is the question of lesbians entering the occupation. Gay women, both avowed and clandestine, probably represent a sizable percentage of the single-woman category.[8] Farming has always attracted utopian separatists (Erasmus 1977), and for women wishing to take up a heretofore male-dominated oc-

8. Precise figures on gay female farmers are difficult to obtain. Unsupported assumptions about the sexual preference of a survey participant are clearly inappropriate. It is certainly possible that some "maiden ladies" or other women in the study are lesbians, but no woman in my sample has been counted as homosexual unless she has described herself as such.

cupation that combines independent thinking with hard work and raising living things, farming is a likely choice. Lesbian farmers vary in the extent to which they express a "male-free" philosophy about their operation. Whether they live alone or with other gay women, lesbian farmers tend to be independent and determined. With no male farmer present to help out, they must be particularly self-reliant and industrious. Some of them pay a high price for their solitude; they may be seriously underinformed as farmers and, lacking the hands they need, inefficient. Others have formed unions for mutual aid, the most common being two women working together, one of them the landowner, the other her helper.

Ruth (age forty-five) runs a purebred Angus operation in south central Iowa. She has always lived on the fringe of her community and is proud to be a flaunter of convention. She has been expelled from several colleges and is a recovered alcoholic. Since her divorce, she has not made a secret of her homosexuality. Ruth grew up on a farm in another part of the state, and her decision to return to the rural life came "out of the blue," she admits. Through a number of jobs and short-term businesses, she and her lover accumulated sufficient cash for the down payment on a farm and moved in. The first year they raised one acre of tomatoes and made $2,000. That year and the next, they learned how to do fieldwork from a hired man who, having six daughters, believed that women could do anything. In the years since, Ruth's lover has left, and Ruth has hired a succession of first male and then exclusively female (and gay) hired hands. The nature of her business has shifted from vegetables to heifers to dairy and now to cattle. Her gay friends jest that Ruth makes the worst hay in the county, but she persists in her farming career, and her friends come to her aid when needed.

## Conclusion

We have seen that what women on matrifocal farms share is their nontraditional occupation and the idiosyncratic status they thus achieve in their communities. Most of them arrive at this status by default, often taking charge after a family crisis, and are thus unprepared and untutored for a job that society deems "men's work." Once they decide to farm, these women must act quickly to make the operation viable. Unsocialized to the image of rugged (manly) individualism attached to their new occupation, female farmers are quick to develop systems of support within the community. They seldom decline help offered by neighbors, nor are they averse to an exchange of labor or goods for tasks they have not mastered. As they become more familiar with the particulars of farming, they also tend to re-design their operations to suit themselves, adjusting acreage, plant-ings, and herd sizes as they see fit. Interestingly, the women farmers I studied tended to be conservative in their planning, generally avoid-ing expansion and large machinery purchases.

Since 1981, favorable changes in federal tax laws have made it economically feasible for inheriting widows to remain on the farm rather than liquidating or transferring ownership to heirs. The growth of other sectors of the matrifocal farming population is more spec-ulative. Certainly, the economic troubles that beset family farming in the wake of increasing economic concentration of agriculture in the hands of fewer farmers means that more male farmers will be forced to seek off-farm employment for supplemental income. Unless there is a dramatic (and unforeseen) reversal of the direction of American farm-ing, then, it is likely that the number of married women operating farms will continue to increase.

This chapter has focused on the personal difficulties of women in agriculture, but the institutional and societal difficulties women face are even more formidable. Foremost among them is bank credit, without which most farming is impossible. Financial assistance can be difficult to obtain for beginning farmers, and when these new farmers are women, local (usually male) bankers are often skeptical. The same bias frequently affects women farmers' dealings with implement com-panies, grain elevator operators, stock dealers, and the like. Such institutional impediments and social constraints are deeply embedded in the rural setting. Whether the matrifocal farm will come to be recognized and accepted as a rural fixture remains to be seen. As it is, thousands of women farm alone despite the many obstacles they must surmount. But without the support of the rural community and its service infrastructure, these female cultivators and ranchers cannot begin to compete successfully with male farmers.

I have suggested here that because of the traditional segregation of men's and women's responsibilities on the farm, women's potential contributions to agriculture have been diminished and the rural econ-omy as a whole has suffered. The exporting of the ideology that a woman's place is in the home similarly minimizes female participation

[161]

in agricultural development programs abroad. My research has shown that thousands of American women have abandoned the domestic arena for the barns and the fields, thus challenging the longheld assumptions about the role of the farmer's wife. I hope that other researchers will continue to study women farmers in other regions so that the myth of female domestication will be banished from the farm and the productive contribution of women will be noticed and analyzed in the United States and in the developing nations of the world as well. Rural women everywhere would be well served by the technical information and support that is currently part of an exclusively male domain. The persistent emphasis on women's domestic functions is inconsistent with the levels of female participation in extradomestic tasks, responsibilities, and decision making on the farm. The burden of carrying on without adequate tools or preparation could be lightened if local, national, and international policy makers address the particular needs of women farmers.

## Acknowledgments

An earlier version of this paper was presented in September, 1983, at the meeting of the Rural Sociological Society in Lexington, Kentucky. I thank Paul Lasley for his advice and Peggy Barlett and Christina Gladwin for their encouragement and comments at that time. I am indebted to Dennis McGilvray, Steven Koester, Paul Shankman, and Michael C. Ehlers for their careful reading and thoughtful criticisms of the paper. Without the keen comments of Michael Chibnik, the paper would never have been produced. Funding for my fieldwork in Iowa was provided by the Iowa Humanities Board, administered through the Iowa Farmers Union.

## References Cited

Beneriá, Lourdes. 1982. Accounting for Women's Work. In *Women and Development: The Sexual Division of Labor in Rural Societies*, ed. Lourdes Beneriá, pp. 119–147. New York: Praeger.

Boserup, Ester. 1970. *Women's Role in Economic Development*. New York: St. Martin's.

Boserup, Ester, and Christina Liljencrantz. 1975. *Integration of Women in Development*. New York: United Nations Development Programme.

Chaney, Elsa M., and Marianne Schmink. 1976. Women and Modernization: Access to Tools. In *Sex and Class in Latin America*, ed. June Nash and Helen Icken Safa, pp. 160–182. New York: Praeger.

Deere, Carmen Diana, and Magdalena León de Leal. 1981. Peasant Production, Proletarianization and the Sexual Division of Labor in the Andes. *Signs* 7:338–360.

Erasmus, Charles J. 1977. *In Search of the Common Good: Utopian Experiments Past and Future*. New York: Free Press.

Gladwin, Christina H. 1982. Off-Farm Work and the Increase in the Florida Farm Woman's Relative Contribution to the Family Farm. Staff paper 213, presented at the Wingspread Seminar on Women's Roles on North American Farms, Racine, Wis.

Hill, Frances. 1981. Farm Women: Challenge to Scholarship. *Rural Sociologist* 1:370–382.

Jones, Calvin, and Rachel A. Rosenfeld. 1981. *American Farm Women: Findings from a National Survey*. Report no. 130. Chicago: National Opinion Research Center.

Kohl, Seena B. 1976. *Working Together: Women and Family in Southwestern Saskatchewan*. Toronto: Holt, Rinehart and Winston of Canada.

Kramer, Mark. 1981. *Three Farms: Making Milk, Meat and Money from the American Soil*. New York: Bantam.

Lyson, Thomas A. 1979. Some Plan to Be Farmers: Career Orientations of Women in American Colleges of Agriculture. *International Journal of Women's Studies* 2:311–323.

Mead, Margaret. 1976. A Comment on the Role of Women in Agriculture. In *Women and World Development*, ed. Irene Tinker and Bo Bramsen, pp. 9–11. Washington, D.C.: Overseas Development Council.

Pearson, Jessica. 1979. Note on Female Farmers. *Rural Sociology* 44:189–200.

Sachs, Carolyn E. 1983. *The Invisible Farmers: Women in Agricultural Production*. Totowa, N.J.: Rowman and Allanheld.

Salamon, Sonya, and Ann Mackey Keim. 1979. Land Ownership and Women's Power in a Midwestern Farming Community. *Journal of Marriage and the Family* 41:109–119.

Semyanov, Moshe. 1983. Community Characteristics, Female Employment, and Occupational Segregation: Small Towns in a Rural State. *Rural Sociology* 48:104–119.

Staudt, Kathleen A. 1979. Class and Sex in the Politics of Women Farmers. *Journal of Politics* 42:492–512.

Tetrault, Jeanne, and Sherry Thomas. 1976. *Country Women: A Handbook for the New Farmer*. New York: Doubleday.

Tinker, Irene. 1976. The Adverse Impact of Development on Women. In *Women and World Development*, ed. Irene Tinker and Bo Bramsen, pp. 22–34. Washington, D.C.: Overseas Development Council.

U.S. Bureau of the Census. 1981. *1978 Census of Agriculture*. Washington, D.C.

PART **III**

# RACIAL AND
# ETHNIC DIFFERENCES

Most anthropologists agree that interethnic differences in economic behavior and social organization originate in historical circumstances specific to particular places and times. There is considerable disagreement, however, about the extent to which these differences persist when the original reasons for their existence are no longer pertinent.

Sonya Salamon's chapter examines how persisting cultural traditions can affect contemporary economic behavior and community character. Salamon compares the extent of social cohesion in two Illinois communities, one inhabited primarily by farmers of German Catholic descent, the other by "Yankee" farmers. She finds that the German community, "St. Boniface," is more close-knit than "Emerson," the neighboring Yankee community. The "yeoman" Germans, she observes, have emphasized community cohesion since they settled the land, and their economic strategies reflect their commitment to passing their farmland on to their heirs. The "entrepreneurial" Yankees, in contrast, have always been more concerned with amassing profits. They stress the importance of individual economic effort and show little attachment to family land.

St. Boniface is about 85 miles north of "Freiburg," the Illinois German Catholic community described in Susan Rogers's contribution to this volume. Most Freiburg farmers raise livestock as well as corn and soybeans, while the Yankees often specialize exclusively in row crops. Thus Freiburg farms are less specialized than those of their Yankee neighbors. The Germans of St. Boniface, however, are less likely to raise livestock (and thus are more specialized) than farmers in neighboring Yankee communities. Nevertheless, both Rogers and Salamon attribute the differences between Germans and Yankees in degree of agricultural specialization to the greater German commitment to keeping farmland in the family.

This seeming paradox results from differences between St. Boniface and Freiburg in soil types, opportunities for off-farm work, land tenure, and inheritance. Some of the effects of these differences are described in Rogers's and Salamon's papers. Others are examined in a recent article by Rogers (1985) comparing Freiburg and St. Boniface and one by Salamon (1985) comparing Freiburg and a neighboring Yankee community.

Lisa Gröger's chapter contrasts land tenure arrangements and intergenerational relationships among blacks and whites in a North Carolina farm community. Gröger reports that ideology and feelings about landownership are similar for blacks and whites. Both groups stress the desirability of owning land, the security it represents, and its importance in keeping the family together. Whites, however, have less difficulty buying land. As a consequence, older whites can help their adult children by providing them with access to land. Older blacks, in contrast, are economically dependent on their children with off-farm jobs, many of whom live in distant cities. The social relations between parents and children are thus quite different for blacks and whites. Unlike Salamon, Gröger does not explain interethnic differences in social and economic behavior with reference to persisting cultural traits. Instead, she emphasizes the effects of the current economic circumstances of blacks and whites in rural North Carolina.

The differences in interpretations offered by Salamon and Gröger may have little to do with their theoretical positions. In the Illinois communities studied by Salamon interethnic differences in wealth are much less pronounced than in the North Carolina area Gröger describes.

### References Cited

Rogers, Susan. 1985. Owners and Operators of Farmland: Structural Changes in U.S. Agriculture. *Human Organization* 44:206–214.
Salamon, Sonya. 1985. Ethnic Communities and the Structure of Agriculture. *Rural Sociology* 50:323–340.

# [6]

# Ethnic Determinants of Farm Community Character

**Sonya Salamon**
*Division of Human Development and Family Ecology*
*University of Illinois at Urbana-Champaign*

In his celebrated study of two California farming communities in the 1940s, Walter Goldschmidt (1978) contended that rural community character was strongly affected by the economic structure of farm operations. According to Goldschmidt, landownership patterns accounted for differences in the index of quality of life—schools, infrastructure, and services—in these communities. Goldschmidt's analysis largely ignored noneconomic factors because he assumed that the two communities shared a common American cultural tradition.

In this chapter I argue that ethnic identity can be as important as landownership in determining community character. I examine two ethnically distinct Illinois farm communities with a common land tenure pattern; some of the land farmed is owned and the remainder rented. Despite the similarity in landownership patterns, the two communities are quite different. One is a commuter bedroom town with boarded-up shops, abandoned houses, deserted streets, and the prairie invading its sidewalks; the other is populated mainly by farm-related residents and retirees and has lively streets and shops, manicured lawns, and busy cafés.

Geographical differences cannot account for the divergence in quality of life in the two communities. Both are twenty-five miles from the same urban center, were adjacent to railroads in the past, and are currently served by interstate highways. Instead, the differences between the communities are linked to ethnic differences in inheritance patterns, church affiliation, and family goals. One community consists of descendants from German Catholic settlers, the other of offspring from "Yankees" (settlers originally from the Protestant British Isles who first settled on the U.S. eastern seaboard and then followed the frontier west). Distinctive farm family ethnic priorities for land, farming, religion, and community have been mirrored in the communities' development over the century since settlement.

The ethnic stock and operation type of the two communities are common in the Corn Belt. In analyses of community development in rural America, cultural factors must be taken into account in addition to the economic forces more frequently described (e.g., Brown 1979; Korsching 1984; Goldschmidt 1978; Nuckton et al. 1982).

**Rural Community Development**

Although few noneconomic explanations have been offered for why some American rural communities have declined while others flourish, cultural and historical factors certainly play a part. Smith (1966) draws an interesting distinction between communities founded upon a "covenant" (a philosophical agreement of purpose) by a relatively homogeneous ethnic and religious group and "cumulative" towns that grow without plan through gradual settling by individuals impelled by economic motives. Over time, according to Smith, covenant towns tend to remain small, true to the covenant of origin, and predominantly agrarian. Cumulative towns, shaped by individual entrepreneurial visions, either boom into commercial cities or erode.

Hollingshead (1937) emphasizes churches as the dominant influence and social centers of communities. Catholics, Lutherans, and Episcopalians were committed to establishing stable farm communities linked to an authoritarian denominational structure in Europe. The first members of these churches in the United States were either first-generation Americans or western European and Scandinavian immigrants. They shared a cultural and religious heritage and tended to settle where ethnic churches had been established.

These centralized churches differed considerably from New World Protestant denominations, whose members were primarily of Yankee stock. The New World churches were more concerned with individual salvation than with creating a permanent organization. Membership fluctuated with the mercurial careers of charismatic leaders; ecclesiastical organization was subordinated to saving souls, and competition for followers was great. These churches did not regard community stability as a particular priority.

Both Smith's and Hollingshead's explanations are helpful in analyzing community differences in Illinois. Families of German and Yankee origin settled in the Corn Belt in substantial numbers between 1840 and 1900 (Kamphoefner 1984). Although traditional farming practices underwent drastic alterations as farmers adapted to midwestern prairie agriculture (Bogue 1963), ethnic traditions regarding kinship, land, and household organization have had surprising persistence (Nelson 1955; Salamon 1984).

The contrasts between farms and families of Germans and Yankees are historically well documented (Schafer 1927; Hansen 1940; Miner 1949; Cogswell 1975; Conzen 1980). Yankee communities were characterized by household self-sufficiency and weak commitment to a particular church or village (Macleish and Young 1942). German communities, in contrast, were settled as people migrated to live near their own relatives; this kinship bound the households together.

In this chapter I use Smith's and Hollingshead's ideas in the construction of a typology of family farm enterprises (see also Salamon 1985a, 1985b). This typology is based on ethnically linked practices concerning farming goals and strategies that evolved to meet these goals. Two predominant midwestern farming patterns make up the typology. The first pattern is the "yeoman" family farm type characteristic of German Catholics. Yeomen seek to reproduce a viable farm and at least one farmer in each generation. The other family farm type, characteristic of Yankees, is "entrepreneurial." The predominant goal is the management of a well-run enterprise that optimizes short-run financial returns. These contrasting goals have implications for farming strategies. Yeomen expand only insofar as necessary to bring family members into the farm; entrepreneurial expansion is limited only by available capital and personal ambition. Yeoman farmers, to fulfill their continuity goal, utilize estate planning; parents assume the major responsibility for intergenerational transfers. Entrepreneurial farmers feel each generation should be responsible for making its own way and use estate planning more for tax benefits than for ensuring continuity (see also Flora and Stitz 1985).

Most important, yeoman and entrepreneurial farming goals reflect different conceptions of family attachment to land. The nature of attachment to land is said to give "the economic and social system its

[169]

central logic" (Bell and Newby 1971:163). Intergenerational maintenance of these contrasting farming patterns are reflected in wider patterns at the community level. The yeoman Germans are typically associated with agrarian, covenanted communities with centralized stable church affiliations; entrepreneurial Yankees are associated with commercially oriented communities that boom or bust according to the economic climate and typically have factionalized, less stable churches.

## Data and Methodology

The Yankee and German Catholic communities described here are located in east central Illinois. Farmers in this "Black Prairie" region have access to the best soils in the state.

"Emerson" is the pseudonym I have given the Yankee community. All the households in the fifty-two contiguous mile-square sections that loosely conform to the consolidated school district were contacted in a door-to-door survey. The community boundaries were defined by an individual born and raised there. In sixty-one (75 percent) of the eighty-one households included in the Emerson survey sample, one or both spouses had some Yankee ancestry. Of the remaining 25 percent, one or both generally were of German origin. A subsample of thirteen households (approximately 20 percent) participated in the intensive phase of the study. The researchers collected genealogies, studied family and land histories, and observed and participated in these families' daily activities (Markan 1981; Penas 1983; Salamon et al. 1986).

In the German Catholic community, "St. Boniface" (also pseudonymous), every farming household in two parishes was contacted. Of the sixty-nine households in the sample, 95 percent included one spouse of German ancestry. In 65 percent of these households both spouses had German origins. Only four households were of Yankee ancestry. Nine households participated in the more intensive phase (Rogers 1985).

Archival materials were also examined. Plat maps of the area, which record both owner's name and size of tract, were used to identify ethnic control of community land. Newspapers, community and church histories, and family-owned documents were drawn upon to place current data in a historical context. Probate records were used to analyze inheritance patterns. These records contain information on estate size and content, location and number of heirs, and whether a will was made (see Carroll and Salamon 1987 for methodological details).

## The Black Prairie Ethnic Farming Communities

### Settlement Patterns

St. Boniface land was originally purchased by Yankees who desired the flat, untimbered terrain to pasture cattle, horses, and sheep. About the time a rail line was put through in the mid-1850s, the first drainage ditch was dug; before that time, only about 20 percent of the land was tillable. Although the railroad company built a large station in anticipation of rapid growth, development proved slow. Around 1865, the first German Catholic immigrants settled, all originating from several Alsatian villages. Through a process of chain migration, in which relatives sponsored other kin from Europe, St. Boniface came to be dominated by the Alsatian farmers.

Because most of the Alsatians did not arrive until twenty years after St. Boniface was founded, only a few of the first ethnic settlers were able to buy cheap land directly from the railroad. Later migrants were forced to buy more expensive already homesteaded acreage, and family stories tell of forebears who worked as hired men before buying their first land. An 1870 county history mentions the industry and enterprise of the German settlers and their achievements in organizing and draining their area of the township. According to a local history (St. Boniface 1976), the community has long been regarded as progressive and neighborly. Locally this reputation is attributed to the neat, orderly farmsteads of Germans and the village's domination by retired ethnic farmers.

The pattern of retirement into town creates close ties between country and village. There are numerous other signs that St. Boniface is a thriving, close-knit community. Volunteer service groups organize a number of community-wide events such as an annual pancake and sausage breakfast fund raiser. An old grocery store, purchased with money raised by the village and remodeled by residents, is used for community meetings and wedding receptions. There is a heavily used ballfield on land donated to the church. The village supports several taverns, a post office, a bank, and its own water company. People are seen on the streets during the day, and farmers meet and gossip outside the local grain elevator and at the bars and café.

St. Boniface's location along an interstate approximately twenty miles from a metropolitan area makes the community attractive to commuters seeking rural ambience. Two small housing developments slipped in before community members took legal steps to forestall other encroachments. The new families do not farm. Explained a fourth generation farm wife: "The real way we tell them apart from everyone else is because they're not related to everyone here, like the rest of us." Community solidarity is also revealed in the depth of feeling regarding sales of previously German-owned land to non-Germans. Commenting on such a transfer, a farm wife complained, "It just kills you to see an outsider working that land, right next to the church, too."

Yankees began to settle Emerson around 1870. Families trickled in independently, often after migrating from New England and stopping off in Pennsylvania or Indiana (Markan 1981). The heirs of the first settler, a large-scale livestock farmer, started to sell off tracts as the vast holdings became too valuable for pasture. Whole sections are still owned by descendants of the first owner; the early generations were considered particularly astute businesspeople (Gates 1932; Bogue 1959). By the 1920s, Emerson was a prosperous village with schools, several Protestant churches, an interurban commuter line connecting it to nearby villages, and a railroad shipping station. The village peaked in population and prosperity (twenty-six businesses) in the 1940s. After that, residents began to commute to growing urban areas to the east and west for shopping, entertainment, and work. Today, although the population has remained a stable 450 to 500, Emerson is primarily a bedroom village. There are a few small businesses—a grocery store, a service station, an auto dealership, a lumber company, and a grain elevator. The village has been unable to support a restaurant or tavern where residents and farmers can congregate.

Community members identify Emerson primarily as a school district. Many point to the local elementary school (children are bused elsewhere in the combined school district for junior and senior high) as the single unifying force in the community. However, one young farmer indicated that when families no longer have school-aged children, there is little that brings townsfolk and farmers together.

Two events are often mentioned to explain Emerson's lack of commercial development. An opportunity for expansion was lost when an interstate was constructed in the 1970s. No one is quite sure why Emerson, alone of area villages, lacks an interchange, but locals say a native absentee owner with political connections successfully fought any plans to take his land. Another reason for stagnation was the closing of a farm implement dealership that at one time employed fifteen people. The closing affected the vitality of other local businesses, particularly a bank and several restaurants. Townspeople blame the closure on farmers going elsewhere to obtain better deals on equipment. Farmers, conversely, claim the townspeople forced out the flamboyant owner-entrepreneur because of his fancy home and grand gestures of civic benevolence. For many years the implement dealer was the organizing force behind the only annual, community-wide social event on the Fourth of July; after he left, it was never revived. The departure of the implement dealer split the community over who was to blame, and neither townsfolk nor farmers have stepped forward to fill the leadership vacuum created by the loss of this pivotal figure. Emerson's decline is thus linked by its entrepreneurial farmers to a lack of local "boosterism." Community vitality is measured by Emersonian entrepreneurs in the health of its commercial institutions (Hatch 1979).

Other potentially unifying links between village and countryside are missing. Farmers live outside the village and tend to disdain nonfarming townsfolk. "Emerson just can't seem to attract a better type of people." A few widows and farm-related families reside in Emerson, but most farmers are reluctant to retire there. "You just don't move to Emerson. There's really nothing much to hold people." Farmers with no resident kin remain detached, not viewing village affairs as their concern. A farmer commented: "Oh, I don't have much to say. None of us farmers do. We're not affected [by current issues of liquor licenses and sewage disposal]. That's the nice thing about living here. You can watch the goings-on and not become involved. 'Course, if someone asks me directly, I say what I think . . . but those of us outside village limits don't have a vote."

As a consequence of weak loyalty and a belief that the village has little to offer, farmers' social activities are dispersed. Far-flung social networks are a source of pride. "We have friends in all walks of life, not just farmers," said an active operator. A married farmer in his early thirties said, "Everybody goes different places. My dad is all wrapped up in the Shrine. The guy next door has his church. Me, oh, I go to the bars mostly." Young mothers who are farm wives feel particularly isolated by the dispersed social networks. One complained that the women's club, whose members were all over age thirty-five, was the only social group available to her in Emerson.

Emersonians do report some local neighborliness. For example, one operator did not buy a desired tract so that another's son could make his first land purchase. Nevertheless, people sense that "everybody is separate and standoffish." A young farmer commented: "I'm friendly with the farmer next over, and we share things some. Same with the farmer that direction. But that's unusual. Oh, people are friendly, but they're not friends. They don't help each other out."

### Religious Affiliation and Commitment

The divergent paths taken by St. Boniface and Emerson result partly from characteristics of the communities' churches. A stable Catholic church in St. Boniface has maintained a strong authoritarian hold on its farm families. In Emerson, Protestant evangelical churches have come and gone, separated and merged.

In 1875, the seventeen German families of St. Boniface first erected their own country church, subsequently administered by Franciscans. A second church was built (1904) to accommodate the increasing numbers of retirees into the village. To understand the character of St. Boniface is to understand the significance of its church. Though the bishop of their predominantly Irish diocese has exerted pressure for consolidation (i.e., closing the smaller village church), most residents want to maintain St. Boniface's two parishes, which in 1982 had a combined membership of approximately 140 families. One farm wife recounted telling the bishop, "Our church is the center of the community . . . it would be disastrous [to close one church] because everyone depends on the church." About twenty years ago, their parochial school was closed, and a yoking of village and country parishes occurred about ten years ago. Though parish size has declined by about 20 percent, it was diocese policy that dictated these changes (Salamon 1982). Long, deep community religious commitment is evident. St. Boniface has produced five priests, eleven nuns, and one brother (St. Boniface 1976).

To assure that their churches will survive in the face of diocese cutbacks and shortages of priests, parish members have assumed many responsibilities. Volunteers perform all bookkeeping, janitorial work, and cemetery upkeep. "That's how we keep the parish going— everyone pitches in and works. . . . We want something we can be proud of." Women are particularly religiously devoted. A young farm- er said his mother watches his attendance: "She'll call up and say, 'Would you like to come over for breakfast after Mass?'"

Churches were established early in Emerson's history, but the con- gregations have not been permanent. The present small Emerson population is divided among at least three churches (in two villages), and loyalty to any one is tenuous. For example, the congregation of a local Baptist church grew dramatically during the tenure of a popular minister, but has diminished under subsequent leadership. Affiliation is chosen pragmatically: "With the kids going to school in Emerson, we felt it would be good to attend church there," was the explanation for a farmer abandoning his childhood church. There is little commu- nity pressure to attend church regularly or to participate in religious organizations. One farmer observed: "The Methodist church does not really serve to pull the community together. We go, but not regularly. When summer comes, lots of people go away every weekend. They don't bother much with church, so the congregation dwindles." Pas- tors exhibit a similar lack of commitment, staying at most five or six years. "Maybe it's too dull for them," joked a farmer. Such turnover is not so characteristic for the centralized St. Boniface Catholic church.

## Farm Family Goals and Farming Patterns

### Attachment to Land

The agrarian covenant of St. Boniface Germans is expressed in their yeoman priorities for continuity of farming and family land ownership. St. Boniface families of German descent hold a deep attachment to their land, and by extension, to the community. A farm wife ex- plained, "Keeping the land you inherit and the land your family has worked is very important." Children expect parents to fulfill an obliga- tion to assure that family land passes intact to the next generation. A farmer related the bitterness of a friend whose family had a large amount of land years ago, but lost it. "If they'd been able to keep it, they would be in a pretty good position today." Blame for the loss of the family's right to farm was placed on a grandfather's drinking and poor management. "[My friend] really wants to farm, but with that land out of the family, it's not easy." From the perspective of German families, landownership is an almost sacred trust: "We're just stewards of the land. We don't really own it. So it upsets me to see people let land go to waste by poor conservation, or just trying to get the most from it without giving anything back. . . . Taking good care of the land was one thing my father always stressed with us."

Attachment to community through family land is said to extend to nonfarming heirs. "Even for children and grandchildren who have moved away, this is home. This is where their roots are, where their parents and grandparents are buried. This is where their land is." Families depend upon their nonfarming heirs who are socialized to cooperate and appreciate the significance of landownership as well. A farmer who transferred some of his land to his children after he retired stressed that "all the kids that inherit need to stick together so that all can keep the land. . . . We knew our kids would stick together when we gave them the land." One part-time operator worries that his sibling's children, a generation removed from the farm, are "college-oriented, not farm-oriented" and are likely to sell inherited land. A young St. Boniface farm wife explained yeoman sentiments regarding farming: "We were both born and raised on the farm. It's a love for the land and farming which keeps us at it; it's sure not the money. We want it to be here for our kids too. So if we both have to work off the farm, plus do all the farming after that just to make it, then it's worth all the hard work so we can stay here."

Yankee attitudes of loose attachment toward land are evident in their comments about the history of their families and property. "Who really cares about it?" was a typical male remark regarding family history. The comments of a son who took over the family farm revealed the lack of oral history passed down with land: "Most of the land I farm belongs to my parents. I know my mother inherited some, but the acreage my father owns, I just don't know a whole lot about it. I mean Dad hardly ever talked about who he bought it from or the circumstances. Dad liked to buy land—that's all I really know." Just as early Yankees were described as lacking an *"amor patriae* which attaches a man to a particular locality, and probably induces him to use means for establishing it as the home for his descendants" (Robert Barclay Allardice, quoted in Gates 1972:52), so Emerson Yankees focus on the challenge and the business aspects of farming, rather than on passing the farm on to the next generation. Said a daughter from a well-established family, "There's not much sense of tie to the land as family land. . . . There's no connection, no 'our family name is on this.' It's kind of, 'This is my land. That's it.'"

Another farmer commented on the unsentimental, commercial family-to-land relationship characteristic of the entrepreneurial Emerson Yankees:

> I'd say we have a pretty good group of farmers around here. . . . What we'd say are poorer farmers have all been weeded out. . . . Well, in the sixties farms were smaller. When it became necessary to get more farmland to pay expenses, some farmers didn't make it. They were bought out pretty quickly if they hadn't added to their operation. Those who are still here saw it coming and expanded. Farming is not just putting seeds in the ground and watching them grow. It takes management skills too, but the poorer farmers don't have those skills.

Attachment to farming accounts for continuity in Emerson, rather than the maintenance of ties to a particular family farm. The core entrepreneurial motivation of Yankees was expressed by an elderly Emerson bachelor farmer, still in the fields: "I guess I'm from the old school, and that means that I think you gotta produce. The whole point is to make it. For me work is a pastime. And it's a challenge; you try to make the most for the littlest cost. In a way it's like a game—but that's the way it is."

## Commitment to Farming as a Way of Life: Yeoman and Entrepreneur

The yeoman priority of continuity as a family goal requires that each generation produce a farmer to assume the family operation (Rogers and Salamon 1983). Among St. Boniface yeoman Germans, carrying on the farm is a responsibility that is not left to chance. A retired farmer who had considered other occupations remembered, "My father, with tears rolling down his cheeks, told me he'd raised me a farmer and that was what he wanted me to do. I had to do it then." St. Boniface families have typically produced at least one farmer: in one family all but one of six middle-aged siblings are farmers.

The mean number of children in contemporary German families is a relatively high 3.3. Before 1900 this figure was 5.2, and in 1930–60 it was 4.8. Although since the turn of the century St. Boniface Germans have had more children per family than Emerson Yankees (Carroll and Salamon 1987), German out-migration has remained low. According to the residence of heirs in the probate record, fewer than one-quarter resided outside of St. Boniface.

Many community young people express a strong desire to farm, even though some are pessimistic regarding their chances. A young man said, "I'd like to get into farming, but it's difficult. . . . There are a lot of big families here. . . . You have to find yourself a girl with land and no brothers." St. Boniface farmers increasingly compete to purchase and rent the same ethnically owned land.

Emersonians do not view farming as destiny, and sons are not coerced to follow fathers (Penas 1983; Salamon et al. 1986). The mean number of children in Emerson families is currently 2.6, a figure much smaller than the 5.3 mean (similar to the German figure) found in probate records before 1900. The mean number of children in Yankee families dropped to 3.8 by the 1930s and soon thereafter reached current levels. Although smaller family size meant that there was less competition among heirs for family land, Yankee children out-migrated at a rate almost twice that of their German counterparts. Many Yankee heirs in probated wills relocated to large midwestern cities and presumably took jobs outside of agriculture. Even those Yankee children who stayed in Emerson reflected nonagricultural occupations in the articles listed in their estate inventories (Carroll and Salamon 1987).

Yankee children are encouraged to obtain an education and to explore nonfarming career alternatives before deciding to farm. Said one parent, "I never pressured them one way or another. I wanted them to make up their own minds. I wanted it to be strictly an option for them." A father who takes a son into the family operation believes the son must prove himself as an entrepreneur, and passing the test is never a certainty (Penas 1983; Salamon et al. 1986). For this reason, sons seem to hold back from becoming too attached to a business that may never be theirs. Because many parents are reluctant to make the sacrifices necessary to bring a son into the operation before they retire, all but the most tenacious sons give up (Penas 1983).

All of this is not to say that Emerson operators are unenthusiastic about farming. Said one Emerson farmer: "Here I'm my own boss—

no one to answer to. If something works, I get the credit. If it doesn't, I know who to blame." But farmers say the occupation of farming, rather than the "family farmstead," is what they are "attached" to, and explains why they farm (Penas 1983).

*Inheritance*

Inheritance traditions shaped by family goals affect land-use patterns (see Salamon 1980). For instance, land fragmentation is a consequence of a partible inheritance system, because all children tend to hold on to and farm any inheritance (Habakkuk 1955). Plat map records (which record owners' names and the size of their tracts in a single county) show how the land has become increasingly fragmented in St. Boniface during the century since settlement (see Table 6-1). In St. Boniface, the average size of German-owned tracts has diminished by 20 percent. Though tract size is not equivalent to farm size (a farm may consist of as many as fifteen or more separate tracts), fragmentation is indicative of smaller amounts of owned land and the necessity of obtaining rental parcels to create a viable operation.

Yankee average tract size and numbers of owners have stayed relatively stable in Emerson over the last century. A fluctuation occurred around 1930, when the number of owners increased and tract size decreased. These changes probably reflect speculation and property loss before and during the Depression. Speculation is evident in the extent of turnovers in landownership; 50 percent of the 1930 Yankee owners appeared on neither the early nor the later plat map.

Emerson has a higher proportion of absentee landlords than St. Boniface. Landowners' names on the latest plat map were compared with those in the local rural telephone directory; in east central Illinois this covers surrounding areas for a distance of twenty to thirty miles. A majority (73 percent) of the seventy-nine Emerson landowners (Table 6-1) were not listed in the phone directory. In St. Boniface approximately half (52 percent) of the landowners were not listed. Less than half (45 percent) of the absentee landlords in St. Boniface were of German origin; the remainder were Yankees. In St. Boniface land is often willed to children who have left the community as well as to those that stay to farm (see Rogers 1985). This atypical practice is one reason the absentee-landlord rate is higher in St. Boniface than in many other German communities in Illinois (Salamon 1985b).

[179]

*Table 6-1.* Ethnic landownership patterns in St. Boniface and Emerson[a]

| German[b] | 1893 | 1930 | 1981 |
|---|---|---|---|
| Total acreage | 5,747 | 5,745 | 5,534[d] |
| Total number of owners | 48 | 47 | 64 |
| Number and (percent) German owners | 14 (29) | 18 (38) | 28 (44) |
| Average size of German-owned tracts (acres) | 105 | 99 | 83 |
| Percent of community land owned by Germans | 26 | 31 | 42 |

| Yankee[c] | 1875 | 1930 | 1978 |
|---|---|---|---|
| Total acreage | 8,338 | 8,023[e] | 8,304 |
| Total number of owners | 75 | 97 | 79 |
| Number and (percent) Yankee owners | 57 (77) | 71 (73) | 59 (71) |
| Average size of Yankee-owned tracts (acres) | 113 | 88 | 106 |
| Percent of community land owned by Yankees | 77 | 76 | 77 |

[a]Data is taken from plat map records of a 25 percent randomly selected sample of all the owners from the area surveyed. The 1930 date is approximate, suggested by the Illinois Historical Survey; maps issued during this period were undated. Ethnicity was determined by verification of the origin of names in genealogical dictionaries of surnames, principally Smith (1956). Several tracts owned by a single landowner were treated as one tract.

[b]Most non-German owners were of Yankee ancestry.

[c]Most non-Yankee owners were of German ancestry.

[d]Loss of acreage due to building of an interstate.

[e]Inaccurate map records account for acreage loss; average tract figure calculated on a base adjusted by the addition of 300 acres.

Although Yankee parents speak abstractly of wanting children to carry on the farm, succession is not made inevitable by parental planning (Penas 1983). Community probate records reveal that a lower percentage of Emerson Yankees (22 percent) than of St. Boniface Germans (56 percent) left wills before 1930. When intergenerational transfers are made without planning, continuity becomes problematic.

Because keeping land in the family is a priority to St. Boniface Germans, they have stressed equal inheritance regardless of which child actually farmed (Rogers 1985). This rule is followed even when families recognize that such a division may create very small farms. In an effort to avoid land fragmentation, however, many farmers have

[180]

passed land undivided to all the children. Or parents in earlier periods left land to their sons and cash to their daughters (Carroll and Salamon 1987).

Yankee families also have a firm belief in dividing land equally among children. They think, however, that disposition of inherited land is an individual's prerogative rather than a family matter. Unlike Germans, Yankees do not feel strongly that heirs should farm or maintain ties to family land. A woman in her late seventies described her father's family: "Dad was from a family of ten kids. In those days a farm, at least a typical farm, was 160 acres. Each of the kids would have inherited about sixteen acres. Dad bought them all out. I guess no one else cared too much for the farming bit. . . . He hated shucking corn, so he just sold it [the farm]. That was the end of the land in the family." Few rentals from siblings were reported by Yankee farmers. Instead, Yankees often sell or trade land to their siblings (Salamon et al. 1986; Salamon 1984). Sales and trades among siblings who have inherited land have kept land holdings undivided within families and have helped to account for the stability of Yankee tract size and the proportion of territory they control in the community (Table 6-1).

Besides farmland, animals, and money, Yankee estates often contain numerous stocks and bonds. German estates, in contrast, contain few nonfarm investments. Because Yankee estates possess more capital, larger amounts of owned acreage (mean 198 acres compared to 155 acres for Germans), and fewer heirs, Germans usually receive smaller inheritances (Carroll and Salamon 1987).

The difference in capitalization and number of heirs, combined with the effects of out-migration, have profoundly affected the amount of real estate controlled by heirs in each community. German heirs have stayed and attempted to farm although they have inherited smaller portions of land and have had less liquid capital to enable them to purchase land or equipment. In Emerson the out-migration of heirs has meant that the land has been less fragmented and the population less dense than in St. Boniface (see Table 6-1), but there has been more absentee ownership.

*Farming Patterns*

Because of their larger families and smaller inheritance portions, St. Boniface Germans typically farm smaller farms than Emerson Yankees (see Table 6-2). Germans also rent a higher proportion of their land

Sonya Salamon

Table 6-2. Types and characteristics of farm operators in the German and Yankee communities

| Operator type[a] | Number | | Percent of sample | | Mean age | | Mean farm size (acres) | |
|---|---|---|---|---|---|---|---|---|
| | German | Yankee | German | Yankee | German | Yankee | German | Yankee |
| Tenant | 13 | 10 | 19 | 12 | 48 | 44.9 | 420 | 616 |
| Part owner | 32 | 35 | 47 | 43 | 51.6 | 46.9 | 502 | 555 |
| Full owner | 5 | 7 | 7 | 9 | 60 | 46.2 | 89 | 163 |
| Landlord | 19 | 29 | 27 | 36 | 69.4 | 65.7 | 159 | 163 |
| Total | 69 | 81 | 100 | 100 | | | | |

[a]Tenants rent all the land they farm; part owners own a portion and rent the remainder of their acreage; full owners own all the land they farm; and landlords are full owners who do not farm their own land.

from other owners. Renters (crop sharers) split profits with their landlords; full owners retain all their returns.

Because German operators work farms that are on the average almost one-third smaller than Yankee farms and own a smaller proportion of the land farmed, some St. Boniface farmers, to stay in agriculture, must adopt strategies that require personal compromises. Many German farms are only marginally profitable, but the households are willing to pay the costs to remain in farming and in St. Boniface. They live modestly, and their farmsteads typically have older buildings. Said one woman whose husband farms with two married sons: "The figures they cite for how much land it takes to make a living are hogwash. Each of our boys started with only eighty rental acres. Even with a family they were each able to make it quite comfortably. It's just a matter of budgeting your money and spending wisely." To manage, their sons work off-farm in slack seasons, and they raise hogs. More important, this extended family cooperates in a manner reminiscent of past farming patterns in other places. The three families pool land, labor, and equipment, "Doing it together is the only way to make it work. . . . Living so close by . . . my husband and the boys can share machinery. Otherwise it would be too expensive for the boys." Joint cooperation is common in St. Boniface. Although the survey did not specifically solicit such information, more than 30 percent of active farm households mentioned joint equipment ownership.

Although their mean operation size is smaller than that of the Yankees, more German households appear involved in each active operation. Cooperation in the form of labor exchange and shared equipment ownership reveals a high level of German family support and interdependence in St. Boniface. Related Yankee families, in contrast, see little reason to cooperate. Yankee farmers tend to deny even the interdependence that inevitably occurs in father-son joint operations (Salamon et al. 1986).

In Emerson, small operations are looked on with some disdain. Farmers think that business cycles force smaller operators out of agriculture and do not view the subsequent loss to the community negatively. One boasted that six operators formerly farmed "what I do now." Emerson farmers frequently mention efficiency and economies of scale. "You don't want to have unused labor or expensive machinery that you're not working to full capacity." Unlike St. Boniface farmers, who often cooperatively own major equipment, Emerson operators prefer to use expensive equipment on a single farm. A son starting out in farming will share equipment with his father, but attempts as quickly as possible to obtain the necessary capital that permits independence. In the words of one son farming his father's land, "I want to prove to myself and my dad that I don't need him."

Some active operators in both communities find that corn and soybeans alone do not provide a satisfactory income. There are pronounced community differences in what options such operators choose. German farmers tend to seek off-farm employment because their smaller inheritances do not allow them sufficient capital to diversify their farming operations. Location near a city makes nonfarm work a viable supplemental income solution. For instance, several farmers work as janitors by night and farm by day. "Three out of four people work off-farm. That's how my dad got through," said one young operator from a family of six children. Table 6-3 shows major secondary-income sources of active operators, excluding landlords. In both communities grain crops are the primary source of income. The divergence in farming strategies appears in what sources are tapped for other income. For secondary income, Germans favor off-farm jobs rather than the on-farm animal production favored by Yankees. No German part owners raised animals as a second source of income, while nine Yankee operators did. Nine German part owners worked off-farm, however, while only four Yankee operators did.

Many Yankee sons, independently of their fathers, have chosen to

Sonya Salamon

Table 6-3. Percent of active operators (excluding landlords) with grain crops, animals, and other businesses as secondary-income sources[a]

| | Grain crops | Animals | Other[a] |
|---|---|---|---|
| German (N = 33) | 21 | 9 | 70 |
| Yankee (N = 42) | 7 | 45 | 48 |

$\chi^2 = 12.546$
2df p = <.001

[a]"Other" includes off-farm jobs, custom work, social security, and additional side businesses. For example, one German household raises worms; a Yankee household sells firewood.

raise livestock as a secondary source of income diversification (Penas 1983; Salamon et al. 1986). "Dad never did really work at the livestock; now I've turned it into a money-making proposition," explained a young farmer. Such livestock production businesses are made possible by substantial amounts of family capital, either provided or inherited.

Because German families have a staunch commitment to farming, it may seem surprising that they have chosen off-farm work rather than animal production as an additional income source. The explanation lies in the small size of their operations and historical circumstances. A young farmer reflected that off-farm work is often the most logical financial strategy: "Animals take the capital investment. I think that's why more [farmers] don't have livestock. It's just easier to find a second job."

Germans rationalize off-farm jobs as a means of maintaining their commitment to farming as a way of life, as a mechanism to deal with incurred expenses resulting from large families and small farms. Explained a wife involved in the farm: "My husband used to work off the farm, and I still do. We did it so we could get the machinery paid off and get the kids through college. It's been a long haul, but I think we're just about paid up, and our youngest is in her last year of college. I think next fall I'll be able to quit."

## Conclusion

The structure of these two communities mirrors the ethnic family bonds; community life is a replication of farming pattern type. The roots of the contrast lie in attitudes toward land, reflected in operation styles and extended to community. German yeoman goals involve commitment to continuity of a particular farm and community; the Yankee entrepreneurial goals do not. An agrarian ethic still motivates the yeoman Germans even a century after settlement.

Logically, the German pattern of working off-farm in nearby cities to supplement farm income from small operations might fragment community bonds and pull families apart. Yet it is among the Yankees, whose operators are farming full-time, that community integration is weak and loyalty nonexistent. The links among German households are many layered, characterized by equipment sharing and labor co-operation—patterns not fostered among Yankees.

German values require preservation of the original agrarian cove-nant which regards farming as a superior way of life. The St. Boniface farmers take off-farm jobs to achieve the yeoman goal of intergenera-tional continuity in agriculture, even when large families, high land values, and fragmentation by past inheritance practices made farms too small to be viable. The Yankees, more concerned with managing profit-maximizing businesses, have little attachment to family land or community. They have been historically more willing than Germans to leave farming and their community, and those Yankees who stay regard farming as a job. Their cumulatively settled village has died because their priorities did not include social investment in its preser-vation.

Yankees farm more diversified operations that may have greater potential to survive as viable farms. However, they lack the added dimension that living in the German cooperative and supportive com-munity provides in daily life. Links among households are weak, and young families sense their isolation. Families perceive no financial benefits from cooperating and therefore make little effort to share on either the household or community level. Because the Yankees build up few social obligations during the course of everyday life, support and cooperation are not readily available when sorely needed. The social and emotional costs are high for Yankee family farmers; so are the financial costs for Germans.

As a consequence of structural agricultural changes, farm commu-nities today must struggle to persist and maintain integration in the face of declining populations. Families must cope with school and church mergers and often must travel distances to obtain goods and services that previously were available locally. These changes have tended to pull apart the fabric of farmers' lives rather than to provide the reinforcement between farm families and rural communities experienced scarcely a generation ago. Rural communities clearly differ in the extent to which they have remained socially cohesive. The communities examined in this chapter suggest that ethnic traditions can explain some of this variability.

## Acknowledgments

The ethnographic fieldwork was conducted by Karen Davis-Brown, Kathleen Markan, Dwight Penas, Emily Rest, and Susan Carol Rogers. Edward V. Carroll carried out the investigation of probate records. Rosemarie Zabel assisted in the computer analysis. This study was part of Projects 60-302 and 60-308 of the Agricultural Experiment Station, College of Agriculture, University of Illinois at Urbana-Champaign. Funding was also provided in part by the University of Illinois Research Board and by U.S. Department of Agriculture Cooperative Agreement No. 58-319S-1-0156X. I am grateful for the comments of Peggy Barlett, Catherine Surra, Michael Chibnik, Roger Sanjek, and Gilbert W. Gillespie, Jr., who read early versions of this chapter.

## References Cited

Bell, Colin, and Howard Newby. 1971. *Community Studies*. New York: Praeger.
Bogue, Allan G. 1963. *From Prairie to Corn Belt: Farming on the Illinois and Iowa Prairies in the Nineteenth Century*. Chicago: Univ. of Chicago Press.
Bogue, Margaret Beattie. 1959. *Patterns from the Sod: Land Use and Tenure in the Grand Prairie, 1850–1900*. Springfield: Illinois State Historical Society.
Brown, David L. 1979. Farm Structure and the Rural Community. In *Structure Issues of American Agriculture*. Agricultural Economic Report no. 438, pp. 283–287. Washington, D.C.: U.S. Dept. of Agriculture, Economics, Statistics, and Cooperative Service.
Carroll, Edward V., and Sonya Salamon. 1987. Share and Share Alike: Inheritance Patterns in Two Illinois Farm Communities. *Journal of Family History* 12: in press.
Cogswell, Seddie, Jr. 1975. *Tenure, Nativity, and Age as Factors in Iowa Agriculture, 1850–1880*. Ames: Iowa State Univ. Press.
Conzen, Kathleen N. 1980. Historical Approaches to the Study of Rural Ethnic Communities. In *Ethnicity on the Great Plains*, ed. Frederick C. Luebke, pp. 1–18. Lincoln: Univ. of Nebraska Press.

Flora, Jan L., and John Stitz. 1985. Ethnicity, Persistence and Capitalization of Agriculture in the Great Plains during the Settlement Period: Wheat Production and Risk Avoidance. *Rural Sociology* 50:341–360.

Gates, Paul W. 1932. Large Scale Farming in Illinois. *Agricultural History* 6(1):14–25.

———. 1972. Problems in Agricultural History, 1790–1840. *Agriculture History* 46:33–58.

Goldschmidt, Walter. 1978. *As You Sow: Three Studies in the Consequences of Agribusiness.* 2d ed. Montclair, N.J.: Allanheld, Osmun.

Habakkuk, H. J. 1955. Family Structure and Economic Change in Nineteenth Century Europe. *Journal of Economic History* 15:1–12.

Hansen, Marcus L. 1940. *The Immigrant in American History.* Cambridge, Mass.: Harvard Univ. Press.

Hatch, Elvin. 1979. *Biography of a Small Town.* New York: Columbia Univ. Press.

Hollingshead, A. B. 1937. The Life Cycle of Nebraska Rural Churches. *Rural Sociology* 2:180–191.

Kamphoefner, Walter. 1984. The German Agricultural Frontier: Crucible or Cocoon. *Ethnic Forum* 4:21–35.

Korsching, Peter F. 1984. Farm Structural Characteristics and Proximity of Purchase Location of Goods and Services. In *Focus on Agriculture*, ed. Harry K. Schwarzweller. Research in Rural Sociology and Development, vol. 1, pp. 261–287. Greenwich, Conn.: JAI Press.

Macleish, Kenneth, and Kimball Young. 1942. *Culture of a Contemporary Rural Community: Landaff, New Hampshire.* Rural Life Studies, No. 3. Washington, D.C.: U.S. Dept. of Agriculture, Bureau of Agricultural Economics.

Markan, Kathleen K. 1981. Farm Family Corporations: Some Implications for Family Relationships. Master's thesis. Univ. of Illinois, Urbana-Champaign.

Miner, Horace. 1949. *Culture and Agriculture.* Ann Arbor: Univ. of Michigan Press.

Nelson, Lowry. 1955. *Rural Sociology.* 2d ed. New York: American Book.

Nuckton, Carole Frank, Refugio I. Rochin, and Douglas Gwynn. 1982. Farm Size and Rural Community Welfare: An Interdisciplinary Approach. *Rural Sociology* 47:32–46.

Penas, Dwight J. 1983. Always Settling, Never Settled: Family Life among Contemporary Yankee Farmers. Master's thesis. Univ. of Illinois.

Rogers, Susan Carol. 1983. Land Tenure and Cash Grain Specialization in Illinois: The Significance of Farmland Ownership and Rental. M.S. thesis. Dept. of Agricultural Economics, Univ. of Illinois, Urbana-Champaign.

———. 1985. Owners and Operators of Farmland: Structural Changes in U.S. Agriculture. *Human Organization* 44:206–214.

Rogers, Susan Carol, and Sonya Salamon. 1983. Inheritance and Social Organization among Family Farmers. *American Ethnologist* 10:529–550.

Salamon, Sonya. 1980. Ethnic Differences in Farm Family Land Transfers. *Rural Sociology* 45:290–308.

————. 1982. Sibling Solidarity as an Operating Strategy in Illinois Agriculture. *Rural Sociology* 47:349–368.

————. 1984. Ethnic Origin as Explanation for Local Land Ownership Patterns. In *Focus on Agriculture*, ed. Harry K. Schwarzweller. Research in Rural Sociology and Development, vol. 1, pp. 161–186. Greenwich, Conn.: JAI Press.

————. 1985a. Ethnic Communities and the Structure of Agriculture. *Rural Sociology* 50:323–340.

————. 1985b. An Anthropological View of Land Transfers. In *Transfer of Land Rights: Proceedings of a Workshop on the Transfer of Rural Lands*, ed. D. Moyer and Gene Wunderlich, pp. 123–144. Washington, D.C.: U.S. Dept. of Agriculture.

Salamon, Sonya, and Shirley M. O'Reilly. 1979. Family Land and Developmental Cycles among Illinois Farmers. *Rural Sociology* 44:525–542.

Salamon, Sonya, Kathleen M. Gengenbacher, and Dwight J. Penas. 1986. Family Factors Affecting the Intergenerational Succession to Farming. *Human Organization* 45:24–33.

Schafer, Joseph. 1927. *Four Wisconsin Counties*. Wisconsin Domesday Book 11. Madison: State Historical Society of Wisconsin.

Smith, Elsdon Coles. 1956. *The Dictionary of American Family Names*. New York: Harper and Brothers.

Smith, Page. 1966. *As a City upon a Hill: The Town in American History*. New York: Knopf.

St. Boniface [pseudonym] Bicentennial Committee. 1976. St. Boniface Village History. Unpublished ms.

# [7]

# The Meaning of Land in a Southern Rural Community: Differences between Blacks and Whites

**B. Lisa Gröger**

*Public Administration Program,*
*North Carolina Central University, and*
*Center for the Study of Aging and Human Development,*
*Duke University Medical Center*

## Introduction

Owning land is one of the loveliest feelings in the world. I'm free right here on my land. I'm calling the shots around here. I just don't know a place in the world that I would trade my land for.

I get so mad sometimes I think I'm going to cut my head off. Me and my wife and my children almost killed ourselves working and got nothing for it. We'd plant flowers and shrubbery, and before we could enjoy them we'd have to move.

What these speakers have in common are their age, their place of residence, and their occupation: both are elderly men retired from farming and living in the same rural community. But here the similarities end. Although they farmed in the same community, their life experiences have been very different because one of them owned the land he worked and the other did not—a difference that resulted in far-reaching consequences in a number of social and cultural domains.

In the literature on the rural elderly, such intracommunal differences are overlooked whenever the rural aged are compared to the urban aged.[1] Many researchers have discussed the problem of providing transportation and other services to the rural elderly and have documented their isolation, deprivation, and loneliness. The rural aged are said to be worse off than their urban counterparts concerning income, transportation, reported physical health, outlook on life, and the impact of industrialization on their communities (Youmans 1977:81).

The United States Bureau of the Census defines the rural elderly as persons aged sixty-five and older who reside in places with fewer than 2,500 inhabitants. This "size-of-settlement" definition has been criticized because it is based on a primitive distinction that "has become more or less universal simply by the weight of tradition and the huge volume of statistics based on it" (Sheldon 1967:118), because it does not take into account where people lived before age sixty-five but assumes "that persons rather suddenly came into existence at the age of sixty-five and at the location where they were found" (Adams 1975:11), and because it ignores the great variation within communities (Glenn and Hill 1977:50). Comparison of rural with urban aged assumes that both locality and age have a homogenizing effect. It ignores the great variation that exists within a category of individuals (the aged), and within a category of places (rural or urban).

This chapter takes a different perspective. It treats a more general phenomenon—resource control—and how it affects the quality of people's lives. The resources people control may take various forms in different settings. The setting I have chosen to study is rural North Carolina, and the major productive resource there is farmland. The idea for this research was inspired by Simmons (1957:58), who found that in societies with well-developed property rights, the aging experience is influenced by whether a person owns property. While the aging do not constitute a cohesive power bloc in the political arena (Binstock 1974:199), their individual power in the private domain of the family can be considerable because of their control of resources. Streib (1976:166) points out that fortunes need not be large in order to represent "powerful 'weapons' in the family and kinship system. . . . [and that] smaller amounts can be a real consideration in the treatment which older persons receive."

1. Some examples are Atchley and Byerts 1975; Bylund et al. 1979; Jackson 1970; Taietz and Milton 1979; Youmans 1967, 1973, 1977.

I will show how access to the major productive resource has affected people's lives—in their youth as well as in their retirement and old age. I will also show how people manipulate their resources, if they have any, and how they manage if they do not. I will describe the consequences of having and not having access to land in a number of economic and social domains.

The analysis is based on farm records and land transactions in a county that I call Piedmont and on participant observation of and interviews with thirty-eight white and thirty-five black people, age fifty-nine to ninety-two, in a township I call Mayfield.[2] A church community within the county became the geographical base for the research among whites, some of whom acted as contacts to blacks, who in turn introduced me to their churches.

Mean farm size in Mayfield is 120 acres. This is small compared to the United States mean farm size of 440 acres (U.S. Bureau of the Census 1977:13) and is actually even smaller because 75 percent of all farmland in Mayfield is wooded, bringing the average arable land per farm to thirty acres. Because of the small farm size, flue-cured or bright leaf tobacco, with its high yield per acre, is deemed the only viable crop in Piedmont County (it is also the most important crop in North Carolina as a whole)[3] Many owners of tobacco allotments are older and rent their allotments to younger growers, who depend on these renting arrangements to keep their farms viable. Thus tobacco allotments are a resource for retired farmers, who in turn depend on these renting arrangements for a part of their income.

I chose the county for this study partly for expediency (it is within commuting distance of Duke University) but also because of the demographic and occupational characteristics relevant to the particular focus of the study. Sixty percent of the county's land and 20 percent of its population are involved in farming. At the same time, the establishment of industry (11 percent of the population of the county works in manufacturing and wholesale) has provided alternatives to farming

2. All proper names of people and places are pseudonyms.
3. Elsewhere I have described the rules and regulations that govern every step of tobacco production and the way in which they affect older farmers (Gröger 1982:126–127). The permission to grow tobacco, known as tobacco allotment, is a government franchise that can be transferred, within a county, through annually renewable rental arrangements. In other words, the farmer who rents an allotment will often grow the crop on his own land; what he rents is the permission to grow a certain number of pounds of tobacco.

and has enabled some of the children of the elderly to remain in the community—an important aspect in the lives of older people.

Mayfield is probably typical of other communities in the rural South. Most people in the community were born in the area and have lived in a rural community all their lives; all come from farming families; most have been farmers, and all have ties to farming and the land. According to the 1970 census, 54 percent of the 2,243 inhabitants of Mayfield were black. While blacks and whites have not had equal opportunity to own land, land has been a major source of income for most people in the study throughout their working lives.

Although I set out to study poor and nonpoor blacks and whites, I could find few poor whites according to income and fewer still when assets such as land and home ownership were taken into account. For blacks it was the other way around. Given the historical exclusion of blacks from access to resources, their relative poverty requires little explanation. That blacks, especially in the rural South, are worse off than whites is a fact that has been documented (Butler 1975:30; Jackson 1974; Kent 1971; Muller 1980). In an attempt to go beyond the simple statement of the fact of economic disadvantages suffered by blacks, this chapter explores how these basic material differences are translated into sociocultural differences that have affected and continue to affect the lives of the elderly in this community.

The absence from the community of whites who live below the poverty level *and* who own neither a home nor land can be explained by the fact that the poor whites could and did better themselves more easily than blacks (before the 1960s) through employment in industry, in nearby federal institutions, and in the area hospitals. In the process of this upward mobility, most hitherto-poor whites moved away from the rural community to the neighboring towns. Those who stayed depended on land as their major productive resource. Land was the basis of security for those who owned it, and landownership was a lifelong goal for those who worked the land but did not own it.


## Landownership

Farming was the main occupation for nine-tenths of the blacks and three-quarters of the whites in the sample. Yet more than half of the blacks never owned any farmland, compared to less than 10 percent of whites. Table 7-1 summarizes the data on differences in landownership, farm size, and size of tobacco allotments.

*Table 7-1.* Landownership among whites and blacks, 1980

|  | Whites (N = 34) | Blacks (N = 35) |
|---|---|---|
| Lifelong farmers | 25 (74%) | 31 (89%) |
| Owned farmland past or present | 32 (94%) | 15 (43%) |
| Never owned any farmland | 2 ( 6%) | 20 (57%) |
| Mean farm size |  |  |
| Farmland | 155 acres | 74 acres |
| Cropland | 45 acres | 18 acres |
| Tobacco allotment | 7.96 acres | 3.3 acres |
| Pounds of tobacco allotted per year | 12,943 | 4,636 |
|  | Whites (N = 32) | Blacks (N = 15) |
| How farmland was acquired |  |  |
| Inherited and/or bought from kin | 26 (81.5%) | 3 (20%) |
| Inherited | 14 (44%) | 2 (13%) |
| Bought from parents | 4 (12.5%) | 1 ( 7%) |
| Bought from other kin | 8 (25%) | 0 |
| Bought from nonkin | 6 (19%) | 12 (80%) |

The size of farms owned by blacks averages less than half that of whites. The difference in tobacco allotments, the most crucial aspect of agricultural production, is equally striking. The size of tobacco allotments owned by blacks is on average less than 40 percent of that of whites.

Differences in how farmland was acquired reflect the disadvantage suffered by blacks. Seven times as many whites (fourteen) as blacks (two) inherited their land. Four whites but only one black farmer bought their land from their parents. A total of twenty-six whites but only three blacks inherited and/or bought land from kin. The majority of the blacks had to buy their farms from nonkin, compared to less than one-fifth of whites. Land purchases from kin were guided by a desire not only to keep the land in the family but also to maintain the relationship between seller and buyer. Thus in most cases, purchase from kin, and especially from parents and siblings, was considered more advantageous than purchase from nonkin.

The full measure of the disadvantages of blacks is illustrated by the history of a black farmer who was able to buy ninety-seven acres. The land he bought was completely wooded, and it took him over three years to clear one acre. Because he could not grow a sufficient amount

[193]

of tobacco for some time, he continued to sharecrop for others. When he stopped sharecropping, he still had not cleared enough of his own land to make a living, and so he turned to renting land from others. Thus he had to work for others while carrying the burden of his investment without getting any return for a long time. The information that he owns ninety-seven acres says nothing about the quality of the land or about the low return on his investment. Black participants in the study stressed repeatedly how difficult it was for them to acquire land. Often they were able to buy land only because the land for sale was of such low quality that no white person competed for it.

Given the hardship of having to buy not very productive land from nonkin (i.e., strangers who wanted to make a profit), blacks also found it more difficult to keep the land, as a few examples will illustrate:

Mrs. B., age eighty-two, still owns farmland. She and her husband were sharecroppers until in 1939 they were able to buy 148 acres through the Farmers Home Administration. In 1969, they had to relinquish fifty-six acres of that land to alleviate their original debt.

In 1943, Mrs. E. and her husband bought eighty acres from their landlord. They could not meet the annual payments of $1,000, and so in 1952 they sold seventy-five of those acres to a doctor in town and then rented the land from him.

Mrs. C. and her husband are sharecroppers who have never owned any land, but her father bought forty-five acres from his landlord. Because he could not pay the taxes on the land, a "white friend" paid the taxes for him. Her father never could repay his friend, and the friend took the land.

Whites, too, have sold land, but for different reasons:

When Mr. A. retired early after a disabling farm accident, he sold his 155-acre farm because he preferred to invest his money in something other than land and because he was "too much of a farmer" not to be working his land.

Similarly, when Mr. I. retired, he sold part of his land. He had owned two farms, a 100-acre farm which he inherited from his parents and which he is keeping, and a 105-acre farm that he bought and later sold to a neighbor upon retirement.

When Mr. F. retired, he sold ninety acres. He kept twenty acres to raise cows because he loves them and because he wanted to continue some of his former activities. He invested money from the land in certificates of deposit and has not regretted the decision.

Mr. E. was one of the biggest landowners. He sold 375 of his 1,200 acres because he thought his money would be better invested else-where. According to his widow, he did later regret the transaction, but it certainly did not ruin him, and his widow continues to own 836 acres of farmland.

Mrs. G. inherited 200 acres from her husband, who, unbeknownst to her, had incurred enormous debts through business ventures. She sold the farm to her son to pay off part of her husband's debts, and she deeded her house to her son to save it from the creditors.

Thus the reasons for selling land were different for blacks and whites. Many blacks had to resell land before they owned it fully simply because they could not meet the payments or the taxes on the land. Whites have used land sales as a resource management strategy, especially at the time of retirement. One could say the sale of Mrs. G's land was motivated by economic necessity, but that necessity had its origin not in a systematic and structural exclusion from the land market, as was true for blacks, but in her husband's poor resource management.

## Consequences of Landownership and Landlessness

### Income

Because of landlessness and land poverty among blacks, their total income comes from fewer sources and is less than half that of whites. None of the whites receive Supplemental Security Income (SSI), while over one-third of black households do. Similarly, more than twice as many blacks as whites have an income below the poverty level, and five times as many blacks as whites expressed a need for food stamps.[4]

---

4. Differences in income between black and white elderly people in the state are less pronounced than between blacks and whites in this sample. Among families with heads of households sixty-five years and older in North Carolina, median income in 1980 was $10,937 for whites and $7,694 for blacks (U.S. Bureau of the Census 1983:84) compared to $10,000 for whites and $3,976 for blacks in this sample. The discrepancy can be explained partly by the fact that this is not a random sample. But it is probably also true that the aggregate census statistics for the larger and more diverse statewide population mask the differences among the rural elderly (see Schulz 1976:564). The differences between blacks and whites in this particular setting are as dramatic as they are because of the nature of their occupations (agriculture) and the systematic exclusion of blacks from owning the major resource (land).

Upon retirement, people in the United States are likely to experience a decline in income (Schulz 1976:567–69; Seltzer et al. 1978:6). This was true of less than half the whites and slightly over half the blacks in the sample. On the other hand, over one-quarter of both blacks and whites reported an increased income upon retirement although for different reasons and with different results. After having worked for low and unpredictable wages from sharecropping or day labor, blacks finally had a regular and predictable income when they received social security. But most of those whose income increased when they retired were still living below the poverty level, even after the increase. For them, the function of social security is very different from what it is for some of the whites, who stated that social security was play money or pin money. The increased income for whites was attributable to their having given up farming and rented out their tobacco allotments, which they said was more lucrative than farming. For whites, land continued to be a source of wealth.

## Home Ownership

The equity of home ownership represents a more important asset for the elderly than savings (Schulz 1976:571–572). Home ownership is highly valued by that generation of the American people (Streib 1976:164).

Table 7-2 shows that 46 percent of blacks surveyed do not own their homes, while only 15 percent of whites do not own their homes. As was the case with landownership, however, the mere fact of whether someone owns a home now does not tell the whole story. Of the five whites who do not own their homes now, four have sold them. One woman sold her big house after her husband's death and returned to the house she grew up in to live with three sisters who had also spent their working lives away from home but decided to return and live together when they retired. Another woman (Mrs. G., mentioned

---

The percentage of households below the poverty level in the sample approaches the national figures for 1970. Forty-seven percent of black elderly and 22 percent of white elderly lived below poverty level nationally (Watson 1983:45), compared to 49 percent of blacks and 21 percent of whites in the sample. (The poverty level was defined in February 1981 as an annual income of $4,850 for two persons on a farm or $5,690 for two nonfarmers. [U.S. Office of the Federal Register 1981:15271]).

*Table* 7-2. Income and home ownership among whites and blacks, 1980

|  | Whites (N = 34) | Blacks (N = 35) |
|---|---|---|
| Income |  |  |
| Mean per household | $11,964 | $5,707 |
| Median per household | $10,000 | $3,976 |
| Mean per person | $ 7,136 | $2,854 |
| Median per person | $ 6,250 | $2,375 |
| Mean number of sources of income | 3.2[a] | 2.4[b] |
| SSI recipients | 0 | 12 (34%) |
| Households below poverty level | 7 (21%) | 17 (49%) |
| Expressed need for food stamps | 4 (12%) | 21 (60%) |
| Income change at retirement |  |  |
| Increase | 9 (26%) | 10 (29%) |
| bringing mean household income to | $13,845 | $4,242 |
| Decrease | 14 (41%) | 18 (51%) |
| bringing mean household income to | $11,865 | $6,347 |
| No change | 11 (32%) | 7 (20%) |
| Home ownership |  |  |
| Do not own home | 5 (15%) | 16 (46%) |
| Value of home to $24,000 | 6 (18%) | 14 (40%) |
| Value of home over $24,000 | 23 (68%) | 5 (14%) |

[a]Typically interest from savings, social security, and land.
[b]Typically social security and Supplemental Security Income (SSI); social security and earnings.

above) transferred the title to her house to her son to shelter it from her husband's creditors at the time of his death, but she continues to live in it. A third woman sold her house after she suffered a stroke and came to live with her daughter. One man sold his house to get some money. He sold it to a nephew "to keep it in the family," but he continues to live in it rent-free. Finally, one woman who never married never did own a house. All her life, she has lived in the house in which she was born and which now belongs to her sister, with whom she lives. Thus only one of the whites never owned a house. All the whites who do not own homes now live rent-free, and four of them live in houses in which they have lived all or most of their lives. The situation is quite different for blacks. None of those who do not own their homes have ever owned one. Three have been taken in by kin; two of them live rent-free, and one is paying rent. The other thirteen blacks who do not own homes have lived in rented, largely substandard housing all their lives.

[197]

Table 7-3. Community stability of whites and blacks

|  | Whites (N = 38) | Blacks (N = 35) |
|---|---|---|
| Born in community | 28 (74%) | 16 (46%) |
| Father born in community | 20 (53%) | 2 ( 6%) |
| Both parents born in community | 13 (34%) | 2 ( 6%) |
| Own birthplace unknown | 0 | 3 ( 9%) |
| Father or mother's birthplace unknown | 0 | 21 (60%) |

## Residential Stability

Through landownership one achieves stability of residence. This stability in turn makes one part of a close-knit community where people help each other. One overwhelming feature in the lives of black sharecroppers is the number of times they have had to move. Among the fourteen survey participants for whom this information is available, the mean number of moves was seven, the maximum fifteen. Several blacks had moved so often they could not remember the exact number of moves. Some of these moves took place within the same township, but the uprootedness of these lives is illustrated by the following (Table 7-3):

1. Three-quarters of whites but less than half the blacks were born in the community where they live now.

2. Ten times as many whites as blacks had a father who was born in the community, and six times as many whites as blacks had both father and mother born in the community.

3. All whites knew both their own and their parents' birthplaces, while 9 percent of the blacks did not know their own and more than half did not know one of their parents' birthplaces.

These differences in residential stability are reflected in the respective "mutual-aid networks" of blacks and whites. Members of the mutual-aid network of whites live in a small geographical area, whereas the members of the mutual-aid network of blacks are more widely scattered and therefore may be mobilized less easily.

## Transfer of Property: The Role of Children

Transfers of property within a family have been considered important in evaluating the economic situations of the elderly (Streib

*Table 7-4.* Economic dependency of white and black children and parents

|  | Whites (N = 35) | Blacks (N = 35) |
|---|---|---|
| Never married | 6 (17%) | 0 |
| Ever married |  |  |
|   Childless | 8 (28%) | 3 ( 9%) |
|   Mean number of all children | 1.7 | 6.5 |
|   Mean number of living children | 1.5 | 5.5 |
|   Parents receive money from children | 1 ( 5%) | 17 (53%) |
|   Parents give money to children | 10 (48%) | 2 ( 6%) |
|  | Whites (N = 17) | Blacks (N = 14) |
| Landowning parents |  |  |
|   Let son use farm (successor to farm) | 8 (47%) | 2 (14%) |
|   Gave land for house to offspring | 9 (53%) | 10 (71%) |

1976:164). Typically in the United States, the flow is from parents to children (Sussman 1965:68, 78), although variations depending on socioeconomic class have been reported (Billingsley 1969; Jackson 1969). In Mayfield, these transfers of property flow in opposite directions and have a different significance for blacks and whites. Among whites, property is transferred from one generation to the next as a kind of anticipatory inheritance that serves to maintain social ties and is symbolic of more to come (Sussman 1976:233–234). In contrast, among blacks it is the children who transfer property to their parents, thereby enabling them to make ends meet. If for most whites interhousehold transfers are a means of sharing property, for many blacks they are a mechanism for mitigating poverty.

All of the white participants have wills. Most blacks do not because they have nothing to bequeath. The most important asset a sharecropper of the current generation of elderly had were his children. The more children he had, the bigger the crop he could grow, the greater the share for the landlord, and therefore the more likely a landlord would be to offer him employment. This was not true of the landowner as long as there was abundant tenant labor available. In fact, too many children were sometimes viewed as a threat to the farm, which someday would have to be divided among them. The different significance of children for the landless (who are predominantly black) and the landed (who are predominantly white) is reflected in their different fertility rates. Seventeen percent of whites never married (all blacks surveyed were married); among those who did marry, a higher percentage of whites than blacks were childless; and when they did have children, whites had fewer than blacks (Table 7-4).

### Economic Assistance

What do these differences mean for people as they get older? Aging landowners, who are predominantly white, remain an important resource for their children. On the other hand, the children of retired sharecroppers remain an important asset for their parents, even though sharecropping as an economic arrangement no longer exists in this community. This reversal is a function of unequal access to land. Given their much higher income, whites are able to—and actually do—give money to their children on a regular basis: half the whites (five times as many as blacks) give money to their children. Because older blacks have much smaller incomes than whites—many blacks, in fact, are teetering on the brink of economic disaster—over half (seventeen) of those who have children depend on money from them. Only one of the white participants receives money from children.

Because of their usually precarious economic situation and because they had more children than did whites, some blacks (whether or not they own land) have encouraged some of their children to leave. It is these children who are sending money to their parents from Detroit, New York, Baltimore, and Washington, D.C. Apart from contributing to the support of their parents, children of blacks represent resources for their parents in other ways, as two examples will show.

Kinton Coley, black, owns no farmland. He farmed for others until 1969, when he started to work as janitor in the local school. In 1980 he retired on disability. He has five children, four of whom live with him and his wife. When his two oldest daughters got jobs, they saved enough money to put a down payment on the house in which the family now lives. They decided that only by pooling their resources could they realize the family's dream of living in their own home. The family considers owning this house, which is modest by most standards, their greatest blessing. Mr. Coley is full of appreciation for his daughters' enterprise and cooperation.

Viola King, black, a fifty-nine-year-old widow, owns nothing. But she has raised nineteen children: ten of her own and nine from her husband's first marriage. She and her husband used to farm for others, and now she works part-time doing housework, which gives her an income of about $100 a month. The difference between what she earns and what she needs is made up by contributions from her children, who "help out, give money, and pay the bills." She lives in a new house that one of her daughters, who lives in a trailer next door, is buying.

## Economic Security: The Farm

Landownership not only affects people's economic situation, but also can enable them to select their neighbors by selling land to individuals of their choosing—for example, their children or other kin. Both black and white landowners have done so. Their children often live in new houses or trailers on their parents' land. These family members are engaged in intense interaction and constant exchanges. Often the older person takes care of grandchildren if members of the middle generation work off the farm, or the older persons may participate in the farm work if a son has taken over the farm. Because more whites than blacks own farmland, this situation is more common among whites; all but two whites live in this kind of arrangement with close kin nearby.

Blacks live in similar arrangements if they have land to do it with and children who want to stay. Of landowners with children, over half the whites and almost three-quarters of the blacks have given their children land for a house. The land owned by blacks, however, is likely to be less extensive and less productive than that of whites, and so fewer blacks are able to set up a son in farming. Almost all of the black farm owners have children, but only two have set up a son in farming, whereas about half of the white landowners have children to succeed them.

White parents are a resource for their children not only because they will eventually bequeath their land to them but also because they turn over property to them gradually over a number of years, thus enabling their children to get a start in farming. Two examples illustrate the ways in which this happens. Fred Cooper, white, owns 180 acres. He has two children, a daughter who is married and lives in another state and a son who has come back to farm. Mr. Cooper

[201]

wanted his son to go to agricultural college, but the son preferred to get a degree in business management instead. When he decided that he wanted to farm after all, his father let him use the farm and tobacco allotment. There are frictions between father and son because the son does not take his father's advice, and the son's mistakes are costing the father $10,000 a year. Yet both parents think that the son will eventually make a go of it.

Milton Quick, white, owns 280 acres of land. He is surrounded by his three sons: His youngest son lives with him and will inherit the "homeplace"; his second son lives next door in a house built on land Milton gave him; his oldest son lives next door on the other side. The eldest son is the one who has received the most—twenty acres of land and money to build a house. Milton also gave him all his farming equipment and rents land and the tobacco allotment in an arrangement that is extremely favorable to his son. Officially he pays his father the going rate, but then the father gives a large part of the money back to his son, thus renting him the allotment as cheaply as possible and helping him save income tax. On the mantelpiece of his living room, Milton keeps a piece of yellow paper. It is his will. On it, he has drawn a map of his land and a plan of how he intends to divide the land among his sons. He was anxious to give each one a fair share and access to the river, and he is glad he discussed the planned division with all of them. The document is permanently displayed in this public place, where it reminds the sons of their stake in the farm. From the wear and tear of the paper, it is clear that it has been unfolded, studied, and refolded many times. Among the many psychological and emotional needs his children fill for him, they give Milton the satisfaction of having someone to whom he can bequeath his property.

## Discussion

What has emerged from this analysis are two categories of individuals who, despite having lived in the same rural environment, have had very different experiences. On the one hand are blacks, most of whom are landless or own little land, all children of sharecroppers, all of whom have experienced economic uncertainty at best and extreme hardship at worst. Apart from their own health, they consider their children their major assets. They are certain that hard work is an absolute necessity for survival; their children have helped them to survive and now continue to safeguard their well-being.

On the other hand are whites, predominantly landowners, all but one the offspring of landowning farmers and artisans. While not all of them have been certain of economic security as such, they are fairly convinced that hard work will lead to economic success. If for blacks economic success meant bare survival, for whites it meant accumulating assets to be enjoyed but also to be passed on to their children.

The children of landless sharecroppers can expect no inheritance from their parents and in fact often help to support their parents, rather than the reverse. Whether we call this role reversal filial maturity (Blenkner 1965) or socioeconomic dependency (Clark 1972), it occurs earlier among blacks than among whites in this community. In the case of blacks who receive money from their children, the timing depends less on the diminishing economic position of the parents, which has always been weak, and more on the establishment of economic independence of their children. The moment children can help their needy parents, they do. In contrast, among whites, this role reversal has not occurred so far because the elderly in this community are relatively secure economically.

While blacks and whites have not had the same opportunities to own land, their feelings and their ideology about the land are strikingly similar. All stressed the desirability of owning land, the living one could make from it, its role in establishing a home, the security it represented, its importance in keeping the family together, and the pride and satisfaction landownership engendered. Land is used to cement family relations. Those who have it attach personal and social significance to it; those who do not have it aspire to obtaining it. Given that white landowners (who sold land as a resource management strategy) were more willing to consider land as a liquid asset than were blacks (who sold reluctantly and out of necessity), one could argue that land as legacy meant more to those who obtained it with greater difficulty.

What happens when the importance of agriculture is eclipsed by industry? Land remains a source of wealth and power, but it is no longer the sole source of livelihood. Access to it no longer has such far-reaching consequences. Land is only one kind of resource, and one can expect other kinds of resources to assume a similar significance and to generate the same kind of divisions and social dynamics as landownership in this community. With the shift to wage labor, the importance of landownership as a differentiating mechanism is declining. Those who have been systematically barred from owning—but confined to working—the land now have other options. Wage labor through industrialization is enabling more young people to achieve what their elders dreamed of: a place of their own and some kind of security.

Whether industrialization is likely to lead to reduced power and wealth differences between whites and blacks in this community is another question. Like land, jobs are a limited resource. Among the next generation of elderly there will be some who were better able than others to exploit this resource. While earning power may replace landownership in determining economic well-being, the difference in access to resources may well continue to coincide largely with race as long as blacks as a group suffer discrimination in education and employment.

As I mentioned earlier in the chapter, resource control takes on different expressions in different settings. The urban counterpart to the land in this community could conceivably be the social security check. In a ghetto, a small but regular income may be more valuable than an unpredictable windfall based on irregular employment. Stack (1974) has shown that small sums of money go a long way in the kin network of the urban poor and that "it is scarcity and not sufficiency that makes people generous" (Sahlins 1963:165). When money is scarce, recipients of (albeit small) social security checks may actually become the pivotal points in the kin network. They might become Big Men of sorts and not unlike Milton Quick, who claimed that "the greatest thing about owning land is that nobody can order me around. I'm not obligated to anyone. Nobody can tell me what to do." He paused; then, smiling, he continued, "They can tell me, but I don't have to do it." For him, not owning anything means submission to the desire of others, while property ownership confers a certain power over others.

## Acknowledgements

This chapter is an expanded version of an article published in *Research on Aging* 5(4):511–526, December, 1983. The research was carried out under a National Institute on Aging postdoctoral fellowship at the Center for the Study of Aging and Human Development, Duke University Medical Center, from June, 1979, to June, 1982. I am grateful to George Maddox for guidance throughout the research and for a critical reading of an earlier draft of this chapter. I also want to thank Corinne Nydegger and the anonymous readers for *Research on Aging* for their helpful suggestions.

## References Cited

Adams, David L. 1975. Who Are the Rural Aged? In *Rural Environments and Aging*, ed. Robert C. Atchley and Thomas O. Byerts, pp. 11–21. Washington, D.C.: Gerontological Society.

Atchley, Robert C., and Thomas O. Byerts, eds. 1975. *Rural Environments and Aging*. Washington, D.C.: Gerontological Society.

Billingsley, Andrew. 1969. Family Functioning in the Low Income Black Community. *Social Casework* 50:563–572.

Binstock, Robert H. 1974. Aging and the Future of American Politics. *Annals of the American Academy of Political and Social Science* 415:199–212.

Binstock, Robert H., and Ethel Shanas, eds. 1976. *Handbook of Aging and the Social Sciences*. New York: Van Nostrand Reinhold.

Blenkner, Margaret. 1965. Social Work and Family Relationships in Later Life. In *Social Structure and the Family: Generational Relations*, ed. Ethel Shanas and Gordon F. Streib, pp. 46–59. Englewood Cliffs, N.J.: Prentice-Hall.

Butler, Robert N. 1975. *Why Survive? Being Old in America*. New York: Harper & Row.

Bylund, Robert A., Charles O. Crawford, and Nelson L. LeRay. 1979. Housing Quality of the Elderly: A Rural-Urban Comparison. *Journal of Minority Aging* 4:14–24.

Clark, Margaret. 1972. Cultural Values and Dependency in Later Life. In *Aging and Modernization*, ed. Donald Cowgill and Lowell Holmes, pp. 263–274. New York: Appleton-Century-Crofts.

Dowd, James J. 1975. Aging as Exchange: A Preface to Theory. *Journal of Gerontology* 30(5):584–594.

Glenn, Norval D., and Lester Hill, Jr. 1977. Rural-Urban Differences in Attitudes and Behavior in the United States. *Annals of the American Academy of Political and Social Science* 429:36–50.

Gröger, B. Lisa. 1982. Peasants and Policy: Comparative Perspectives on Aging. In *Holding on to the Land and the Lord*, ed. Robert L. Hall and Carol B. Stack, pp. 121–130. Athens, Ga.: Univ. of Georgia Press.

Jackson, Jacquelyne Johnson. 1969. Negro Aged Parents and Adult Children: Their Affective Relationships. *Varia*, spring, pp. 1–14.

———. 1970. Aged Negroes: Their Cultural Departures from Statistical Stereotypes and Rural-Urban Differences. *Gerontologist* 10(2):140–145.

————. 1974. NCBA, Black Aged and Politics. *Annals of the American Academy of Political and Social Science* 415:138–159.

Kent, Donald P. 1971. The Negro Aged. *Gerontologist* 11(1):48–51.

Muller, Charlotte F. 1980. Economic Roles and the Status of the Elderly. In *Aging and Society*, ed. Edgar Borgatto and Neil G. McCluskey, pp. 17–41. Beverly Hills, Calif.: Sage.

Sahlins, Marshall D. 1963. On the Sociology of Primitive Exchange. In *The Relevance of Models for Social Anthropology*, ed. M. Banton, pp. 139–236. London: Tavistock.

Schulz, James H. 1976. Income Distribution and the Aging. In *Handbook of Aging and the Social Sciences*, ed. Robert H. Binstock and Ethel Shanas, pp. 561–591. New York: Van Nostrand Reinhold.

Seltzer, Mildred, Sherry L. Corbett, and Robert C. Atchley, eds. 1978. *Social Problems of the Aging*. Belmont, Calif.: Wadsworth.

Sheldon, Henry D. 1967. Distribution of the Rural Aged Population. In *Older Rural Americans*, ed. E. Grant Youmans, pp. 117–143. Lexington: Univ. of Kentucky Press.

Simmons, Leo W. 1957. Aging in Pre-Industrial Cultures. In *Aging in the Modern World*, ed. Clark Tibbits and Wilma Donahue, pp. 70–83. Ann Arbor: Univ. of Michigan Press.

Stack, Carol B. 1974. *All Our Kin*. New York: Van Nostrand Reinhold.

Streib, Gordon F. 1976. Social Stratification and Aging. In *Handbook of Aging and the Social Sciences*, ed. Robert H. Binstock and Ethel Shanas, pp. 160–185. New York: Van Nostrand Reinhold.

Sussman, Marvin B. 1965. Relationships of Adult Children with Their Parents in the United States. In *Social Structure and the Family*, ed. Ethel Shanas and Gordon F. Streib, pp. 62–92. Englewood Cliffs, N.J.: Prentice-Hall.

————. 1976. The Family Life of Old People. In *Handbook of Aging and the Social Sciences*, ed. Robert H. Binstock and Ethel Shanas, pp. 218–243. New York: Van Nostrand Reinhold.

Taietz, Philip, and Sande Milton. 1979. Rural-Urban Differences in the Structure of Services for the Elderly in Upstate New York Counties. *Journal of Gerontology* 34:429–437.

U.S. Bureau of the Census. 1977. *County and City Data Book*. Washington, D.C.

————. 1983. *1980 Census of the Population*. Vol. 1, *Characteristics of the Population*. Ch. C, General Social and Economic Characteristics. Part 35, North Carolina. Washington, D.C.

U.S. Office of the Federal Register. 1981. General Characteristics of Community Action Programs: CSA Income Poverty Guidelines. *Federal Register*, Mar. 5, 1981, vol. 46, no. 43, pp. 15271–72.

Watson, Wilbur H. 1983. Selected Demographic and Social Aspects of Older Blacks. In *Aging in Minority Groups*, ed. R. L. McNeely and John L. Colen, pp. 42–49. Beverly Hills, Calif.: Sage.

Youmans, E. Grant, ed. 1967. *Older Rural Americans*. Lexington: Univ. of Kentucky Press.

————. 1973. Perspectives on the Older American in a Rural Setting. In *The Neglected Older American*, ed. John G. Cull and Richard E. Hardy, pp. 65–85. Springfield, Ill.: Thomas.

————. 1977. The Rural Aged. *Annals of the American Academy of Political and Social Science* 429:81–90.

PART **IV**

# LEGAL AND POLICY ISSUES

The lives of American farmers are profoundly affected by government legislation and private contractual agreements. Laws and contracts regulate bank lending, specify land use rights and obligations, set price supports, and provide money for land-grant universities.

The chapters in this section examine the social settings within which laws, public policies, and contracts are established and enforced. The authors emphasize neither legal technicalities nor abstract considerations of right and wrong. Instead, they focus on the cultural norms and economic and social relations influencing political behavior and organizational decision making.

Miriam Wells's paper compares the sharecropping arrangements of cotton farmers in the post–Civil War South, grain farmers in the Midwest in the second half of the nineteenth century, and strawberry producers in contemporary California. She notes that two broad perspectives have dominated analyses of sharecropping in the United States and elsewhere. Some writers explain sharecropping as a predictable consequence of market forces; others regard it as part of a repressive sociopolitical system in which tenants have little power. Wells argues that neither position is altogether correct because sharecropping systems vary greatly. Careful ethnographic and historical analyses of relations between landowners and laborers are necessary prerequisities to understanding sharecropping systems in particular places and times. Wells points out that tenants exercise some control over the form of sharecropping arrangements in all three cases she examines.

In many densely populated areas, prime farmland is being converted to nonagricultural use. This conversion has led to political, legal, and economic conflicts between farmers and nonfarmers. In her contribution, Frances Aaron Brooks describes conflicts caused by the depredations of trespassers on New Jersey farms. She notes that suburbanites view farmland as public open space rather than as private property. Nonfarmers in the area Brooks studied thus do not regard trespassing as a serious crime. Brooks argues that policymakers and judges seem to share this perception because trespass laws are weak and offenders are seldom punished severely.

In the final chapter, Gerald Britan, a specialist in ethnographic analyses of bureaucracies, describes the effects of yearly budgetary negotiations, formal organizational structures, and informal cultural understandings upon agricultural science policies. He examines an attempt under the Carter administration to reorganize the agricultural science bureaucracy in order to give a larger voice to consumer, environmental, labor, minority, and urban constituencies. Bureaucratic infighting and pressure brought by powerful lobbying groups resulted in government-funded research continuing to concentrate on problems of interest to agribusiness and farmers with large-scale, capital-intensive enterprises.

# [8]

# Sharecropping in the United States: A Political Economy Perspective

**Miriam J. Wells**

*Department of Applied Behavioral Sciences*
*University of California, Davis*

American sharecropping is poorly understood. Despite its popular association with the postbellum South and despite assertions from a range of economic standpoints that sharecropping is inefficient and likely to disappear in advanced capitalist systems (Lenin 1899; Marshall 1890; Marx 1894; Mill 1848; Smith 1869), share contracts have been a significant feature of American agriculture since the early 1800s. Not only does sharecropping persist outside the South, but much of the impressive gain in agricultural productivity in the United States has occurred in regions where share tenancy is dominant (Bray 1963:25). Moreover, in recent years sharecropping has reemerged in highly rationalized fruit and vegetable industries that had long used wage labor (Wells 1984).

There are two dominant theoretical perspectives on share tenancy. The first emphasizes free choice and explains sharecropping in terms of the rational laws of the competitive market (Cheung 1969; Reid 1979a). The second emphasizes extraeconomic coercion and attributes sharecropping to a repressive sociopolitical system that exploits tenants and fosters economic stagnation (Lenin 1899; Marx 1894). These perspectives differ on several key issues: whether sharecropping is the result of individual decisions or of a particular socioeconomic system; whether it is the result of economics or politics; and whether the relations between landowners and share tenants reflect coercion or complementarity of interests. Finally, these schools of thought differ about the distributional justice and the long-term economic consequences of this institution. While these are not the only ways to view share tenancy, the preponderance of contemporary work takes one of these two views, both of which have distinct limits as tools of analysis.

I argue here that the relative accuracy and utility of these analytical perspectives depends in large part on the sharecropping system considered. Although generally treated as a single phenomenon, American sharecropping has in fact taken many forms. It has no single set of causes, nor does it have a single impact on efficiency or a single role in socioeconomic development. What is needed is a framework within which the range of empirical cases can be analyzed. Such a framework must be sensitive to historical fluctuations and change, not only because sharecropping depends on conditions that are subject to change, but because when sharecropping is coercive, the resulting tensions can themselves generate change. What is needed is an understanding of the actual interrelations between landowners and sharecroppers, the purposes that drive them, and the ways they are affected by their wider operating contexts. The processes of sharecropping are as important as the structures they establish because they reveal the flexibility in contracts and the life cycle mobility of contractors.

The intent of this chapter is not to provide an exhaustive study of sharecropping in the United States, but rather to demonstrate its variability and to present a framework for its analysis. With this framework, we can reevaluate traditional analyses of sharecropping and clarify the determinants and diversity of contemporary American share tenancy. I will examine sharecropping arrangements as "forms of production" in terms of: (1) the relations within the production unit, in particular the distribution of control over the means of production and the social relations among participants, and (2) the dynamics of the wider social formation.[1] In doing so, I will focus on the concrete relations between landowners and share tenants in particular regions and crop industries, as they are shaped by changes in the political and economic environment. I will also specify the diverse combinations and interrelations of economic and political variables and of individual action and structural constraint.

---

1. See Harriet Friedmann's insightful development of the "form of production" concept (1978). The notion of the "social formation" is defined by Althusser and Balibar (1979:313) as the complex whole of society including economic, political, and ideological components.

I will first examine the two traditional approaches in more detail and present my proposed political and economic framework. Next I will describe the demography of share tenancy in the United States and consider three historic examples: cash grain sharecropping in nineteenth-century Iowa, cotton sharecropping in the postbellum South, and strawberry sharecropping in post-1960s California. In the first case, the vast majority of sharecroppers were whites of European extraction. In the second case, emphasis will be placed on black share tenants, who operated in a distinct web of sociopolitical constraints. In the third case, the sharecroppers are Americans of Mexican descent, almost all of whom speak only Spanish.

## Sharecropping and Social Theory

### The Complementarity Perspective

Traditional neoclassical economists saw sharecropping as inefficient and unlikely to persist because it fosters the underinvestment of labor and capital. John Stuart Mill (1848), Adam Smith (1869), and Alfred Marshall (1890), for example, all argued that because the sharecropper receives only half of the fruits of his labor, he will tend to apply his resources only until they total half the value of his marginal output. Landowners will similarly tend to underinvest in land assets. More recently, neoclassical scholars have reevaluated this traditional point of view, arguing that under certain market conditions not only is sharecropping efficient, but it offers definitive advantages. Steven Cheung, for example, holds that if there is competition among landowners for labor and among laborers for land, and if landlords and tenants freely negotiate contracts, then sharecropping will be efficient and will provide a fair return to both parties (Cheung 1969). Moreover, Cheung argues, because share contracts distribute risk between landowner and tenant, they will be preferred in especially risky or uncertain situations.

While there is evidence that the risk perceived by the contracting parties (Stiglitz 1974:219, 230) and the uncertainty of inputs such as labor (Albert 1982; Newbery and Stiglitz 1979) are significant motivators of share farming, not all sharecropping occurs in risky environments. Moreover, other means can be used to disperse risk (Bardhan and Srinivasan 1971:8; Rao 1971:586–587; Reid 1973:12; Roumasset

[213]

1976:94; Wright and Kunreuther 1975:544). Another motivation for sharecropping is the potential to pool resources. For example, tenants who lack the production expertise, entrepreneurial ability, or capital necessary to shoulder all the risk as cash renters and landlords who lack labor but have managerial expertise, land, and capital can reach mutually advantageous agreements (Reid 1979a; Hallagan 1978).

The division of benefits and risks between landowners and tenants may also have a desirable impact on production. A number of authors argue that because both parties suffer or profit from the same overall endeavor, they both have optimal motivation to increase efficiency (Reid 1976b:574; Stiglitz 1974:242). Share contracts can also have a salutary impact on the climate of trust (Murrell 1983:290; Waswo 1977:25–30). This consequence is especially advantageous in agriculture, argues Joseph Reid, because farming involves a high degree of sequential uncertainty—that is, uncertainty whose negative effects can be minimized by flexible responses over the course of the season. In such situations sharecropping may actually reduce risk in that it provides motivation for landowners and tenants to modify production plans in agreed-upon ways (Reid 1975:434–435; 1976b:575).

The characteristics of a particular crop industry may also encourage sharecropping. For example, in production processes in which effort (in terms of pace, thoroughness, efficiency, or inventiveness) is important and cannot be easily observed, direct supervision may be costly or ineffective. Under such conditions, a self-motivated labor force can reduce supervisory costs and enhance efficiency (Murrell 1983:284–285, 287; Stiglitz 1974:219, 242). Consequently, sharecropping may be especially well suited to industries in which hand labor comprises a relatively high proportion of production costs, the quality of labor is important, and the landlord wants, without undue supervisorial costs, to specify cropping practices and to include provisions protecting soils, perennial plants, and other assets (Caballero 1982:10). One would expect sharecropping to increase as managerial complexities and risk increase (Reid 1975:437–438) and to be especially well suited to crops whose production can be subdivided among families (Paige 1975:58–60). Sharecropping landlords have at their disposal a variety of measures to increase their control over production. For example, they can directly vary the share rate with the rate of labor input, contractually stipulate the kinds and amounts of labor that sharecroppers provide, vary their own contributions (seed, fertilizer, etc.), vary the amount of land allotted to tenants, and renew share leases frequently (Johnson 1950:118–119).

[214]

The "complementarity perspective" just elaborated views share-cropping as a rational response to market conditions, given certain reciprocal needs and capacities of landowners and tenants and certain production problems and patterns characteristic of agriculture in general and of some crop industries in particular. While it is undisputedly important to explore market conditions and the fit of landowner and tenant interests, this viewpoint neglects political and ideological factors that enter into market conditions. In some cases such "externalities" may actually create the market conditions and shape the distribution of human and physical capital that makes sharecropping advantageous. By ignoring these political and ideological factors, this perspective places some of the most important causes of sharecropping outside the pale of analysis. In addition, the latitude of tenants especially and landlords as well to choose among alternatives may be underrepresented. In this sense the complementarity approach may assume market conditions that are contrary to empirical fact.

### The Coercion Perspective

The "coercion perspective" explicitly disagrees that unfettered factor markets, efficiency, and free, rational choice are characteristic of sharecropping systems. Proponents of this school of thought agree with the traditional neoclassical position that sharecropping is inefficient, but attribute this inefficiency not to the structure of share contracts, but to the operation of wider social and political institutions. This point of view is grounded in the seminal works of Marx (1894) and Lenin (1899), who viewed share farming as an actual historical stage in the transition from feudalism to capitalism. According to this perspective, because share tenants are exploited, they would not remain in this status on the basis of free, rational economic choice. In fact, the hallmark of sharecropping systems, as opposed to competitive capitalist markets in wage labor and contracts, is the prevalence of extra-economic coercion. This coercion takes the form of legal and political institutions and of illegal practices such as terrorism which circumscribe the rights and alternatives of tenants. Also important are societal ideologies such as racism, which rationalize and perpetuate tenants' subordinate status (Marx 1894:2ff., 324ff.). Tenants are also prevented from moving to more advantageous situations by being allotted subsistence plots of land, so that they are tied to the landowner's estate and provide a pool of tractable labor (Lenin 1899:191).

[215]

The proponents of coercion perspective also argue that because production methods and implements in such systems are in the hands of impoverished and uneducated direct producers, technology is stagnant and productivity is low (Lenin 1899:192). As a result share farming cannot compete with more productive capitalist enterprises. Sharecropping is expected to disappear when the political constraints on share tenants weaken and when competitive markets and transportation erode the boundaries of closed, self-sufficient feudal economies (Lenin 1899:202, 207–218; Marx 1894:795, 802–813). Where share tenancy does persist, it is seen as an anachronism perpetuated temporarily through isolation (Marx 1894:789).

In short, this point of view holds that the economic alternatives of share tenants as a group are so heavily circumscribed that their individual latitude for choice is negligible. In addition, landowners are motivated by irrational traditional values, such as racism, which encourage economically irrational decisions. As a result, sharecropping can best be explained in terms of share tenants' categorical oppression by sociopolitical institutions and practices.

While this approach is valuable in directing attention toward the role of domination and the level of social systemic constraints, as a single analytical framework this perspective, too, has limitations. First, its view of direct producers as passive players in the march of history whose fate is predetermined may underrepresent the initiative that they in fact exercise and the extent to which they have mobility and choice. Second, the assumption that sharecropping landlords are irrational does not allow for the possibility that extraeconomic domination may be economically rational and that share farming may be technologically advanced and productive. Third, although it identifies coercive sociopolitical institutions, this approach generally fails to examine the mechanisms through which, and the extent to which, political constraints affect market conditions. As a result, the invalidity of a microeconomic approach is not proved.

## The Political Economy Framework and Class Struggle

Because each of these two perspectives views sharecropping as determined by a single category of variables (either political or economic), neither takes into account the variable weighting and interpenetration of political and economic forces as they affect share farming. Nor do they help us understand the roles that sharecropping has played in the evolution of rural class relations. I will show that sharecropping arrangements are quite varied; one may be empirically closer to the coercion characterization and another to the complementarity characterization. That is, sharecropping arrangements may be grounded in systemic constraints or in individual initiative, the result of political or of economic considerations, depending on the circumstances. As a result, these systems can be analyzed with varying degrees of success by one approach or the other. In many cases, both approaches are useful in analyzing a particular situation. More appropriate is a political economy framework that examines relations within the production unit and within the wider social formation, which can help clarify the diversity of causation and outcome in sharecropping systems. Using such a framework, I will examine the role of sharecropping in rural class relations and the causes and consequences of sharecropping systems.

## Sharecropping in the United States

Sharecropping has played a major role in American agricultural history. Although data on share farming were not systematically recorded until 1880, narrative accounts before that time describe sharecropping in colonial New England, in the antebellum South, and on the middle and far western frontiers (Gates 1973; Innes 1976; Reid 1976a). In 1880 the federal census first reported the tenure status of farm operators, and it continued to do so through 1974. The census defines a share tenant as a person who works land owned by another, to whom he pays a share of the crops, and/or of the livestock or livestock products, in rent.

As Table 8-1 indicates, 17.5 percent of the farm operators in the United States were share tenants in 1880. The distribution of share farmers varied by region, ranging from a high of 24.4 percent in the South to 13.4 percent in the North and 8.5 percent in the West. Although share tenancy was most common in the South, it was more prevalent than cash rental in all regions. Share tenancy increased nationwide until 1930, when depression farm foreclosures brought it to an all-time high, and then it began to subside. By 1974 share tenants comprised only 5.6 percent of farm operators in the country, and regional distribution had shifted. Share tenancy is now more

[217]

Table 8-1. Percentage distribution of farm operators by region and tenure, 1880–1974

| Region | Tenure | 1880 | 1890 | 1900 | 1910 | 1920 | 1930 | 1940 | 1950 | 1959 | 1964 | 1969 | 1974 |
|---|---|---|---|---|---|---|---|---|---|---|---|---|---|
| United States | Owners and managers | 74.4 | 71.6 | 64.7 | 63.0 | 61.9 | 57.6 | 61.3 | 73.2 | 80.2 | 82.9 | 89.8 | 88.7 |
| | Tenants | 25.6 | 28.4 | 35.3 | 37.0 | 38.1 | 42.4 | 38.7 | 26.8 | 19.8 | 17.1 | 10.2 | 11.3 |
| | Cash | 8.0 | 9.9 | 13.1 | 13.0 | 10.1 | 7.8 | 8.4 | 4.0 | 2.9 | 3.2 | 2.0 | 3.0 |
| | Share | 17.5 | 18.4 | 22.2 | 24.0 | 28.0 | 34.6 | 26.8 | 19.9 | 15.5 | 11.5 | 5.6 | 5.6 |
| | Other and unspecified | NA[a] | NA | b | b | b | | 3.5 | 2.9 | 2.4 | 2.4 | 2.6 | 2.7 |
| North | Owners and managers | 80.8 | 77.9 | 73.8 | 73.5 | 71.8 | 70.0 | 68.9 | 78.9 | 80.9 | 83.0 | 87.4 | 86.0 |
| | Tenants | 19.2 | 22.1 | 26.2 | 26.5 | 28.2 | 30.0 | 31.1 | 21.1 | 19.1 | 17.0 | 12.6 | 14.0 |
| | Cash | 5.8 | 7.7 | 9.5 | 9.8 | 9.2 | 8.2 | 8.3 | 3.3 | 2.6 | 2.8 | 3.3 | 2.8 |
| | Share | 13.4 | 14.4 | 16.7 | 16.7 | 19.0 | 21.8 | 20.3 | 16.0 | 14.7 | 12.4 | 6.3 | 8.7 |
| | Other and unspecified | NA | NA | b | b | b | c | 2.5 | 1.8 | 1.8 | 1.8 | 3.0 | 2.5 |
| South | Owners and managers | 63.8 | 61.5 | 53.0 | 50.4 | 50.4 | 44.4 | 51.8 | 65.9 | 77.7 | 81.5 | 85.0 | 88.8 |
| | Tenants | 36.2 | 38.5 | 47.0 | 49.6 | 49.6 | 55.6 | 48.2 | 34.1 | 22.3 | 18.5 | 15.0 | 11.2 |
| | Cash | 11.7 | 13.4 | 17.5 | 14.6 | 10.1 | 7.4 | 8.5 | 4.5 | 3.0 | 3.4 | 3.3 | 4.4 |
| | Share | 24.5 | 25.1 | 29.5 | 33.0 | 38.5 | 48.2 | 35.2 | 26.0 | 16.2 | 12.0 | 6.7 | 3.6 |
| | Other and unspecified | NA | NA | b | b | 1.0 | | 4.5 | 3.6 | 3.1 | 3.1 | 5.0 | 3.2 |
| South, white | Owners and managers | NA | NA | 63.9 | 60.8 | 61.1 | 53.4 | 59.5 | 74.2 | 83.5 | 85.6 | 88.9 | 90.2 |
| | Tenants | NA | NA | 36.1 | 39.2 | 38.9 | 46.6 | 40.5 | 25.8 | 16.5 | 14.4 | 11.1 | 9.8 |
| | Cash | NA | NA | 10.0 | 8.7 | 6.4 | 6.0 | 8.2 | 3.8 | 2.5 | 3.0 | NA | NA |
| | Share | NA | NA | 26.1 | 28.9 | 31.4 | 40.6 | 28.5 | 18.7 | 11.4 | 8.9 | NA | NA |
| | Other and unspecified | NA | NA | b | 1.7 | 1.1 | | 3.8 | 3.8 | 2.6 | 2.5 | NA | NA |

| | | | | | | | | | | | | |
|---|---|---|---|---|---|---|---|---|---|---|---|---|
| **South, nonwhite** | | | | | | | | | | | | |
| Owners and managers | NA | NA | 25.4 | 24.7 | 23.8 | 20.7 | 25.5 | 34.6 | 48.0 | 55.4 | 71.7 | 87.5 |
| Tenants | NA | NA | 74.6 | 75.3 | 76.2 | 79.3 | 74.5 | 65.4 | 52.0 | 44.6 | 28.3 | 12.5 |
|   Cash | NA | NA | 36.7 | 29.3 | 19.3 | 11.1 | 9.5 | 7.1 | 5.6 | 6.5 | 5.4 | NA |
|   Share | NA | NA | 37.9 | 43.2 | 56.2 | b | 58.1 | 53.8 | 40.8 | 31.7 | 15.5 | NA |
|   Other and unspecified | NA | NA | b | 2.8 | 0.7 | 68.2 | 6.9 | 4.5 | 5.6 | 6.4 | 18.4 | NA |
| **West** | | | | | | | | | | | | |
| Owners and managers | 86.0 | 87.9 | 84.1 | 86.1 | 82.3 | 79.1 | 78.7 | 82.3 | 88.1 | 88.7 | 87.2 | 87.9 |
| Tenants | 14.0 | 12.1 | 15.9 | 13.9 | 17.7 | 20.9 | 21.3 | 17.7 | 11.9 | 11.3 | 11.8 | 12.1 |
|   Cash | 5.5 | 5.0 | 8.7 | 7.4 | 8.2 | 8.1 | 8.9 | 3.5 | 4.1 | 4.5 | 4.6 | 4.7 |
|   Share | 8.5 | 7.1 | 7.3 | 6.6 | 9.5 | 12.8 | 10.2 | 12.0 | 6.0 | 5.1 | 5.2 | 4.8 |
|   Other and unspecified | NA | NA | b | b | b | c | 2.2 | 2.2 | 1.8 | 1.7 | 3.0 | 2.6 |

a NA = data not available.

b Other and unspecified included with cash tenants.

c Figures for standing renters (renters paying a fixed quantity of products) were included with "other tenants" in 1930 and 1925; in 1920 they were included with "other tenants" for the southern states only, and with "cash tenants" for the northern and western states.

Sources: Computed or taken directly from the following sources: 1880–1890, *Eleventh Census of the United States*, vol. 5, pp. 4, 116; 1900, *Twelfth Census of the United States*, vol. 5, pt. 1, Tables LXV and LXVI (p. lxvi), XCVIII (p. xcviii), and C (p. c); 1910, *Thirteenth Census of the United States*, vol. 5, Table 25, p. 199, Table 28, pp. 202–203, Table 30, pp. 210, 215; 1920, *Fourteenth Census of the United States*, vol. 5, Table 16, pp. 214–215; *Farm Tenancy in the United States: 1920* (Census Monograph 4), Table 53, pp. 145–147; 1930, *Fifteenth Census of the United States*, vol. 4, Table 19, pp. 162–163, Table 20, p. 170; 1940, *Sixteenth Census of the United States Agriculture*, vol. 3, Table 22, pp. 30, 32, 34, 36; 1950, *United States Census of Agriculture: 1950*, vol. 2, Table 21, pp. 956–958; 1959, *U.S. Census of Agriculture: 1959*, vol. 2, Table 24, pp. 1116, 1118; 1964, *U.S. Census of Agriculture: 1964*, vol. 2, Table 11, pp. 769–775, Table 18, p. 784; 1969, *U.S. Census of Agriculture: 1969*, vol. 2, Table 39, p. 105; 1974, *U.S. Census of Agriculture: 1974*, vol. 2, Table 39, pp. 1–45, 1–46, 1–47, 1–48, Table 53, pp. 1–84, 1–86, Table 59, p. 1–93.

common in the North (8.7 percent) and the West (4.8 percent) than in the South (3.6 percent). The decrease in the South is attributable largely to the mechanization of cotton production and its exodus to new producing regions.

Sharecropping has been and still is concentrated in certain crop industries: cotton, cash grains (primarily corn), tobacco, permanent-tree fruit and nuts, and more recently labor-intensive fruit and vegetable crops. In the North, sharecropping has centered in the north central states and has been negligible on the northeastern seaboard. Sharecroppers in the North have produced primarily cash grains and more recently cucumbers as well. In the South sharecropping has been associated mainly with cotton and more recently with cash grain. In the far West it has been associated with cash grain and permanent-tree fruit and nuts and more recently with strawberries (Reed and Horel 1980; Reid 1979a; Wells 1984). Crop characteristics alone cannot account for the use of share contracts, however. For example, although strawberries and pickling cucumbers were profitably farmed with wage labor for most of the post–World War II period, many landowners have recently switched to share contracts (Wells 1984). Similarly, although most corn-farming tenants pay rent in crop shares in the middle and far West, in the postbellum South, corn was less likely than cotton to be sharecropped (Reid 1979a:295–296). As will be seen, while commodity-related constraints such as risk, labor-intensiveness, and the character of labor processes make sharecropping useful in the United States, commodity characteristics are only necessary preconditions. It is the changing sociopolitical dynamics of the wider social formation that provide the sufficient conditions for share farming.


*Iowa: Cash Grain Sharecropping, 1850–1900*

Share farming in Iowa from 1850 to 1900 approximates the representations of the complementarity model. That is, the benefits to individual landowners and tenants, whose economic choices were not significantly constrained by sociopolitical factors, largely account for share tenancy. Sharecropping has been the dominant form of tenancy in Iowa throughout most of its history, and cash grain has been the product of choice. The period between 1850 and 1900, which saw the transition from frontier settlement to established commercial agri-

Table 8-2. Percentage distribution of farm operators by tenure, Iowa, 1880–1974

| Tenure | 1880 | 1890 | 1900 | 1910 | 1920 | 1930 | 1940 | 1950 | 1959 | 1964 | 1969 | 1974 |
|---|---|---|---|---|---|---|---|---|---|---|---|---|
| Owners and Managers | 76.2 | 71.9 | 65.1 | 62.2 | 58.3 | 52.7 | 52.4 | 61.9 | 65.0 | 68.6 | 74.1 | 78.6 |
| Tenants | 23.8 | 28.1 | 34.9 | 37.8 | 41.7 | 47.3 | 47.6 | 38.1 | 35.0 | 31.4 | 25.9 | 21.4 |
| Cash | 4.5 | 12.4 | 19.5 | 21.7 | 22.0 | 21.4 | 13.9 | 6.4 | 4.7 | 5.1 | 3.8 | 3.9 |
| Share | 19.3 | 15.7 | 15.4 | 16.1 | 19.7 | 25.9 | 31.4 | 29.6 | 28.5 | 24.7 | 17.1 | 13.9 |
| Other and unspecified | b | b | b | b | b | c | 2.3 | 2.1 | 1.8 | 1.6 | 5.0 | 3.6 |

For footnotes and sources, see Table 8-1.

culture, is richly documented. Iowa became a state in 1846, and between 1850 and 1890 the population increased from two hundred thousand to two million. Settlers spent much of the early period breaking sod and readying farmland for agriculture; by 1890 the area was largely settled, and agricultural specialization by region had begun (Winters 1978:10–11). Tenancy was common from the earliest years, ranging from 11.6 percent to 22.1 percent of farm operators in 1850 and consisting largely of share agreements (Winters 1977:384). Federal census data on tenancy in Iowa were recorded beginning in 1880. These data show a high proportion of share rental in 1880 when the frontier was still being settled (19.3 percent of farmers), a declining but still considerable proportion through the end of the century, and an increasing proportion after that date until 1950 (see Table 8-2).

Most share tenants in Iowa grew corn, and by the 1890s share tenancy was concentrated most heavily in the north central and northwestern counties, which specialized in cash grain production (Winters 1977:400–405). Tenant shares of the net proceeds varied from one-fourth to three-fourths, with one-third and one-half being the most common. How the shares were divided depended on the crop farmed and on differences in the landlord's inputs. Share-renting landlords were more involved than cash-renting landlords in their tenants' farms: they generally oversaw farm operations and provided implements, work animals, and sometimes part of the cost of fertilizer, seed, and threshing. Most contracts lasted for one year, a term that was agreeable to tenants, who could move on to possibly better lands after a year, and to landlords, who may have wanted to seek better tenants. In Iowa, as elsewhere in the Corn Belt, share contracts included stipulations to ensure efficient production, the wise husbandry of property, and the collection of rents (Bogue 1959:169–170, 182–183; Socolofsky 1950:347). For example, contracts commonly required share tenants to haul out and spread manure regularly and prohibited them from burning or removing straw and cornstalks from the fields. Some contracts specified crop rotation patterns, forbade the growing of soil-depleting crops such as flax or Hungarian millet, and specified methods of plowing, harvesting; and weed control. There were protective clauses for the care and maintenance of improvements and for the timely delivery of the rent (Winters 1978:69–73).

These protective clauses seem to have guarded the landlords' interests effectively because they got about the same return on their capital as owner-operators did (Winters 1978:69ff.). Share rents were higher than cash rents, a differential attributed to landowners' inputs, enforcement costs, and assumption of risks (Gray and Lloyd 1920:28–32). Then, as now, share tenants earned a somewhat lower income than they would with cash rental if market prices were high, but they also got more protection from unstable markets. Landlords received an income that paralleled changes in living costs and was not vulnerable to tenants' bankruptcies in years of crop failures and price drops (Wallace and Beneke 1956:3–4, 58).

Landlords and tenants in Iowa preferred cash grains over other crops for several reasons. In contrast to livestock and dairy production, the other major farm industries in Iowa, cash grain farming permits easy calculation and payment of shares, gives regular and quick returns, and ensures an intensive use of the rented land. Although both cash and share tenants produced primarily corn, share tenants grew slightly more wheat than did cash tenants. This preference for corn can be attributed to the greater risks of wheat, which was more subject than corn to diseases and pests and more vulnerable to harsh weather (Winters 1978:38–46, 64).

In the frontier period, risk dispersal and reduction seem to have been the primary motivations for sharecropping. Newly arrived settlers were unfamiliar with the most profitable uses and the production potential of the land. Throughout the Corn Belt, many settlers sought out established landowners to orient them and to share the risk. Risk dispersal was particularly important in north central and northwestern Iowa, where poor drainage increased the likelihood of crop damage from rains (Hibbard 1911; Holmes 1923). Sharecropping also provided many with an income while settlers located desirable lands for purchase or broke the sod on virgin land (Bogue 1963; Bogue 1959; Gates 1973; Ross 1951:37; Winters 1977:388). Thus sharecropping was more common in recently settled counties than in mature counties (Winters 1978:60). Access to the managerial expertise of the landowner does not seem to have been such an important motivation for sharecropping in this period because production techniques were fairly simple (Winters 1978:66–67). But because share rental required more involvement by the landlord than fixed rental, it was more likely to be preferred by landlords who were willing and able to provide that input.

The overall decline of sharecropping over the course of the nineteenth century as frontier-associated risk diminished is understandable. Sharecropping continued in the late 1800s, however, partly because of skyrocketing land prices. Some historians have argued that political factors caused rising land prices in the Corn Belt in that federal land policies permitted unlimited purchase by large speculators and special interest groups such as railroads and canal companies, who then withheld the land from the market and drove up its price (Gates 1973). Others emphasize the role of unscrupulous creditors and frontier banks in forcing foreclosures on indebted farmers (Murray 1946; Shannon 1945). Most scholars who have studied nineteenth-century Iowa, however, agree that land speculation and foreclosure were not significant causes of tenancy and the rising cost of land in that state and period. Rather, prices rose as a consequence of supply and demand factors, specifically the completed settlement of the frontier (cf. Bogue 1963; Cogswell 1975; Swierenga 1968; Winters 1978:76). It was tenants' shortage of capital, and their consequent inability to purchase land or to shoulder all the risks of cash tenancy, that accounted for the continuation of share farming (Bogue 1963; Ross 1951:38–39).

In the 1880s, sharecropping became increasingly a young man's institution and a life-cycle phenomenon. By 1890, as in capital-intensive twentieth-century corn farming, Iowa sharecropping was often a starting point for young farmers, who rented land from relatives until they could purchase their own land (Heady and Kehrberg 1952:654). Although much controversy surrounds the thesis that farmers in the United States have historically moved easily from share tenancy to cash tenancy to encumbered ownership to debt-free ownership (the agricultural ladder hypothesis; see Cox 1944:100–104; Gates 1945: 206), there is considerable evidence that share tenants in this period and region did follow this pattern of mobility (Bogue 1963:56; Cogswell 1975:30–41; Winters 1978:78–91).

Sharecropping in nineteenth-century Iowa did not lock particular categories of people into a situation of diminished control and returns. Settlers in this region were native- and foreign-born persons of European origin. Interestingly, foreign-born tenants moved more rapidly into landownership over the course of the century than did native-born tenants (Cogswell 1975:154–155). Moreover, although one might expect that immigrants would be more in need of a landowner's credit recommendations or capital contributions or the landowner's knowledge of agriculture in the region, immigrants were in fact less likely to sharecrop than were native-born farmers (Winters 1978:65). This phenomenon is probably related to the widely noted desire of this immigrant population for landownership and independence, to the farming experience and capital that many immigrants brought with them (Cogswell 1975:155–156), and to the fact that sharecropping in this region offered relatively less autonomy than did cash rental.

### Southern Black Sharecropping: 1865–1900

Much controversy has surrounded black sharecropping in the postbellum South. The literature divides generally between those who view sharecropping as efficient and as the product of a competitive market that was not skewed by the existence of racism in sociopolitical relations (DeCanio 1974; Higgs 1977; Reid 1973) and those who argue that sharecropping is primarily a consequence of coercion by racist planters, politicians, law enforcement officials, and merchants, who are often considered to be economically irrational as well (Banks 1905; Ransom and Sutch 1977; Taylor 1970; Woodward 1951). An exhaustive review of this rich and diverse literature is impossible here. Rather I hope to show that although southern black sharecropping in some regions and periods approached the coercion pole, blacks were not simply pawns in the generation of labor relations; nor were all parts of the South identical in the distribution and form of contracts. An understanding of the relations between landowners and suppliers of labor, and of the political and economic context in which these relations took shape, helps clarify the nature and causes of sharecropping in the aftermath of slavery. Again, in order to tie the analysis to particular historical conditions, I will limit discussion to a circumscribed period, 1865 to 1900.

Emancipation released some four million slaves into the southern labor market and challenged plantation owners to find a new means of meeting their need for a disciplined labor force (Thompson 1975:55, 70). In the first years after the Civil War, planters tried to establish slave-style work gangs that were paid in crop shares or in wages plus rations and garden rights. By 1867, however, the majority of southern plantations had turned to share or cash tenancy (Reid 1973). The census and historical analyses show that blacks were far more likely than whites to be share tenants and less likely to be farm owners or managers (see Table 8-1 and Higgs 1977:478–479). As Table 8-1 shows, the South had the highest share tenancy rate in the nation by 1880 (24.5 percent), and that rate increased to 29.5 percent by 1900.

[225]

Share contract terms and crop choice reflected to some extent the interests and resources of freedmen, planters, and their creditors. Contracts varied according to the contributions of each party and the crops farmed. When planters provided the land, seed, agricultural equipment, work animals, and feed, plus other expenses, black share tenants received one-third of the crop, or one-quarter if rations were provided. When freedmen shared expenses and contributed half of the inputs excluding land, they received one-half of the crop. If the planter supplied only the land, the freedmen received two-thirds of the crop. Planters usually advanced funds for the purchase of supplies and often provided a house, a subsistence garden plot, the privilege of gathering firewood, and the right to use the landlord's animals and tools on the tenant's private garden plot. The principal crops specified in share contracts were cotton, rice, corn, peas, potatoes, fodder, wheat, oats, and rye, with cotton being by far the most prevalent. For small grain crops tenants were paid either a fixed wage or a share of the crop that was smaller than the share they received with other crops (see Reid 1973:108–109; Schlomowitz 1979:561). Sharecropping families were responsible for labor on a specific plot of land, and they delivered the crop to the landowner. Planters did not relinquish interest in the operation of their plantations. They did supervise their sharecroppers to some extent, although less than they did wage laborers. In addition, they varied the terms of contracts according to the value of the land and the abilities and contributions of the tenants (DeCanio 1974:app. B; Ransom and Sutch 1977:ch. 8).

Limited capital and assets prevented freedmen from becoming cash tenants, which would have required at the very least purchase of a mule and tools (Wright 1979:103). They preferred sharecropping to wage labor because it enabled the entire tenant family to balance a variety of tasks over the year, including housekeeping, education of the children, fishing and hunting, leisure, livestock raising, and crop tending. Perhaps most important, it gave freedmen a greatly desired measure of independence from heavy supervision and also access to the land (Reid 1973:123; Davis 1981). Sharecropping also permitted an advantageous blending of blacks' knowledge of farming but limited physical capital with white landowners' capital and credit recommendations, which were essential in a racist credit market (Higgs 1977).

The choice of cotton as a crop was related to risk and labor demand, as well as to the economic constraints on tenants and their creditors. Producing cotton was more labor-intensive than producing corn or wheat but also allowed freedmen to use their children as workers as they could not in corn, and to schedule their time flexibly (Reid 1979b:46). In addition, because landowners limited share tenants to small plots in order to encourage the intensive use of land, cotton was the only crop that generated enough cash on a small plot to pay for supplies, fertilizers, and other expenses. Subsistence production fell because it was not possible to secure enough cash income and enough food crops from small amounts of land (Wright and Kunreuther 1975:548–551). The rural merchants who were the tenants' main sources of credit also encouraged cotton production as payment for their loans, because cotton had lower transaction costs than other crops since it was as easily handled as money when it was resold by the merchants. In fact, Bureau of Labor Statistics reports at the time stated that in some regions merchants refused to lend to those who planned to plant other crops (Goldin 1979:26–27).

While it is clear that black sharecroppers, landowners, and creditors had some complementary interests in this period, this observation begs the question whether the opportunities were established by the free market or by sociopolitical constraints. Scholars of this period do find evidence for the operation of a competitive market, including: (1) labor mobility in some regions by freedmen seeking higher wages and/or better working conditions; (2) planters' competition and awareness of competition for labor; (3) rising wages after the Civil War as would be expected with the influx of free labor; and (4) alternative employment opportunities for blacks and whites (DeCanio 1974:51–76; Reid 1979b).

There are indications, however, that labor mobility, the alternatives of freedmen, and landlord competition for labor are overstated in these studies, and that in particular states and periods, they were significantly limited by sociopolitical pressures. For example, observers have documented: (1) laws in most southern states restricting the labor mobility and ability of black workers to seek out employment at the highest offered wages; (2) extralegal intimidation and laws that kept blacks from leaving the plantations, ensured that they worked in a certain manner, and prevented them from organizing; (3) planter collusion to depress workers' wages and to bend the operation of government agencies to enforce exploitative contracts; (4) planters' consciousness of sharecropper exploitation; (5) legal and informal attempts to prevent the flow of job information to freedmen; (6) use of various forms of forced labor; and (7) the restriction of employment

[227]

outside agriculture for blacks (DeCanio 1974:16–50; Wiener 1978: 35ff.; Woodman 1979).

Although this evidence challenges the notion that the options of black sharecroppers were set by the free market, it does not establish a uniformly coercive economic environment, nor does it demonstrate that blacks were the passive and defenseless victims of an order established entirely by whites. Rather, examination of the actual relations between freedmen and their former masters reveals that many of the features of postbellum society were forged by active struggle between these groups. This struggle was not only individual but collective and institutionalized, and its outcome varied with the political and economic resources available to each, in particular periods, regions, and cropping systems.

Because the United States was unique among postemancipation societies in immediately granting freedmen the right to vote, the political arena quickly became a locus for contention over the rights, privileges, and social role of blacks. Variations in the tenor of state and national political administrations were critical to the outcomes of political struggle. The immediate postwar period, termed Presidential Reconstruction (1865–1867), restored planters to local power and employed the Union Army to control the plantation labor force. Under Radical Reconstruction (1867–1877), governments in the southern states aggressively protected the civic and legal rights of freedmen, working closely with organized black constituencies. By 1877, the conservative governments of the Redeemer period had regained control of southern politics and returned political and economic authority to planters (Foner 1983:45–47). Examination of several key issues of contention illustrates the extent to which the options of share tenants were an outcome of class struggle.

First, sharecropping itself was not a form of labor control freely chosen by planters. Whatever the hypothetical advantages of sharecropping for freedmen, in point of historical fact freedmen refused gang wage labor and did not have the resources for fixed rent tenancy. On the plantations and in the legislative halls, blacks demanded sharecropping because it gave them the independence and access to land that they so passionately wanted (Davis 1981:156–158; Wiener 1978:66). Planters preferred the gang labor system and tried to enlist the army and the Freedmen's Bureau to bind workers to it. However, to a degree that varied with the regional availability of economic alternatives, freedmen migrated away from their former slave plantations and sought alternative employment, creating significant regional labor shortages (Wiener 1978:43–44).

Access to land and credit was also the subject of active struggle. Freedmen eagerly supported the Freedmen's Bureau Bill of 1865, which promised to distribute confiscated or abandoned plantations, as well as the Southern Homestead Act, which allowed blacks to file for homesteads before whites. President Johnson vetoed the Homestead Act, however, and planters' pressure was sufficient that little confiscated land was actually distributed to blacks (Wright 1982:171). The Freedmen's Bureau early granted priority to sharecroppers and laborers in being reimbursed from crop liens, which were the major basis of rural credit. In practice, however, after 1877 planters succeeded in establishing priority for their own claims. This action had a significant impact on the ability of freedmen to move up the rungs from tenancy to landownership (Wright 1982:173–174).

Laws protecting labor conditions and mobility were also hotly debated. In 1865–66 almost all former Confederate states enacted laws, called Black Codes, that, among other things, punished vagrancy, required apprenticeship with one's former master, prevented enticement of workers by other employers, and reinforced labor contracts regardless of their equity. Blacks were forbidden to rent land in many rural areas, and any white person was empowered to arrest any black who deserted the service of his employer (Foner 1983:48ff.; Wiener 1978:59–62). Freedmen found ways to circumvent these laws, however, and black leaders opposed them, calling on the Freedmen's Bureau and the Civil Rights Act of 1866 (Cohen 1976; Daniel 1979; Novak 1978; Woodman 1979). Under Radical Reconstruction (1867–77) the remnants of the Black Codes were repealed, and laws were passed protecting blacks from arbitrary dismissal and ensuring wage payment. After 1877, however, many coercive laws were reinstituted. Although not all of these laws applied only to blacks, the important point is that their enforcement centered on blacks (Foner 1983:52).

Property rights, including the right to subsistence, were also the subject of political struggle. Freedmen thought that in emancipation they should have at least the rights they had as slaves. During Presidential Reconstruction, however, legislative efforts were begun to punish and prevent thievery, foraging, hunting and fishing, and grazing on the land of another: all practices that were accepted perquisites of slaves. Freedmen actively fought these laws, most of which were repealed or unenforced during Radical Reconstruction, and reenforced and added to during Redemption (Hahn 1982a, b; King 1982). Beyond these examples, immigration and taxation policy also involved active struggle on the plantations and in the civic arena over political limitations on black economic options.

In sum, the enforcement of repressive legislation, the extent of terrorist intimidation, the tenancy status of freedmen, and the extent to which blacks had alternatives to sharecropping varied by period and region in the South (DeCanio 1974; Reid 1979b:43; Rosengarten 1975; Wharton 1965). In addition, as Eric Foner's study of the rice plantation district of South Carolina shows, certain crop systems gave freedmen more leverage and autonomy. Gang labor and sharecropping were never used for rice production in South Carolina, and freedmen were able to insist on a wage labor parcel system that ultimately resulted in a higher degree of black landownership (Foner 1983:ch. 3).

## Strawberry Sharecropping in California since 1964

California strawberry sharecropping falls between the complementarity and the coercion models of sharecropping and between the empirical examples of Iowa and the postbellum South. Here sociopolitical and economic as well as systemic and individual factors are all important. While technical and economic conditions make strawberry production amenable to share farming, it was actually changes in the balance of power between landowners and suppliers of labor that led to its adoption. While landowners and tenants both stood to gain from sharecropping, this mutuality was created largely by political factors (elaborated later in this section). Political restrictions on the sharecropping population are not as overtly coercive here as in the South, and the collective actions of farm laborers themselves have created one of the major political motivations for share farming.

Strawberries are only one crop produced by sharecroppers in California; sharecropping dominates the grain, tree fruit, and nut industries (Reed and Horel 1980). Since World War II share tenancy in California has declined, however, and the percentage of sharecroppers among all farmers continues to be lower than for the country as a whole (see Table 8-3).

The extent of strawberry sharecropping is largely unrecognized. The data and analysis presented here are drawn from a larger study I

Table 8-3. Percentage distribution of farm operators by tenure, California, 1880–1974

| Tenure | 1880 | 1890 | 1900 | 1910 | 1920 | 1930 | 1940 | 1950 | 1959 | 1964 | 1969 | 1974 |
|---|---|---|---|---|---|---|---|---|---|---|---|---|
| Owners and Managers | 80.2 | 82.2 | 76.9 | 79.4 | 78.6 | 69.5 | 78.7 | 82.3 | 88.1 | 88.7 | 87.2 | 87.9 |
| Tenants | 19.8 | 17.8 | 23.1 | 20.6 | 21.4 | 15.2 | 21.3 | 17.7 | 11.9 | 11.3 | 11.8 | 12.1 |
| Cash | 8.9 | 8.6 | 12.5 | 12.8 | 12.5 | 8.7 | 8.9 | 3.5 | 4.1 | 4.5 | 4.6 | 4.7 |
| Share | 10.9 | 9.2 | 10.6 | 7.8 | 8.8 | 6.6 | 10.2 | 12.0 | 6.0 | 5.1 | 5.2 | 4.8 |
| Other and unspecified | NA[a] | [b] | [b] | [b] | [b] | [c] | 2.2 | 2.2 | 1.8 | 1.7 | 3.0 | 2.6 |

For footnotes and sources, see Table 8-1.

conducted between 1976 and 1985.[2] This study focused on the central coast region, including the Salinas, Watsonville, and Santa Maria districts, which have 42 percent of the state's berry acreage and the highest per-acre yields in the world (PSAB 1983). California strawberry production is highly rationalized, expensive, and profitable. California is the world leader in strawberry production and productivity, and it markets 76 percent of the national crop (PSAB 1983). Strawberries are grown primarily in the sunny, ocean-cooled, coastal valleys, and the harvest stretches from February through November. As a result, while the yield per acre for the nation excluding California is 4.05 tons, California averages 27.4 tons and some central coast growers produce 60 tons per acre (Cultural Practices 1978; PSAB 1983). Until the late 1960s, the strawberry industry relied on crews of migratory Mexican wage laborers. Beginning in the mid-1960s, however, many larger growers in the central coast region began to turn to share rental. By 1980 an estimated 55 percent of the strawberry acreage on the central coast and one-quarter of the acreage statewide was sharecropped.[3]

Share contracts assign to each family a specific series of plots totaling between 2.5 and 3.5 acres. Contracts typically last for one year, but the owner can terminate them for poor performance within a matter of days. Landlords provide the land, plants, fertilizer, pesticides, land preparation supplies and equipment, and marketing facilities. The employees prepare the land and often plant the plants. Sharecroppers provide no tools other than knee pads, small hoes, and the occasional carts that wage workers would also supply. Like wage laborers, they are responsible for all labor in plot maintenance and harvest; but unlike wage laborers, they are empowered to hire and fire any assistants they may need beyond their own families. Given a harvest labor requirement of 2.5 to 3 persons per acre, all must hire workers. They typically hire friends and relatives—often illegal immigrants from Mexico.

The landowner provides detailed specifications on cultivating and

2. This research on the changing organization of California agriculture was supported by the Agricultural Experiment Station, College of Agricultural and Environmental Sciences, University of California, Davis.
3. See Wells (1984:3–5) for a detailed discussion of the nature and limitations of sources and methodology. There are no formal statistical sources that discriminate the extent of strawberry sharecropping. The figures given here are based on the author's surveys plus the estimates of county agricultural commissioners, Department of Labor officials, and farm advisers.

harvesting practices and hires supervisors to enforce them. Supervisors advise sharecroppers when and how to fertilize, water, weed, spray for diseases, and harvest. The exact spacing of plants in the beds, the timing of planting, and the packing and grades of the berries are specified by the landowner and enforced by the supervisors. If sharecroppers arrive in the fields late or have too few workers on their plots, the supervisors tell them so. According to the testimony of sharecroppers and one supervisor in a recent lawsuit, sharecroppers never disobey the supervisor's "recommendations" because they believe they will be fired if they do (Real v. Driscoll Strawberry Associates 1976, 1977). Tenants must deliver the crop to the landlord, and in return they receive from 50 to 55 percent of the net market proceeds, minus certain assessments.

It is clear that technical and economic constraints on California berry production render share contracts potentially beneficial to growers in this industry. First, the quality of labor is crucial to profitability and is also expensive and difficult to enforce. Labor demand fluctuates daily and over the season. Planting, maintenance, and harvest must be performed at scientifically determined times, or production is depressed. To maintain yields, workers must remove runners, weeds, and substandard berries as they pick; but because this maintenance takes time away from filling the trays for which they are paid, wage laborers tend to shirk maintenance. Moreover, the care with which berries are selected, handled, and packed is a major determinant of market price. In short, share contracts can increase incentives to work efficiently and thus increase profit levels in this industry.

Second, hand labor is currently the most costly production input, constituting 53.5 percent of total costs in the first year of production on the central coast (Welch and Beutel 1980:4–5). The industry has not mechanized the harvest process because rough, plant-destroying machines cannot be used on fruit that is to be sold to the profitable and higher priced fresh fruit market, on which about three-fourths of the California crop is sold (Berry Mechanization 1977). The cost of labor is key to growers, who cannot control the rising costs of land, finance, transportation, and supplies. Monopoly has not been a means of increasing returns in the relatively competitive commodity market, and product differentiation into fresh and processed fruit has not significantly increased demand. Finally, California's tremendous productivity edge makes relocation to lower-wage regions undesirable. Thus, to the extent that sharecropping could improve the quality and reduce the cost of hand labor, it was potentially advantageous to California berry growers.

It was changes in the political context that led to its actual adoption, however. These developments have been set forth in detail elsewhere (Wells 1984), but will be outlined briefly here. The first change was the termination of the Bracero Program, an agreement reached during World War II between the United States and Mexico that lasted until 1964. Under this program the government recruited and set the wages for crews of Mexicans to be hired in American agriculture. Virtually all strawberry workers were braceros during this period. This program, initiated under joint pressure from California growers and southern cotton producers, enabled growers to externalize the costs of controlling the quality of labor (Jones 1970; Hawley 1966). The central coast growers interviewed uniformly called braceros the most inexpensive, problem-free labor force they had used. In 1964, however, after southern cotton farmers withdrew support from the program and the growing farm labor movement rallied forces to oppose it, the Bracero Program was terminated (Bach 1978).

At the same time, farm workers in California were becoming increasingly organized. The United Farm Workers (UFW) union was founded in the early 1960s, and in 1970 it began to focus on the central coast region. Although large lettuce firms were the direct targets of the UFW, strawberry workers also walked off the job when the union called a general strike in August 1970. The central coast berry industry suffered a $2.2 million crop loss because of the three-week strike (Federal-State 1972:30). This walkout plus the subsequent bankruptcy of the single berry firm that signed a contract with the UFW dramatically demonstrated berry growers' vulnerability to unionization. The central coast continues to be the major focus of union activity in the state, and UFW contracts have raised wage rates throughout the region (Martin et al. 1984).

The third political change is the extension of protective legislation to agricultural workers, who were explicitly excluded from most prior labor protections. It was only in the 1960s and 1970s that farm workers, largely through the efforts of the UFW, were guaranteed a minimum wage, overtime pay, unemployment and disability insurance, workers' compensation payments, the right to organize and bargain collectively, and protection against child labor and unfair labor practices (Wells 1984:115–116). These state and federal measures are funded largely through employers' contributions, and they restrict employer latitude in deploying labor.

Spurred by these political developments, and in the presence of favorable commodity characteristics, many larger California berry growers began to turn to share farming after the mid-1960s. Significantly, almost all sharecropping is found on the central coast, the heart of union activity. There is virtually no strawberry sharecropping in the southern producing region where the proximity of the Mexican border and the consequent ease of labor replacement render both the UFW and threats to labor control weaker. The legal status of share-croppers is particularly advantageous to growers. Because sharecrop-pers are deemed "independent contractors" by their contracts, and because they can hire and fire workers, they are not covered by labor legislation and are ineligible for membership in the UFW. Their il-legal employees, fearful of dismissal and bound to the sharecroppers by ties of ethnicity, kinship, and friendship, tend not to participate in the union either. Sharecropping thus subdivides larger farms into family-managed units in which share contracts and personal ties with hired workers ensure loyalty and efficiency. Sharecropping in this way undermines the solidarity of farm workers in the region, stratifying the work force into categories with differing rights and often conflict-ing interests and allegiances.

It is important to note that political pressures also shape workers' interest in share farming. Most sharecroppers were previously bra-ceros for the same growers. When the Bracero Program ended, their only legal option was to return to Mexico, where underemployment and unemployment were rampant and only a few family members could find work. Joining the ranks of illegal Mexican migrants pro-vided a fragile source of sustenance, especially given the regional surplus of farm workers. Only those with the guarantee of a job in the United States could obtain a cherished "green card," which enabled them to work legally in California. Sharecropping contracts provided ex-braceros with citizenship papers and the chance to bring their families from Mexico and employ them.

Sharecroppers find themselves pulled between identification with workers and with farm owners. The fact that they are by contract "their own bosses" is a matter of great pride to them, although they constantly bemoan the limits of their autonomy. In periods of intense regional labor conflict, however, sharecroppers have identified with striking field workers who wish to organize against landowners. In fact, sharecroppers on one farm organized and used a UFW negotiator to obtain a greater share of the market returns. In two cases, share-croppers directly challenged their legal status in the courts, charging

[235]

that they are in fact disguised wage laborers and as such deserve labor protections. A number of sharecroppers attend UFW meetings and rallies. Although few individuals have moved from share farming to independent ownership, many are hopeful.

## Conclusion

This chapter has demonstrated that sharecropping in the United States takes many forms, to which the two dominant economic theories about sharecropping apply unevenly. In the history of American sharecropping, we can find examples that resemble the characterization of the complementarity model, such as Iowa cash grain sharecropping between 1850 and 1900. In such cases tenants and landlords chose share contracts in a relatively unencumbered competitive market, basing their choices primarily on the risk environment and labor demand of a particular crop industry and on their own possession of human and physical capital. In such situations a focus on the microeconomic arena of individual decision making surfaces most of the variables critical to the choice and character of share tenancy. Black sharecropping in parts of the South between 1865 and 1900 comes closer to the characterization of the coercion model. Here sociopolitical constraints seriously restricted the economic mobility and alternatives of blacks, as well as their ability to strike advantageous bargains with landowners and creditors. In the most exploitive of such situations, the focus on sociopolitical rather than economic determinants, and on systemic constraints rather than individual initiative, effectively explicates share tenancy.

While some sharecropping systems approach these polar extremes, many fall somewhere in between. Political regulations and relations thoroughly penetrate contemporary agriculture, in many cases altering market conditions (Buttel and Newby 1980). Moreover, few social systems are so repressive that they eliminate all possibility of individual choice. Even within the postbellum South, for example, the extent of mobility and sociopolitical coercion varied by locality and period of time. In addition, a form of social relations that neither approach allows for, that of struggle between self-conscious and organized agrarian classes, is a major cause of sharecropping in some areas and a component of its dynamics. California strawberry sharecropping, for example, is strongly influenced by farm labor unionization and by the involvement of the state in regulating immigration and

[236]

protecting farm workers. The struggles between freedmen and planters in the postbellum South provide an example that highlights the importance of universal suffrage as an economic resource. In all three cases the technical and economic constraints of particular crop industries affect the interests and options of landowners and tenants. Finally, the social dynamics and causal factors of sharecropping change over time. For example, black southern sharecropping became more repressive after 1900 (Wright 1979:104–105), and currently the extreme mechanization and capital intensivity of the cash grain industry make it amenable to sharecropping (Heady 1955:502–503).

The framework presented here incorporates all of these patterns and clarifies their changing causes and consequences. This approach focuses on the concrete interrelations between landowners and tenants and on the ways that these shape and are shaped by wider political and economic forces. In this analysis three key variables have emerged as determinants of sharecropping systems: (1) the technical and economic constraints characteristic of particular crop industries, (2) the options offered to landowners and laborers by their political and economic environment, and (3) the level of organization of landowners and suppliers of labor. This analysis reveals that more and less coercive systems appear to be distinguished by a central contrast: the extent to which access to factors of production depends on the categoric identities of prospective tenants, such as their race or immigration status, rather than on their changing personal circumstances. Where sociopolitical institutions and practices differentially benefit or burden sets of economic actors, sharecropping tends toward the coercion pattern, and consideration of extraeconomic variables is crucial to understanding the system. When categorical identity does not significantly disadvantage share tenants, sharecropping is more likely to be a relatively equitable form of production, and one amenable to microeconomic analysis.

It is important to delineate the contrasts among the three sharecropping patterns treated here. For the most part, all three systems are called sharecropping or share tenancy by participants and in the literature.[4] They are, however, quite different forms of production.

---

4. The Census Bureau distinguishes a subtype of share tenants called "croppers," who are reported only for the sixteen southern states and Missouri. According to the census, croppers tend to work under closer supervision than do other share tenants, their landlords furnish all the work animals or tractor power, and they are often part of a multi-unit operation (U.S. Bureau of the Census 1962:xxxiv).

The relations within the production unit in each case vary in terms of the distribution of control over the means of production and the social relations among participants, and the production units have differing connections to the wider social formation. Sharecropping in the most coercive pockets of the postbellum South bore many similarities to sharecropping in post-feudal Europe and in contemporary Third World countries. These sharecroppers were not free wage laborers. They and their families had access to the means of production and they provided all labor, basing production relations on kinship rather than on the wage contract. This form of sharecropping had many of the semifeudal features expected to hinder economic efficiency: exploitive, paternalistic dependence on a landowner, a mobility-preventing subsistence plot of land, a low level of technology in the early years, much of it controlled by impoverished direct producers, and underdeveloped factor and product markets in the wider society.[5]

Post 1960s strawberry sharecroppers, by contrast, are more like wage laborers with a share feature to their labor contract. That is, their share constitutes wages paid by the landowner for the use of their labor. They provide only labor and the simple equipment laborers supply, they have no access to subsistence plots, and personal ties to landlords do not hinder their employment mobility. California sharecropping is part of a fully rationalized commodity system that is technically refined and fully integrated into factor and product markets and that involves a careful division of responsibilities to ensure efficiency. Iowa cash grain sharecroppers between 1850 and 1900 were essentially renters with a share feature to their rental contract. That is, they paid for the use of the landlord's land and other inputs by means of a share of the market proceeds. They acquired possession and control over the land plus other inputs, subject to agreed-upon restrictions on their operations, for the term of the contract. These share tenants, and most of their present-day counterparts, were relatively independent agricultural operators who provided or secured labor and capital themselves and who significantly shared production risks. Their operations were highly productive and fully integrated

5. Space limitations preclude examination of the extensive literature on the efficiency of share tenancy. There is substantial evidence that contemporary American sharecropping, and even postbellum southern sharecropping, have been economically profitable. The southern planters' extensive control of tools and production technology has been considered a contributing factor to this efficiency. See Higgs (1973) and Reid (1979b) for discussion of this issue and for references to other sources.

into the market. In contrast to the previous two types, there was considerable equality between the contracting parties in this pattern.

I suggest that we reserve the term *sharecropping* for the most coercive, paternalistic systems which elicited the initial literature and claims about sharecropping. The forms characteristic of cash grain and permanent-tree fruit and nut production are most appropriately called *share tenancy;* and the types currently emerging in some labor-intensive fruit and vegetable industries are most aptly termed *share labor.* Rather than look for a universal origin and role of sharecropping in socioeconomic development, we need to study further its variability in the United States and around the world.

# References Cited

Albert, Bill. 1982. Yanaconaje and Cotton Production on the Peruvian Coast: Sharecropping in the Canete Valley during World War I. Unpublished paper, School of Economic and Social Studies, Univ. of East Anglia, Norwich, Great Britain.

Althusser, Louis, and Etienne Balibar. 1979. *Reading Capital.* London: Verso.

Bach, Robert L. 1978. Mexican Immigration and U.S. Immigration-Reforms in the 1960s. *Kapitalistate* 7:63–80.

Banks, Enoch M. 1905. The Economics of Land Tenure in Georgia. *Studies in History, Economics and Public Law* 23:1–142.

Bardhan, Prnab K., and T. N. Srinivasan. 1971. Cropsharing Tenancy in Agriculture: A Theoretical and Empirical Analysis. *American Economic Review* 61:48–64.

Berry Mechanization Studied. 1977. *The Packer.* Oct. 22, p. 12.

Bogue, Allan G. 1963. *From Prairie to Corn Belt: Farming on the Illinois and Iowa Prairies in the Nineteenth Century.* Chicago: Univ. of Chicago Press.

Bogue, Margaret Beattie. 1959. *Patterns from the Sod: Land Use and Tenure in the Grand Prairie, 1850–1900.* Springfield: Illinois Historical Society.

Bray, James O. 1963. Farm Tenancy and Productivity in Agriculture: The Case of the United States. *Food Research Institute Studies* 4(3):25–38.

Buttel, Frederick H., and Howard Newby. 1980. *The Rural Sociology of the Advanced Societies.* Montclair, N.J.: Allanheld, Osmun.

Caballero, José M. 1982. Sharecropping: A Review of Issues. Paper presented at the 44th International Congress of Americanists, Manchester, England, September.

Cheung, Steven N. S. 1969. *The Theory of Share Tenancy: With Special Application to Asian Agriculture and the First Phase of Taiwan Land Reform.* Chicago: Univ. of Chicago Press.

Cogswell, Seddie. 1975. *Tenure, Nativity, and Age as Factors in Iowa Agriculture*. Ames: Iowa State Univ. Press.

Cohen, William. 1976. Negro Involuntary Servitude in the South, 1865–1940: A Preliminary Analysis. *Journal of Southern History* 42(1):31–60.

Cox, LaWanda. 1944. Tenancy in the United States, 1865–1900: A Consideration of the Validity of the Agricultural Ladder Hypothesis. *Agricultural History* 18(July):97–105.

Cultural Practices Gave One Grower 60 Tons Per Acre. 1978. *Western Fruit Grower* 98(April):13, 48.

Daniel, Pete. 1979. The Metamorphosis of Slavery, 1865–1900. *Journal of American History* 66(1):88–99.

Davis, Ronald L. F. 1981. Labor Dependency among Freedmen, 1865–1880. In *From Old South to New: Essays on the Traditional South*, ed. Walter J. Fraser and Winfred B. Moore, pp. 155–165. Westport, Conn.: Greenwood.

DeCanio, Stephen J. 1974. *Agriculture in the Postbellum South: The Economics of Production and Supply*. Cambridge, Mass.: M.I.T. Press.

Federal-State Market News Service. 1972. *Marketing California Strawberries, 1967–71*. San Francisco: U.S. and Calif. Depts. of Agriculture.

Foner, Eric. 1982. Reconstruction Revisited. *Reviews in American History* 10(4):82–100.

———. 1983. *Nothing but Freedom: Emancipation and Its Legacy*. Baton Rouge: Louisiana State Univ. Press.

Friedmann, Harriet. 1978. World Market, State, and Family Farm: Social Bases of Household Production in the Era of Wage Labor. *Comparative Studies in Society and History* 20(4):545–586.

———. 1980. Household Production and the National Economy: Concepts for the Analysis of Agrarian Formations. *Journal of Peasant Studies* 7(2):158–184.

Gates, Paul. 1945. Frontier Landlords and Pioneer Tenants. *Journal of the Illinois State Historical Society* 38(June):142–206.

———. 1973. *Landlords and Tenants on the Prairie Frontier*. Ithaca, N.Y.: Cornell Univ. Press.

Goldin, Claudia. 1979. 'N' Kinds of Freedom. *Explorations in Economic History* 16(1):8–30.

Gray, L. C., and O. G. Loyd. 1920. Farm Land Values in Iowa. *USDA Bulletin* 874:1–45.

Hahn, Steven. 1982a. Common Rights and Commonwealth: The Stock-Law Struggle and the Roots of Southern Populism. In *Region, Race, and Reconstruction*, ed. J. Morgan Kousser and James M. McPherson, pp. 51–88.

———. 1982b. Hunting, Fishing, and Foraging: Common Rights and Class Relations in the Postbellum South. *Radical History Review* 26:37–64.

Hallagan, William. 1978. Self-Selection by Contractual Choice and the Theory of Sharecropping. *Bell Journal of Economics* 9(2):344–354.

Hawley, Ellis. 1966. Politics of the Mexican American Labor Issue. *Agricultural History* 40:157–176.

Heady, Earl O. 1955. Marginal Resource Productivity and Imputation of Shares for a Sample of Rented Farms. *Journal of Political Economy* 63:500–511.

Heady, Earl O., and Earl W. Kehrberg. 1952. Relationship of Cropshare and Cash Leasing Systems to Farming Efficiency. *Research Bulletin of the Agricultural Experiment Station* 386:634–683, Iowa State College, Ames.

Hibbard, Benjamin H. 1911. Farm Tenancy in Iowa. *Publications of the American Statistical Association* 12(Mar.):469.

Higgs, Robert. 1973. Race, Tenure, and Resource Allocation in Southern Agriculture. *Journal of Economic History* 33:149–169.

————. 1977. *Competition and Coercion: Blacks in the American Economy, 1865–1914.* Publ. no. P163. New York: Hoover Institution.

Holmes, C.F. 1923. *Relation of Types of Tenancy to Types of Farming in Iowa.* Agricultural Experiment Station Research bull. no. 214, Iowa State College, Ames.

Innes, Stephen. 1976. Land Tenancy and Social Order in Springfield Massachusetts 1636–1702. Mimeographed. Dept. of History, Northwestern University, Evanston, Ill.

Johnson, D. Gale. 1950. Resource Allocation under Share Contracts. *Journal of Political Economy* 58(Apr.):111–123.

Jones, Lamar B. 1970. Labor and Management in California Agriculture, 1864–1964. *Labor History* 11(1):23–40.

King, J. Crawford. 1982. The Closing of the Southern Range: An Exploratory Study. *Journal of Southern History* 48(1):53–70.

Lenin, Vladimir I. 1899. *The Development of Capitalism in Russia.* Reprint. Moscow: Foreign Languages Publishing House, 1956.

Marshall, Alfred. 1890. *Principles of Economics.* 8th ed., 1930. London: Macmillan.

Martin, Philip L., et al. 1984. Changing Patterns in California's Harvest Labor Force. *California Agriculture* 6:8.

Marx, Karl. 1894. *The Process of Capitalist Production as a Whole.* Vol. 3 of *Capital,* ed. Frederick Engels. Reprint. New York: International Publishers, 1977.

Mill, John Stuart. 1848. *On Metayers.* Vol. 2 of *Principles of Political Economy,* ed. Sir W.J. Ashley. Reprint. London: Longmans, Green, 1929.

Murray, William G. 1946. *A Century of Farming in Iowa: 1846–1946.* Ames: Iowa State College.

Murrell, Peter. 1983. The Economics of Sharing: A Transaction Cost Analysis of Contractual Choice in Farming. *Bell Journal of Economics* 14(1):283–293.

Newbery, David M. G., and Joseph E. Stiglitz. 1979. Sharecropping, Risk Sharing and the Importance of Imperfect Information. In *Risk, Uncertainty, and Agricultural Development,* ed. James A. Roumasset et al. New York: Agricultural Development Council.

Novak, Daniel A. 1978. *The Wheel of Servitude.* Lexington: Univ. of Kentucky Press.

Paige, Jeffery M. 1975. *Agrarian Revolution: Social Movements and Export Agriculture in the Underdeveloped World.* New York: Free Press.

Processing Strawberry Advisory Board (PSAB). 1983. *Manager's Annual Reports.* Watsonville: PSAB.

Ransom, Roger, and Richard Sutch. 1977. *One Kind of Freedom.* New York: Cambridge Univ. Press.

Rao, C. H. H. 1971. Uncertainty, Entrepreneurship, and Sharecropping in India. *Journal of Political Economy* 79(3):578–595.

Real v. Driscoll Strawberry Associates. 1976. U.S. District Court, Northern District of California. San Jose, Calif., no. C 75-661 LHB, Nov. 8. Deposition of Kazumasa Mukai.

Real v. Driscoll Strawberry Associates. 1977. U.S. District Court, Northern District of California. San Jose, Calif., no. C 75-661 LHB. Jan. 3. Declaration of Rosalio Vela.

Reed, A. Doyle, and Lynne A. Horel. 1980. *Leasing Practices for California Agricultural Properties.* Division of Agricultural Sciences, Univ. of California, Davis.

Reid, J. D., Jr. 1973. Sharecropping as an Understandable Market Response: The Postbellum South. *Journal of Economic History* 33:106–130.

———. 1975. Sharecropping in History and Theory. *Agricultural History* 44(2):426–439.

———. 1976a. Antebellum Southern Rental Contracts. *Explorations in Economic History* 13:69–83.

———. 1976b. Sharecropping and Agricultural Uncertainty. *Economic Development and Cultural Change* 24(3):549–576.

———. 1979a. Sharecropping and Tenancy in American History. In *Risk, Uncertainty and Agricultural Development,* ed. James A. Roumasset et al., pp. 283–308. New York: Agricultural Development Council.

———. 1979b. White Land, Black Labor, and Agricultural Stagnation: The Causes and Effects of Sharecropping in the Postbellum South. *Explorations in Economic History* 16(1):31–55.

Rosengarten, Theodore. 1975. *All God's Dangers: The Life of Nate Shaw.* New York: Knopf.

Ross, Earle D. 1951. Farm Tenancy in Iowa. *Annals of Iowa* 3(31):36–40.

Roumasset, James. 1976. *Rice and Risk.* Amsterdam: North-Holland.

Shannon, Fred A. 1945. *The Farmer's Last Frontier: Agriculture, 1860–1897.* New York: Holt, Rinehart, and Winston.

Shlomowitz, Ralph. 1979. The Origins of Southern Sharecropping. *Agricultural History* 53(3):557–575.

Smith, Adam. 1869. *Wealth of Nations.* Reprint. New York: Modern Library, 1937.

Socolofsky, Homer. 1950. The Scully Land System in Marion County. *Kansas Historical Quarterly* 18(Nov.):337–375.

Stiglitz, Joseph E. 1974. Incentives and Risk Sharing in Sharecropping. *Review of Economic Studies* 41(126):219–255.

Swierenga, Robert P. 1968. *Pioneers and Profits: Land Speculation on the Iowa Frontier.* Ames: Iowa State College Press.

Taylor, Paul S. 1970. Slave to Freedman. Southern Economic History Project, working paper no. 7, Univ. of California, Berkeley.

Thompson, Edgar T. 1975. *Plantation Societies, Race Relations, and the South: The Regimentation of Populations*. Durham: Univ. of North Carolina Press.

U.S. Bureau of the Census. 1962. *U.S. Census of Agriculture: 1959*. Vol. 2, *General Report: Statistics by Subjects*. Washington, D.C.

Wallace, James J., and Raymond R. Beneke. 1956. *Managing the Tenant-Operated Farm*. Ames: Iowa State College Press.

Waswo, Ann. 1977. *Japanese Landlords: The Decline of a Rural Elite*. Berkeley: Univ. of California Press.

Weiner, Jonathan. 1978. *Social Origins of the New South: 1860–1995*. Baton Rouge: Louisiana State Univ. Press.

———. 1979. Class Structure and Economic Development in the American South: 1865–1955. *American Historical Review* 84(1):970–992.

Welch, Norm, Art Greathead, and J.A. Beutel. 1980. *Strawberry Production and Cost in the Central Coast of California*. Cooperative Extension, Univ. of California, Berkeley.

Wells, Miriam J. 1984. The Resurgence of Sharecropping: Historical Anomaly or Political Strategy? *American Journal of Sociology* 90(1):1–29.

Wharton, V. 1965. *The Negro in Mississippi, 1865–1890*. New York: Harper & Row.

Winters, Donald L. 1974. Tenant Farming in Iowa, 1860–1900: A Study of the Terms of Rental Leases. *Agricultural History* 48:130–150.

———. 1977. Tenancy as an Economic Institution: The Growth and Distribution of Agricultural Tenancy in Iowa, 1850–1900. *Journal of Economic History* 37(2):382–408.

———. 1978. *Farmers without Farms: Agricultural Tenancy in Nineteenth Century Iowa*. Westport, Conn.: Greenwood Press.

Woodman, Harold D. 1979. Post–Civil War Southern Agriculture and the Law. *Agricultural History* 53:319–337.

Woodward, C. Vann. 1951. *Origins of the New South, 1877–1913*. Vol. 9 of *A History of the South*, ed. W. Holmes and E. M. Coulter. Baton Rouge: Louisiana State Univ. Press.

Wright, Gavin. 1979. Freedom and the Southern Economy. *Explorations in Economic History* 16:90–108.

———. 1982. The Strange Career of the New Southern Economic History. *Reviews in American History* 10(4):164–180.

Wright, Gavin, and Howard Kunreuther. 1975. Cotton, Corn, and Risk in the Nineteenth Century. *Journal of Economic History* 35(3):526–551.

# [9]

# Conflicts between Commercial Farmers and Exurbanites: Trespass at the Urban Fringe

**Frances J. Aaron Brooks**
*Research Associate*
*New Jersey Farm Bureau*

Since World War II, millions of acres of agricultural land in the United States have been converted to nonfarm uses in metropolitan and nonmetropolitan areas. Between 1959 and 1970, at least 500,000 acres of farmland were converted annually, and approximately 1 million acres were converted each year during the 1970s (Fishel 1982). The major causes of conversion have been the decentralization of manufacturing and service-related employment, changes in residential preferences and the growth of retirement facilities, recreational activities, and state colleges and universities (Beale 1975).

The same characteristics that make land desirable for agriculture— its modest slope and deep, well-drained, soils—make it desirable for nonfarm uses as well. When parcels of agricultural land are developed, they are typically not contiguous and create a scattered pattern referred to as "buckshot urbanization" or "leapfrog" development (Little 1979).

There are many reasons agricultural land is sold. Farmers cannot make a living, they lack heirs who want to take over the business, or their land is condemned for rights-of-way, sewage treatment plants, or other local infrastructure. Other farmers may voluntarily choose to retire, farm elsewhere, or pursue another occupation (Keene et al. 1976; Keene 1979).

Most studies of the effects of urban development on agriculture describe the geographical pattern of urban expansion in farming areas and the consequences of urban development for different types of farming.[1] Other studies focus on land use, but also identify social, political, legal, and economic problems farmers must contend with when nonfarmers move into rural and semirural farming areas.[2] These problems are commonly called "spillover effects." They include increased property taxes to meet the higher costs of urban-level services required by new residents (e.g., schools, roads, and sewerage), condemnation of farmland for newly generated public needs,[3] and competition between farm and nonfarm uses for resources such as water.[4] Nonfarming residents may complain about common elements of farm life such as odors, dust, or noise. Consequently, municipalities may impose ordinances to regulate normal farming practices—for example, limiting the hours when farm machinery can be used or restricting the types of products sold at farm retail markets (Coughlin 1979; Hunter and Holt 1981).

In this chapter I examine the causes and consequences of trespassing, another spillover effect encountered by farmers. The ethnographic materials presented come from interviews with twenty-six commercial family farmers in Burlington County in south central New Jersey.

## Burlington County

Burlington County was founded in 1677 by a group of English Quakers fleeing religious persecution. Beginning in the 1700s and continuing through the colonial period, groups of non-Quaker En-

---

1. See, for example, Berry 1979; Berry et al. 1976; Bryant 1975; Coughlin and Berry 1977; Davies 1953; Dill and Otte 1971; Hart 1976; Mattingly 1972; Otte 1974.

2. See, for example, Coughlin 1979; Coughlin and Keene 1981; Fletcher 1978; Gregor 1970; Lesher and Eiler 1977; Press and Hein 1962; Scott and Chen 1973; Stansberry 1963; Toner 1981.

3. Condemnation or eminent domain "is the power of government to take private land for a public use, without the owner's consent, on the payment of just compensation" (Rose 1979:419). Government at all levels uses the power to acquire land for roads, schools, public buildings, and parks. Public utilities are also authorized to exercise this power, but only in some situations.

4. See, for example, Berry 1978; Berry and Plaut 1978; Gregor 1970; Griffin and Chatham 1958; Moore and Barlowe 1955.

glish, Swedish, Irish, Scottish, German, and French migrants settled in the county. Except for a small group of Italians who migrated to the county just before and after the two world wars, the majority of farmers are descendents of these early settlers. The immigrants quickly learned that the rich, fertile, sandy loam soils were well suited for growing a wide variety of crops. Rye, wheat, oats, barley, and hay for pasturage were grown along with cabbage, lettuce, turnips, cucumbers, carrots, onions, and fruits (Schmidt 1973).

For much of the county's history, agriculture was the primary industry. Following World War II, however, it declined in economic and social importance. The baby boom and the decentralization of population from the nearby cities of Philadelphia and Camden created a demand for suburban residential housing. Between 1940 and 1960, the population of the county increased from 97,013 to 224,910. By the 1960s, manufacturing, retail trade, and service industries were well established. By 1983, the population of the county was 373,600 residents (Office of Demographic and Economic Analysis 1978, 1985).

Beginning in the 1960s, an agricultural transformation occurred in Burlington County. Severe farm labor shortages, rising production costs, and increasing taxes brought about major changes in agricultural enterprises and the economic importance of certain crops. In particular, many farmers shifted from vegetable and fruit production and dairying to growing field crops (Bruch and Koch 1977). In 1959, there were 1,351 farms and approximately 185,000 acres of farmland, which represented 35 percent of the land area in the county. By 1982, the county had 743 farms and 112,689 acres of farmland, 21.5 percent of the county land area (U.S. Bureau of the Census 1961, 1984).

While farms and farmland declined, landownership patterns in Burlington County changed dramatically. More of the land is now concentrated in the hands of nonfarm landowners, including 5,400 acres owned by foreign investors representing countries such as Panama, the Netherlands, Canada, and West Germany (Rural Advisory Council 1981). Farmers may own as little as 10 percent of the ground they farm. The majority of this land is owned by nonfarmers.

Currently, the county ranks first in the state in the production of soybeans, barley, and sweet corn; second in apples, blueberries, and number of hogs; third in strawberries and corn for grain; and fifth in milk production, number of cattle, peaches, all hay, cabbages, peppers, and tomatoes. A wide variety of other vegetables, fruits, field crops, and nursery products are also produced. These include asparagus, broccoli, spinach, squashes, horseradish, melons, cranberries, white and sweet potatoes, wheat, barley, and rye. Sheep and lambs are also raised, along with horses, turkeys, and chickens (New Jersey Crop Reporting Service 1983; U.S. Bureau of the Census 1984).

## The Ethnography of Trespassing

Farmers consider trespassing to be any entry onto their property without permission, whether by a person or a domestic animal such as a dog or horse. Trespassing occurs on land rented by farmers as well as on farmland they own—on open fields, along field roads, in farm buildings such as barns, sheds, and farm stands, as well as on woodlots and around irrigation ponds.

Farmers routinely post "no trespassing" signs on their land. Although trespassers are rarely caught, it is legally necessary to post such signs in order to prosecute them if caught and to reduce liability in the event a trespasser is injured on the property.[5] Signs are placed along fences, edges of woodlots, and in and around fields and irrigation ponds. Posting is, however, a source of extreme frustration for farmers because people regularly steal or vandalize signs.

The farmers surveyed named eight types of trespassing that they considered serious: theft, vandalism, driving motor vehicles on farmland, horseback riding on farmland, hunting, using farms as thoroughfares, loose domestic animals, and litter and dumping. People jogging or walking dogs on their farm property were also mentioned, but were considered less serious problems. I will devote the remainder of this discussion to the major forms of trespassing described by growers.

## Theft

### Crops

Farmers reported that crop stealing takes place during the production season and the off-season. Peaches, apples, sweet corn, peppers,

---

5. This research was conducted between 1981 and 1983. In January 1984, Governor Kean signed into law trespass legislation, which among other things, eliminated the posting requirement for farmland.

[247]

tomatoes, cantaloupes, and pumpkins are among the crops regularly stolen at harvest time. Field crops, such as bales of hay and straw, are stolen during the off-season, although less frequently than other crops.

Crops are usually stolen along the perimeters of fields where they are most accessible. But it is not unusual for a farmer to discover plants stripped of vegetables or trees stripped of fruit or to discover that crops are missing in the interior of fields during harvesting or other fieldwork. One farmer described a typical situation: "There are always people who help themselves to corn and tomatoes. Last summer we were out picking sweet corn. We came through an area of the field and my men said: 'Look, no corn!' For about seventy-five feet there was no corn, about three or four rows."

People living in homes adjacent to farm fields also steal crops. For the most part, farmers can identify the thieves. Speaking of a small housing development next to his fields one farmer remarked: "Down here where I have [a field] next to this housing development we have people come in all the time stealing peaches. Then we plant sweet corn down there, and they just walk in and take what they want." People also stop along roads and pick crops out of fields. "I had a peach orchard down there and we really had trouble. . . . It's along the road. People stop, and just take two or three baskets and think nothing of it," said a farmer.

In addition, farmers say that people are not inhibited about stopping and going into fields to steal baskets full of recently harvested fruits or vegetables. Said one farmer: "We had peppers planted right along this road, and the men were out there picking them, and they were lining them up along the road. They were beautiful. [A] lady in this Cadillac pulls up alongside and puts four baskets in her car."

Nor are field crops immune to theft. Bales of hay and straw stored in barns are easy targets for thieves. Farmers discover their losses when they are ready to "truck out" the bales to sell them.

Moreover, farmers say that the degree of difficulty is no deterrence to theft. People will dig potatoes out of the ground or cut wood from woodlots on farm property. During the Christmas season, it is not uncommon for farmers to lose fir trees.

Some people go so far as to steal whole plants to use in their home gardens. One farmer described his situation: "Sometimes they'll take fifty plants. It just messes up the whole field. Like you've got nice rows of tomatoes, and they'll take a little scoop and take a hunk of dirt with them. They'll take the nicest plants—four or five in this row and maybe four or five in that row. They scatter around. . . . If you re- plant them, they're a couple or three days behind the other plants."

Burlington County farmers distinguish between theft for consump- tion and theft for resale. They believe that stealing for home consump- tion is committed by neighbors or families "out on a Sunday drive." Usually only small quantities are taken. According to growers, howev- er, stealing for resale is not uncommon. It is the work of unknown people who resell the crops to roadside stands or sell the produce along the road themselves. Some farmers reported that they have lost as many as 3,000 ears of corn a night. Farmers who raise livestock along with crops also reported that these animals are targets for thieves, who probably steal them for resale rather than home consumption.

## Equipment

Theft of equipment usually involves tools, parts, and implements, rather than large pieces of machinery, from buildings and tractors in fields. Growers tend to minimize these losses, however, because they have so much equipment that they cannot keep track of it all. Bat- teries, belts, and alternators are regularly stolen from tractors in fields as well as from machinery parked near homes or barns. Batteries, along with other parts, are stolen year-round. It is common for farm- ers to lose four or five batteries a year.

Once I had two tractors on one farm. It was in the wintertime. . . . They took three batteries in one night, and this was tractors in the barn, in a building, put away. They were heavy duty batteries in a John Deere tractor. They took them and yanked the posts right out of the tractor, so they probably took them for junk.

You've got to put up with the weather—that's bad enough; that's some- thing you can't help. But people stealing stuff when you're ready to work. . . . I go out one morning to combine because you have to keep going in good weather . . . so I go out there and turn the key and there's nothing, dead. When I get up there to look, there's the battery stolen right out of the combine.

[249]

During the production season, pumps, pipes, fittings, sprinklers, and other parts of irrigation systems are stolen. Pumps are located next to irrigation ponds or streams and may run throughout the season, depending on rainfall. Unlike tractors, which can be brought back to the home farm nightly, irrigation pumps are not removed at night. Moreover, irrigation ponds and streams are rarely within "watching" distance of the farm, and so it is almost impossible for farmers to keep track of such equipment at night.

Also stolen are "birdbangers," or "scareaways," as they are commonly called. These are devices that make shotgun-like popping noises at regular intervals. Although farmers question their effectiveness, they use them to keep grackles, pigeons, and other birds off farm fields. Birds uproot young plants as they begin to sprout in order to get at the kernel, and they feed on berries. They create the most damage, however, when they feast on the tips of sweet corn just reaching maturity.

Farmers lose scareaways from fields adjacent to housing developments. They believe that people in the developments are responsible for the theft. The propane tanks used to run the scareaways, which can also be used to fuel barbecue grills, are also stolen.

## Supplies

Except for gasoline, supplies such as fertilizer and pesticides are not stolen, most likely because people have little use for them. Empty baskets and crates may be removed from fields or barns during the production season, but farmers say these losses are minimal. Gasoline is stolen most often from tractors, but it is also removed from trucks, storage drums in fields, and tanks at the farm year-round. Generally, diesel fuel is not stolen, presumably because people have little use for it. Farmers pointed out that people have no trouble removing gasoline from tractors because of the way they are designed.

> One of my combines is gas and one is diesel. . . . I had them both parked in a field there, and we finished up and came back the next day to service them. They didn't touch the diesel. The gas combine, they tried to get gas out of it but it had a funny neck on it . . . so they proceeded to beat off the glass bowl [the fuel filter] underneath, which is where the gas is, and they drained the whole thing. . . . The tank was empty. [They took] maybe twenty or thirty gallons.

[250]

They drove right up to the back of the building. The car came right across the field, and the ground was frozen in the wintertime. They were taking cans and I didn't know it. I thought my wife was burning a lot of gas in the car. . . . They were putting it in five-gallon cans and taking it right across.

## Roadside Stands

Stealing is a major problem for farmers with roadside stands. There are several different styles of stands ranging from permanent to temporary. Many farmers sell their produce from a wagon with minimal decoration. Usually, it is open on all four sides and has a canopy or roof to keep off the sun or rain. These wagons are nonpermanent structures that are brought in after the season is over. Other stands are elaborate, permanent structures—enclosed buildings with garage style doors or entrances that are closed and locked at night. These stands are often open ten months of the year. Burlington County farmers sell items they have produced themselves as well as items produced elsewhere. It is common to find a wide variety of fresh fruits and vegetables from out of state such as oranges and grapes. In addition, farmers may sell pies, jellies, jams, honey, milk, eggs, barbecued chickens, dried flowers, christmas wreaths and trees, and other nursery products.

Permanent stands are targets for thieves who steal nonfarm products such as jams, jellies, and snack foods as well as eggs and produce. Farmers have also lost cash registers and electronic scales. Growers with temporary stands, on the other hand, report that they do not have a theft problem. This is so for several reasons. First, the stands are always staffed during the season. Second, farmers usually do not leave farm products on them when they close at night. Finally, these stands are often set up quite close to the farm house, a location that seems to deter thieves.

## Topsoil

Theft of topsoil, although it happens occasionally, is not a major problem for most growers. A few farmers said that every once in a while they could see that people, presumably from nearby houses, had scooped six or eight inches off the top.

Frances J. Aaron Brooks

## Vandalism

### Crops

During the growing and harvesting season people enter fields and randomly pull up entire plants. Youngsters playing in fields rip up sweet corn plants when the plants reach two or three feet. Orchards are also subject to vandalism. People pull whole trees out and leave them strewn throughout the field. Late in the growing season when rye plants are high, children pull straw out of the ground and build little houses to hide and play in. Children also steal crops from fields and roadside stands and smash them on roads or throw them at cars, trains, and houses. Cantaloupes, watermelons, and pumpkins are particularly susceptible.

### Equipment

Extensive equipment vandalism occurs year-round. Equipment parked in farm fields is most vulnerable. People rip out wires and break gauges and lights on tractors and trucks and put nails in or simply let the air out of tractor and truck tires. They also shoot holes in radiators and dump sand in fuel tanks.

Irrigation equipment and bird scareaways are frequently vandalized. Wires, belts, and gauges are ripped out, cut out, or destroyed. Detachable parts such as irrigation pipe, elbow joints, or pumps are often thrown into irrigation ponds or woods. Equipment that moves, such as winch-driven irrigators, is intentionally jammed to prevent movement. Vandals throw logs onto a "water winch," to break the unit that drives the equipment across the field.

Farmers normally set aside an area to store older equipment or pieces of machinery they use only for spare parts. It is almost impossible to save old equipment and vehicles because vandals destroy windshields and engines.

Even electric fences around pastureland are vandalized. Farmers use these fences to ensure that cows, steers, or other livestock do not escape. Animals wander out of such enclosures, however, because "the kids go out there, and they throw things at the metal fence. If you put a metal rod up against an electric fence, the electricity goes into the metal rod and into the ground. . . . Now them cows of mine [will]

[252]

push through the fence and go into people's lawns . . . and they get back to me and holler, 'Your cows are on my lawn!' "

### Buildings

Vandalism of buildings is not as widespread as vandalism of crops and equipment. Nonetheless, barns, roadside stands, tenant houses, and irrigation pump houses are heavily damaged. Wood is stripped from vacant barns on rented land, and windows are broken in used and abandoned buildings by juveniles who throw rocks through them or shoot at them.

### Supplies

Farm supplies are also vandalized. For example, one farmer said when he went for lunch, he left a fifty-gallon gas drum on a truck near his irrigation pump. When he returned no more than an hour later, someone had opened the drum and emptied the gasoline all over the road. The same farmer, on another occasion, went to take care of another task and left a load of fertilizer bags stacked on a truck. When he returned shortly thereafter, he found all the bags cut open and fertilizer dumped on his field.

### Arson

Another form of vandalism, although not widespread, is arson. People set barns, trailers, and fields on fire year-round. The buildings are generally not empty or abandoned, but are used for storage of crops or as packing houses. Moreover, fire fighters and spectators ride over fields and crops.

## Motor Vehicles

Motor vehicles are a constant and serious problem for farmers. People, usually teenagers, trespass year-round in cars, four-wheel drive vehicles, jeeps, minibikes, motorcycles, and, during the winter, snowmobiles. Open fields, field roads, wooded areas, and even home sites are vulnerable. A typical example follows:

> There's acres of woods back there where [people] can run their motorcycles, but why they have to go through my fields I don't know. . . . I looked up, and I see these three motorcycles going right across my cornfield. The corn was [two feet] high. They then went right cater-corner through my tomatoes, peppers, eggplants, and the late tomato plants. All you could see was green tomatoes flying up in the air and peppers flying off the vines. They went into the corn field and made a big U-turn and cut right through the field again.

## Horseback Riders

Horseback riders and riding-school classes also trespass year-round on farmers' property. Most riders keep to field roads, but it is not uncommon for people to ride through fields planted with crops. People rarely ask permission to ride on farm property, and farmers rarely give it when they ask. This is so for two reasons. First, farmers believe that if they let one or two people onto their property, then they will be inundated with riders. Second, they worry about their liability if someone should get hurt on their farm.

## Hunters

Unlike horseback riders, hunters are a problem only during October and November, when the hunting season for small game such as raccoons, pheasants, and rabbits coincides with the period when growers still have crops including soybeans or greens in the fields.[6] Hunters walk all over planted fields and do not keep to field lanes or wooded areas. They take four-wheel drives into standing crops and drive randomly over fields, run over irrigation equipment, and shoot bottles, scattering glass on farm fields and field roads. It is not uncommon for farmers to rent their ground to hunt clubs when the hunting season does not interfere with crop harvesting. Farmers obtain agree-

6. Hunters, however, can be a problem for livestock farmers during deer season. Survey participants related stories about other farmers who have said that hunters deliberately shoot cows, horses, sheep, and other livestock in pastures.

ments that give them liability protection in case of accidents and that protect them from crop and fire damage.

## Using Farms as Thoroughfares

Many farmers complained that people take shortcuts through their farms year-round. They walk through planted and unplanted fields as well as planted areas around the house. It is not unusual for drivers to cut through a farm in order to avoid traffic. For example: "The past five years have been driving us out of our minds with people coming off Orangeville Road, coming right through the back, down the edge of [our house] here, and coming in front of the farm market on Tulip Avenue. . . . They come off this road and [drive] between the two posts where it says 'no trespassing.'"

## Loose Domestic Animals

Unleashed dogs and loose horses also cause problems when they run over fields and gardens. Farmers explained that it is quite common for many of their nonfarming neighbors to keep a horse or two for pleasure riding. The animals become a problem when they break free and run over fields. Moreover, farm animals are particularly vulnerable to dogs. "Everybody that moves to the country thinks they have to have a dog. People just turn their dogs loose. We almost lost one of our sheep. A German shepherd got loose and chased it around the pasture, got hold of it, and ripped it."

## Litter and Dumping

Littering and dumping occur year-round. Although throwing refuse from a car is technically not trespassing, farmers consider it an intrusion. Growers differentiate between littering and dumping. They classify bottles, cans, and paper products, such as fast food wrappers that blow onto their property, as litter. The deposition of bagged or unbagged refuse from garden, kitchen, or home, old mattresses, cars, bricks, or wood is considered dumping.

People throw bottles, cans, and paper products from cars as they

[255]

pass by. Sometimes refuse lands on the shoulder of the road or falls in a field ditch. It also catches in hedgerows bordering fields. If there is no ditch or planted barrier, most litter lands in the field itself or along a strip of land bordering the field.

Litter accumulates on farm property in other ways as well. People, generally young adults and teenagers, congregate and party on farmland. Farms are considered a good, "safe" place to go if one is underage and wants to drink. Teenagers leave piles of empty bottles strewn around the party area, smash or shoot at bottles, and leave broken glass scattered on fields and field lanes. They throw bottles through building windows, which shatter on the inside of the building. Some growers also complained about debris blowing onto their fields from new construction projects.

Farmers find bagged refuse along the shoulder of the road, edges of fields, and strips of land bordering fields. They speculate that this type of refuse is dumped by people driving by on the public roads. People also trespass onto farm ground to junk old motor vehicles, tires, metal containers, refrigerators, and similar items. Often such objects are found in or near wooded areas on the farm. It is not uncommon, however, for people to throw unbagged trash, garden debris, metal and wire objects, old clothes and toys, Christmas trees, and building materials into planted fields as well. Although both neighbors and nonneighbors are responsible for the dumping, farmers say that it is most common for neighbors adjacent to farm ground to deposit this type of debris and trash.

## The Consequences of Trespassing

### Financial Costs

Burlington County farmers tried to reckon the economic costs associated with trespass problems. It was generally easier for them to recall how much a piece of equipment cost than to remember how much money they spent repairing damaged equipment or the market value of stolen crops. For example, one farmer said that a new tractor he bought to replace one destroyed by arson cost $12,000. Batteries for a combine can cost $100.

Farmers are able to obtain additional insurance to cover losses due to vandalism and theft of harvested crops, farm machinery, and livestock. Growers generally do not purchase this coverage because they cannot justify the additional expense when they weigh it against the costs of their losses. Moreover, they emphasized repeatedly that financial losses were far less important than the extra time and labor expended to correct a problem, the physical damage, and the psychological effects of trespassing.

## Time and Labor Costs

The time and labor required to rectify a problem are major concerns. One farmer said, "There's half a day shot because you have to buy a new battery someplace. It's not always what they steal, but how much time you waste." Said another, "You go out and find your irrigation pump all torn up. Maybe it costs you twenty-five or thirty dollars for parts, but you got hours and hours of work replacing them—a good, solid day's work."

Many farmers spoke about the extra time and labor they and their field hands spend picking up bottles and cans on farm fields and roads. They have to pick up litter in the spring before plowing and planting. Farmers frequently have to stop and get off equipment while cultivating or harvesting to pick up bottles and cans. Some farmers could quantify the time they spent collecting bottles and cans:

> I usually get my workers out to the fields with some baskets in the spring. It takes them about three to four hours. It's usually before the grain begins to grow, and you can still see them—they're easy to find. Winter is a bad time because people just throw it out all winter long. [There are] enough bottles to fill a [bushel] basket, and you can do that every couple of months.

> Every time you go out to work a field you have to pick up bottles. At least once or twice a week you've got to clean up . . . and on all the [public roads] you've got beer bottles you have to pick up, hundreds of them.

Farmers pointed out that the costs associated with these problems can go beyond the time and labor needed to correct them. If fixing the problem diverts them from the task at hand, particularly if weather conditions change for the worse, the incident can make the difference between getting a field harvested on time and into the market for sale at a good price and having to delay harvesting and possibly getting a lower price for a crop or losing the crop entirely.

> Say you have five acres [of soybeans], and you want to get it off because it's supposed to rain the next day. Say, for five acres, it takes you an hour to pick up bottles. You don't get the field done, and it rains the next day. Then the field's so muddy you can't do it, and you've got five hundred dollars worth of beans out there [which] you can't get . . . because you [were] out picking bottles up.

## Physical Damage to Crops, Equipment, and Fields

Another consequence of trespassing is the potential and actual physical damage to farm fields, crops, machinery and buildings. Motor vehicles and motorcycles cause extensive damage by knocking plants down and crushing crops. The extent of the damage depends on the time of the growing season and the crop. For example, if a motorcycle knocks down green plants early in the grain season, the plants may recover and spring back. Vegetable plants, however, cannot withstand the buffeting and will break and thus be ruined when vehicles run through the rows.

Motor vehicles also run over equipment, such as irrigation pumps, pipes, and hoses. Growers also noted that vehicles damage equipment left out in fields after the production season. In general, the damage is irreparable. The greatest damage is done to aluminum irrigation pipe because it is placed throughout the field and hidden from view by standing crops. It does not take much pressure to bend or crack irrigation pipe, which at one dollar per foot (1980–1981 price) is costly to replace. Some farmers pointed out that if the damage is localized, they can salvage pieces of pipe by removing the damaged piece and replacing the fittings on the remaining pipe. But this requires additional time and labor that farmers do not usually have at the time of the incident.

Moreover, as motor vehicles zigzag over farm fields, their tires put ruts into the soil. These can seriously affect the planting and harvesting operations, the machinery, and the condition of the field. When ruts are made on sloping areas, the crop is torn from the ground, leaving soil exposed to the elements. During heavy rains, these areas are subject to erosion, which can lead to a "washout."

Farmers also explained that planting machinery cannot seed the field rows properly if the field is rutted. The evenness of field rows is disturbed because the ruts change their shape and depth. As the planter moves along and encounters a rut, the planter wheels sink in and rise unevenly. Consequently, the planter does not drop the seed into the center of the furrow and it ends up on the top or side. One farmer described the action of a planter in ruts made by four-wheel-drive vehicles:

> Say [the vehicle] sinks in a foot deep, and there's a mark here and a mark two feet ahead, and marks beyond, and I'm going to [plant] right there. The planter hits that first rut, and the wheels hit it and . . . bounce up. The section where my tire hits his wheel mark is not going to be planted . . . because as [the planter] goes up in the air, it throws the seed on top of the ground. I get ready to plant again and hit the other rut, and [the planter] flies up in the air again. I'd say [for] roughly ten [feet in the row] you aren't going to hardly get nothing [planted].

If the seed does not drop precisely in the furrow, the height of the mature plant will differ from the correctly seeded plants. This variation in height creates harvesting problems because modern machinery is designed to harvest even stands of crops. Thus if a soybean or corn plant does not grow at the requisite height, the crop is not picked up by the "header" and is left in the field.

Poor harvesting in turn affects crop sales and returns. Farmers pointed out that "every bean counts," particularly with field crops such as soybeans, because "you need a lot to make any money." "You take beans," said one farmer. "They're expensive. You're talking about twelve or thirteen cents a pound. You don't get many pounds per acre, so each pound counts."

Ruts create actual physical damage to machinery as well. Machinery parts may snap or bend as they hit ruts. When such damage occurs, farmers have to stop their routine and spend extra time and labor to correct the problem. The rocking motion of the machinery as it bounces around makes it unwieldy to drive and thus increases the chances of an accident.

For the most part, pickups, cars, or motorcycles are responsible for damage to fields and crops. However, one farmer said fire trucks unnecessarily ruined his crops and put ruts in the fields in their haste to put out an arson-related fire.

[259]

Horses and dogs also cause crop and field damage. Horses' hooves leave depressions in unplanted fields or in the unplanted areas of planted fields. Plants are either ripped out of the soil or crushed when horses travel across fields. "You got something planted, and wherever the horse gallops across the field, everything will die." Dogs also rip and crush plants as they race over fields or roll on the ground. Moreover, they can damage plants, making it difficult for machine harvesters to pick them. Carrots, for example, are harvested by a machine that loosens the soil around the carrot, then pulls the carrot out by the top. Said one farmer: "If those tops are broken off or damaged, you lose the carrot. . . . Last year I rented some ground and put carrots in. [The nearby neighbor] had two big retrievers. They ran around down there. . . . I must have lost three or four tons of carrots from them rolling around."

Litter and dumping also have serious consequences for growers. Not only can debris damage machinery, but some types of debris can run through machinery such as combines and be processed with the crop. For example, glass can be picked up by machinery and mixed in with hay. Although the glass is heavier than the hay and more often than not shakes out, farmers express concern about selling the bales because some glass might go undetected. Weeds, sticks, and stones will travel through, but wire hangers and the like, for example, can jam machinery causing extensive damage.

Bottles were more of a problem for farmers than metal cans, although both can damage equipment and kill animals.[7] Glass bottles cut tractor and truck tires as farmers travel from parcel to parcel on public roads. Farmers have to be especially vigilant as they ride the shoulder because these areas are usually strewn with broken glass and bottles. Tires are also cut in and along the sides of fields because farmers often cannot see bottles or pieces of glass.

If the damage is extensive, the tires have to be replaced. Certain tractor tires can cost upwards of $1,000. Some farmers spoke of spending $2,000 each season replacing cut tires. Even if the tires are not permanently damaged, the farmers must spend extra time and labor

---

7. Farmers described why metal cans are extremely harmful to livestock: As crops such as alfalfa are harvested for silage, cans can be picked up inadvertently by machinery and turned into "shrapnel" as they are processed along with the crop. Dairy cows then eat the silage and ingest the metal pieces. The metal can rip the cow's stomach, thus killing the animal. Broken glass can have the same effect on cows if ingested along with the feed.

to remove, patch, and repair them. According to one grower, "It's the time you waste taking it off, getting it fixed, and getting a new one. You can't just change it like a car tire—it takes a while to do it."

*Psychological Costs*

Although they are not quantifiable, there are also psychological costs associated with trespassing. Farmers regularly use terms such as "aggravation" and "worry" when discussing trespassing. "It's very aggravating to have to get out of a piece of equipment to pick up this litter," said one farmer. "It's just more aggravation having to clean up after somebody when nobody has the right, nobody should do that." Farmers also spoke about the frustration they felt because they could not control the problems. "It's stuff like that I have to put up with all the time!" "The fire company, they don't do nothing about that [the field damage]; they had a good time putting the fire out. It's what I've got to put up with afterwards!" Much of their worry concerns their potential liability if someone should get hurt playing on or around machinery or an irrigation pond or entering a recently sprayed field. "They are doing a small amount of damage. Whether I can measure it in tens or hundreds . . . of dollars, I don't know. It's hard to put a dollar figure on it. The money that it cost me . . . is probably insignificant compared to my worry of what is going to happen if some kid gets hurt and some smart lawyer gets involved."

## Conclusions

Demand for raw land is mushrooming as home owners, industries, and businesses choose to locate in Burlington County. Development alarms nonfarm residents because it usually eliminates the pastoral environment that attracted them to the county in the first place. Nonetheless, the conversion of agricultural land to residential and other nonfarm uses will continue as long as demand for land in rural and semirural areas remains high. Continued migration and development most likely will only intensify existing trespass problems.

The financial costs of trespassing are significant. In New Jersey, a special committee appointed by the governor in 1983 to study trespass estimated that damage from trespassing costs at least $1 million annually. Considering that net farm income in 1983 was $112.9 million, losses from trespassing represent 0.9 percent. Not surprisingly, the costs have not been sufficient to put farmers out of business or cause them to sell out.

Although the financial costs cannot be minimized, the primary significance of this problem is that it reflects changes in the social and political structure of rural communities. The newcomers to rural communities bring with them a particular type of social organization and set of attitudes and values. They have "certain needs, competencies, and resources, and of course, their own ideas about the good life" (Schwarzweller 1979:16). As carriers of a new kind of social organization, they often become advocates of change and seek to influence community affairs by imposing their expectations on their new surroundings (Fliegel et al. 1981).

Political changes occur as the new migrants assume key positions on local councils and community boards. Municipal policies are framed to suit the needs, goals, and values of these new residents. Regulations increase in number and shift in focus to support the values and goals of these newcomers. Farmers suggest that there is no longer a municipal will to address their problems. As these new residents have taken a greater role in directing community affairs, they say, the status and position of farmers has changed. Farmers' influence at the local level has diminished, and their views, needs, and interests have become less important.

From the farmer's perspective, at the heart of trespass problems is the nonfarmers' perception of farmland. Suburbanites tend to view farmland as public open space, and they use it as such, rather than as private property for agriculture. It is apparent to farmers that these migrants come to the country with values and attitudes that are not consonant with farming and an agricultural way of life. "The migrants see all this open space," said one fellow, "and think it belongs to them." "There's something required there as far as educating some of them. . . . I don't think they really know that there's even a crop out there."

The view that farmland is public open space is reflected in the courts as well. Farmers who have been fortunate enough to catch trespassers have gained little monetary or psychological satisfaction by prosecuting them. Trespass laws are weak, and judges are often uninformed and unsympathetic. Farmers reported that judges rarely fined trespassers who were caught stealing crops, for example, because they felt that farmers could not possibly "miss a few vegetables or bales of hay."

For the most part, the study of North American farmers and agricultural policy has been left to agricultural economists, while planners and bureaucrats have led preservation efforts. Yet anthropologists have much to contribute to these endeavors. In anthropology, there is a growing emphasis on the identification and examination of the actual problems people face, their consequences, and how people respond to them (Vayda and McCay 1975; McCay 1978; Morren 1980). Vayda (1983) rightly proposed that such examinations should focus on policy questions. Research should lead to concrete findings that are useful and easily conveyed to decision makers to meet their need "to define some piece of the human predicament on which to act" (Mulhauser 1975).

An understanding of the nature of the conflicts between farmers and nonfarm residents is essential if we are to implement coherent and practical programs for farmland preservation. Currently, various land use controls, land purchase techniques and tax remedies are in effect which help prevent direct conversion of farmland to nonfarm use. Although these measures can slow conversion of farmland, they do not cause nonfarmers to reevaluate their beliefs and attitudes about farmland as public open space. If legislators and administrators of farmland preservation programs agree (and I believe they do) that agricultural land and open space are different, they must focus attention not only on the preservation of land, but also on the behavior of people on the land. Policy makers must be knowledgeable about the problems generated by urban development and their consequences from the perspective of commercial farmers.

Anthropologists can address specific questions about the actual social, economic, and political problems farmers experience, their effects on farm operations, and what farmers are doing about the problems. The results of such research have clear implications for policy making. Such research can contribute to legislative, judicial, and educational actions designed to complement existing programs to prevent agricultural land conversion.

### Acknowledgments

Research for this chapter was part of a project funded by the National Science Foundation (grant no. BNS-8020833), Wenner Gren

Foundation for Anthropological Research (grant no. 4070), the New Jersey Agricultural Experiment Station (grant no. 26400), and the Women's National Farm and Garden Society. I thank Stuart A. Brooks, Anna Kline, and Michael Chibnik for their valuable comments on earlier drafts of this chapter.

## References Cited

Beale, Calvin. 1975. *The Revival of Population Growth in Nonmetropolitan America*. Agricultural Economic Report no. 605, Economic Research Service. Washington, D.C.: U.S. Dept. of Agriculture.

Berry, David. 1978. Effects of Urbanization on Agricultural Activities. *Growth and Change* 9:2–8.

————. 1979. The Sensitivity of Dairying to Urbanization: A Study of Northeastern Illinois. *Professional Geographer* 31:170–176.

Berry, David, and Thomas Plaut. 1978. Retaining Agricultural Activities under Urban Pressures: A Review of Land Use Conflicts and Policies. *Policy Sciences* 9:153–178.

Berry, David, Ernest Leonardo, and Kenneth Bieri. 1976. *The Farmer's Response to Urbanization: A Study of the Middle Atlantic States*. Discussion paper, series no. 2. Philadelphia: Regional Science Research Institute.

Bruch, Robert H., and A. R. Koch. 1977. *The Influence of Labor, Capital, Investment Requirements and Regulations on the Type of Agricultural Commodities Produced between 1960 and 1976 in New Jersey*. Report no. AE-374. New Jersey Agricultural Experiment Station, Rutgers, The State University, New Brunswick, N.J.

Bryant, William R. 1975. *The Effects of Urban Expansion on Farming in Wayne County, New York*. Research paper no. 75-28. Dept. of Agricultural Economics, Cornell Univ., Ithaca, N.Y.

Coughlin, Robert E. 1979. Agricultural Land Conversion in the Urban Fringe. In *Farmland: Food and the Future*, ed. Max Schnepf, pp. 29–47. Ankeny, Iowa: Soil Conservation Society of America.

Coughlin, Robert E., and David Berry. 1977. *Saving the Garden: The Preservation of Farmland and Other Environmentally Valuable Land*. Philadelphia: Regional Science Research Institute.

Coughlin, Robert E., and John C. Keene. 1981. *National Agricultural Lands Study: The Protection of Farmland*. Washington, D.C.: U.S. Dept. of Agriculture.

Davies, Ivor. 1953. Urban Farming: A Study of the Agriculture of the City of Birmingham. *Geography* 38:296–302.

Dill, Henry W., Jr., and Robert C. Otte. 1971. *Urbanization of Land in the Northeastern United States*. Agricultural Economic Report no. 485, Economic Research Service. Washington, D.C.: U.S. Dept. of Agriculture.

Fishel, William A. 1982. The Urbanization of Agricultural Land: A Review of the National Agricultural Lands Study. *Land Economics* 58:236–259.

Fletcher, Wendell W. 1978. *Agricultural Land Retention: An Analysis of the Issue, A Survey of Recent State and Local Farmland Retention Programs, and a Discussion of Proposed Federal Legislation.* Washington, D.C.: Congressional Research Service.

Fliegel, Frederick C., Andrew J. Sofranko, and Nina Glasgow. 1981. Population Growth in Rural Areas and Sentiments of the New Migrants toward Further Growth. *Rural Sociology* 46:411–429.

Gregor, Howard F. 1970. Urban Pressures on California Land. *Land Economics* 33:311–325.

Griffin, Paul F., and Ronald L. Chatham. 1958. Urban Impact on Agriculture in Santa Clara County, California. *Annals of the Association of American Geographers* 48:195–208.

Hart, John Fraser. 1976. Urban Encroachment on Rural Areas. *Geographical Review* 66:3–17.

Hunter, John, and Laura Holt. 1981. *An Analysis of Municipal Zoning Ordinances Defining or Restricting Agricultural Use.* Special report 60. Dept. of Agricultural Economics and Marketing, Rutgers, The State University, New Brunswick, N.J.

Keene, John C. 1979. A Review of Governmental Policies and Techniques for Keeping Farmers Farming. *Natural Resources Journal* 19:119–144.

Keene, John C., et al. 1976. *Untaxing Open Space.* Washington, D.C.: Council on Environmental Quality.

Lesher, William G., and Doyle A. Eiler. 1977. *Farmland Preservation in an Urban Fringe Area: An Analysis of Suffolk County's Development Rights Purchase Program.* Research paper no. 77-3. Dept. of Agricultural Economics. Cornell University, Ithaca, N.Y.

Little, Charles E. 1979. *Land and Food: The Preservation of U.S. Farmland.* Washington, D.C.: American Land Forum.

McCay, Bonnie J. 1978. Systems Ecology, People Ecology, and the Anthropology of Fishing Communities. *Human Ecology* 6:397–422.

Mattingly, Paul F. 1972. Intensity of Agricultural Land Use Near Cities: A Case Study. *Professional Geographer* 24:7–10.

Moore, E. Howard, and Raleigh Barlowe. 1955. *Effects of Suburbanization upon Rural Land Use.* Technical bulletin 253. Agricultural Experiment Station, Michigan State Univ., East Lansing.

Morren, George E. B., Jr. 1980. The Rural Ecology of the British Drought of 1975–1976. *Human Ecology* 8:33–63.

Mulhauser, Frederick. 1975. Ethnography and Policymaking: The Case of Education. *Human Organization* 3:311–314.

New Jersey Crop Reporting Service. 1983. *New Jersey Agriculture 1983.* Circular 503. Trenton: N.J. Dept. of Agriculture.

Office of Demographic and Economic Analysis. 1978. *New Jersey Population Trends, 1790–1970.* Trenton: N.J. Dept. of Labor and Industry.

————. 1985. *Population Estimates for New Jersey*. Trenton: N.J. Dept. of Labor and Industry.

Otte, Robert C. 1974. *Farming in the City's Shadow*. Agricultural Economic Report no. 250, Economic Research Service. Washington, D.C.: U.S. Dept. of Agriculture.

Press, Charles, and Clarence J. Hein. 1962. *Farmers and Urban Expansion: A Study of a Michigan Township*. Agricultural Economic Report no. 59, Economic Research Service. Washington, D.C.: U.S. Dept. of Agriculture.

Rose, Jerome G. 1979. Eminent Domain. In *Legal Foundations of Land Use Planning: Textbook/Casebook and Materials on Planning Law*, ed. Jerome G. Rose, pp. 419–461. New Brunswick, N.J.: Center for Urban Policy Research.

Rural Advisory Council. 1981. *Agricultural Land Sales in New Jersey*. 4th report. Trenton: N.J. Dept. of Agriculture.

Schmidt, Hubert G. 1973. *Agriculture in New Jersey: A Three-Hundred-Year History*. New Brunswick: Rutgers Univ. Press.

Schwarzweller, Harry K. 1979. Migration and the Changing Rural Scene. *Rural Sociology* 44:7–23.

Scott, John T., Jr., and C. T. Chen. 1973. Expected Changes in Farm Organization When Industry Moves into a Rural Area. *Illinois Agricultural Economics* 13:41–47.

Stansberry, Robert R., Jr. 1963. *The Rural Fringe and Urban Expansion*. Agricultural Economic Report no. 43, Economic Research Service. Washington, D.C.: U.S. Dept. of Agriculture.

Toner, William. 1981. *Zoning to Protect Farming: A Citizen's Guidebook*. Washington, D.C.: U.S. Dept. of Agriculture.

U.S. Bureau of the Census. 1961. *U.S. Census of Agriculture, 1959*. Vol. 1. *State and County Data*. Part 30, New Jersey. Washington, D.C.

————. 1984. *U.S. Census of Agriculture, 1982*. Vol. 1. *State and County Data*. Part 30, New Jersey. Washington, D.C.

Vayda, Andrew P. 1983. Progressive Contextualization: Methods for Research in Human Ecology. *Human Ecology* 11:265–281.

Vayda, Andrew P., and Bonnie J. McCay. 1975. New Directions in Ecology and Ecological Anthropology. *Annual Review of Anthropology* 4:293–306.

# [10]

# The Politics of
# Agricultural Science

### Gerald M. Britan
*Agency for International Development*

## Introduction

The high productivity of American agriculture, envied by much of
the world, is due in large part to the successful application of agricultural science. This success has been achieved through a historically
unique partnership among federal, state and local governments cooperating in a loosely defined agricultural research and extension system
that encompasses federal laboratories, land-grant universities, state
experiment stations, state and county extension offices, and more than
a million extension volunteers. The federal agricultural research and
extension budget alone totals more than a billion dollars a year.

Agricultural scientists have developed new plant and animal
breeds, cures for plant and animal diseases, techniques for preventing
soil erosion, machines for planting and harvesting, and a variety of
other technologies that have dramatically increased the productivity
of farming. During the 1970s, however, agricultural science came
under increasing scrutiny. Farm workers complained that the development of new agricultural machines was threatening their livelihood.
Environmentalists worried that new pesticides, insecticides, fertilizers, and other chemicals were endangering the quality of food and of
life. Minorities protested their limited involvement in agricultural
science. Public interest groups demanded a much clearer focus on the
needs of the urban majority.

When Jimmy Carter became president, some of agricultural science's severest critics were appointed to senior posts in the Department of Agriculture. New federal agencies were organized. New programs were created. New forums were convened. Agricultural science, it was said, would be reoriented to better meet the needs of all Americans (USDA 1979, 1981). But despite the rhetoric, corporate, university, and bureaucratic interests continued to dominate research and extension planning. After Ronald Reagan was elected in 1980, the veneer of organizational change was quickly removed.

This chapter draws on my experience as a participant in and observer of two organizations—the National Agricultural Research and Extension Users Advisory Board and the Science and Education Administration—which were created to reorient agricultural science. My goal in analyzing the development, operation, and eventual demise of these two organizations is not to assess particular agricultural science policies, but rather to describe the policy-making process and its implications for policy change.

## Historical Background

Despite a turbulent early history, by the 1920s research and extension services in the United States were functioning smoothly (Cochrane 1979). By the mid-1960s, researchers had developed cures for plant and animal diseases, high-yielding and widely adopted hybrids, new planting and harvesting technologies, and modern management approaches to the business of farming. Student enrollments at agricultural universities peaked. Research funding reached an all-time high. Federal, state, and local governments and industry combined their resources in a closely cooperating alliance. Production and productivity soared, and a growing population was fed by fewer and fewer farmers.

By the mid-1960s, agricultural science had also become increasingly parochial. Intellectually, it was a curious amalgam of basic and applied research that cross-fertilized little with mainstream scientific disciplines. There were colleges, laboratories, and experiment stations devoted to agricultural science, as well as separate scientific, professional, trade, and social organizations; distinct federal, state, and local bureaucracies; special magazines and journals; and clearly identifiable constituencies.

By the mid-1960s agricultural science was also coming under increasing scrutiny. In 1962 Rachel Carson's *Silent Spring* presented a nightmare vision of an agricultural science establishment that was destroying the environment in a narrow-minded quest for chemical and technological gimmicks. By the mid-1970s agricultural research was being criticized as an "island empire" (Mayer and Mayer 1975) that produced record profits for industrial agribusiness but "hard tomatoes" and "hard times" for everyone else (Hightower 1978).

Meanwhile, American agriculture was also changing. By the late 1970s agriculture was no longer a "unique" social and economic sector (Paarlberg 1980). Farm populations were declining, rural and urban lifestyles were becoming more similar, the boundaries between agricultural and mainstream science were blurring, and national action agencies were reaching into the rural heartland. The number of part-time farmers increased dramatically. Farming was becoming more a business and less a way of life.

At the same time, labor, consumer, minority, environmental, and urban groups, recognizing their stake in agricultural science, became increasingly vocal (Brazzel and Nielson 1980). Soon many of agricultural science's longstanding assumptions were being questioned. Should the government develop new harvesting machines that eliminated farm workers' jobs? Was research meeting the needs of small farmers? Were researchers paying sufficient attention to problems of human nutrition and the food needs of inner cities? Were opportunities for urban gardening, organic farming, integrated pest management (which de-emphasizes the use of chemical pesticides), and other less intrusive farming methods being adequately considered?

By the mid-1970s, agricultural scientists themselves began worrying that the research and extension system was becoming too inbred and lethargic. Committees were formed, conferences were held, policies were charted, and programs were begun, but the substance of research and extension services changed very slowly. After Carter was elected with the support of the "new constituencies," the momentum increased. In 1977 a new farm bill was passed that centralized previously independent research and extension agencies into a new Science and Education Administration (SEA). The farm bill also established a National Agricultural Research and Extension Users Advisory Board (UAB) as a vehicle through which a broader range of research and extension service users could influence agricultural science policy.

Gerald M. Britan

## The Organizational Context of Policy Change

Agricultural research and extension policy is formulated within a loosely defined network of agencies, individuals, institutions, and interest groups whose informal interaction only partially mirrors formal bureaucratic structures. A wide range of groups are involved in this "open system": the United States Department of Agriculture (USDA), other federal agencies, congressional committees and offices, state agencies, land-grant universities, farmers and farm industry interest groups, and a variety of other public and private institutions. Basically, then, the agricultural research and extension system encompasses four kinds of institutions: traditional state and federal bureaucracies, White House offices, Congress, and outside interest groups. These groups have varying degrees of influence on program and budget decisions within the USDA, the state experiment stations, and the state extension services. The media of exchange within this system are people, money, and information.

Agricultural research and extension policy is greatly influenced by the shared experiences, values, and understandings of policy makers. Staff members rotate among positions with congressional committees, executive branch agencies, private industry, and interest group associations. The same person who writes the farm bill may well become the government executive implementing it or the private-sector manager affected by it. Richard Lesher, for example, the senior Senate Agriculture Committee economist responsible for much of the 1977 farm bill, became assistant secretary of agriculture for economics in 1981 before leaving to join a private agribusiness firm in 1984. Such organizational relationships are reinforced by the shared experience and background of participants, nearly all of whom graduated from or taught at land-grant universities or worked in state extension services or experiment stations. With few outsiders allowed, agricultural science has developed a unique organizational culture.

Agricultural research and extension issues rarely surface within the office of the president. The agricultural science budget is simply too small and too unimportant compared with such politically sensitive topics as farm subsidies. Historically, research and extension constituencies—the land-grant colleges, agribusinesses, and farm groups—have also been well organized and politically well connected, and therefore ideologically unopposed at senior government levels.

Although the secretary of agriculture is the cabinet officer who is ultimately responsible for federally supported agricultural research and extension, the role of the secretary's office is usually limited to final budget decisions. Responsibility for planning and implementing federal programs is delegated to the assistant secretary for science and education (formerly the director of science and education) and to the heads of the semi-independent federal research and extension agencies, who work closely with other federal agencies and state and local partners.

This core research and extension bureaucracy includes key officials in the USDA's science and education agencies (the federal Extension Service, the Cooperative State Research Service, and the Agricultural Research Service); other USDA agencies, such as the Forest Service, the Economic Research Service, the Food and Nutrition Service, and the Food Safety Information Service; other federal agencies, such as the National Science Foundation and the National Institutes of Health; the state land-grant universities; and state agriculture and extension agencies. The federal agricultural science and education agencies directly employ nearly five thousand scientists and professionals throughout the United States, but also provide substantial funding for state experiment stations and extension services that employ tens of thousands of additional workers and more than a million volunteers.

The management of agricultural science is complicated. In part, this complicatedness stems from the number of federal agencies involved in agricultural research and extension services. In part, it reflects the close collaboration between federal scientists and their university colleagues, who sometimes work together at the same facilities. Perhaps most important, the management of agricultural science is complex because the federal science and education budget funds a number of independent institutions—the state experiment stations, the land-grant universities, and the state extension services—that receive only a portion of their budgets from federal sources. These "state partners" are concerned about the federal research and extension budget, and they are politically powerful.

The formal goal of the USDA's science and education agencies is to discover, develop, and disseminate new knowledge. As bureaucracies, however, these agencies must justify their existence in yearly budget negotiations with the secretary of agriculture's office, the Office of Management and Budget, and Congress. Because of their close partnership with the land-grant universities, state experiment stations, and state extension services, the science and education agencies also represent and advocate the interests of the state partners, of the professional societies through which both state and federal scientists are represented, and of a variety of agricultural and other lobbying groups.

The shared understandings of agricultural scientists are reflected in historically long-standing priorities, programs, and procedures. The bulk of the federal agricultural research and extension budget is passed from federal bureaucrats to state extension services and experiment stations through a legislatively mandated funding formula. Most remaining federal funds are targeted to particular projects selected by legislators or scientists—tobacco research in Georgia, for example, or irrigation services in north Texas. Federal research and extension service bureaucrats advocate state interests in federal budget negotiations, and state partners lobby for federal bureaucrats in turn. This cooperation is facilitated by a dense network of workshops, conferences, task forces, and committees that plan research and extension priorities and activities.

Congressional interest in the food and agricultural sciences centers around the House and Senate appropriations committees and the four House and Senate legislative committees dealing with agriculture and human nutrition. Research and extension services represent only a portion of these committees' responsibilities, but given the importance of research and extension services in farming states, some members of Congress have given them special attention. Committee staff members, in particular, are knowledgeable and experienced in agricultural science policy—many, after all, have held jobs with the USDA, land-grant universities, or agribusiness.

Congressional influence is also manifested through quasi-independent agencies, such as the Office of Technology Assessment, the General Accounting Office, the Congressional Research Service, and the Congressional Budget Office. While these organizations rarely analyze agricultural research and extension issues, their occasional reports and recommendations are extremely influential.

Agricultural science policy is influenced most strongly by organizations representing the state partners, such as the National Association of State Universities and Land Grant Colleges; associations representing non-land-grant colleges of agriculture; agriculture-related professional societies; and the national and regional organizations representing state extension and state experiment stations. These organizations prepare widely circulated reports, make presentations at congressional hearings, and participate directly in departmental planning.

Other special interest groups traditionally concerned about research and extension policy include representatives of energy, chemical, and forest industries; food processing, marketing, and transportation; farmers; agricultural equipment producers; and farm workers. Although these groups have well-established lobbyists who can significantly affect congressional and USDA decisions, they rarely take a direct role in science and education planning.

Newer public interest groups concerned with small-farm owners, appropriate technology, energy, science policy, the environment, nutrition, and consumer affairs were peripheral to agricultural research and extension decision making until quite recently. However, after several public interest lobbyists joined the USDA during the Carter administration, these public interest groups began playing a more active role, and their members developed close personal and professional ties with particular research and extension programs. But the influence of public interest groups on agricultural science never became particularly strong and declined sharply again after President Carter's defeat.

## The Emergence of the Users Advisory Board

The draft farm bill approved by the House Agriculture Committee in 1977 included provisions to establish a new "National Agricultural Research, Extension and Teaching Policy Advisory Board." The board as initially proposed was to include fifteen members, appointed by the president, representing farm groups, forestry organizations, commodity associations, transportation organizations, nutrition groups, consumer groups, and the like. The board was intended to provide a forum through which people affected by research and extension activities could influence programs and policies. The Senate Agriculture Committee endorsed the principles embodied in the House proposal, but sought to enhance the role of new agricultural research and extension constituencies by expanding their representation on the proposed advisory board.

Concerned that their power was being eroded, federal bureaucrats, land-grant organizations, and groups representing the interests of traditional agricultural industries and operators of larger farms mounted an extensive lobbying campaign. Responding to this pressure, the joint House-Senate conference committee eventually compromised on a three-part advisory structure: a federal interagency coordinating committee on food and renewable resources; a joint council of federal, state, and local research and extension providers; and what was now called a National Agricultural Research and Extension Users Advisory Board (UAB). Congress mandated that the UAB include both traditional and nontraditional research and extension constituencies, including four food and fiber producers, four food processors, two food marketers, two environmentalists, one expert on rural development in the United States, two human nutritionists, one animal health expert, one agricultural transporter, one farm labor representative, and one expert on international agricultural development. To increase federal coordination and better focus research and extension on "national priorities," the farm bill also reorganized previously independent federal research, state research, and extension agencies into a new Science and Education Administration headed by a joint planning and evaluation staff. This new organizational and advisory structure became law with the passage of the farm bill on September 27, 1977.

The lobbying continued after passage of the farm bill, and it took nearly fourteen months of jockeying among USDA bureaucrats, congressional staff, and outside interest groups before the first seventeen members of the Users Advisory Board were appointed. Although the Carter administration was sympathetic to new constituencies, traditional farming groups used their political and bureaucratic ties to assure that they were strongly represented. At the board's first meeting in December of 1978, a sharp split was already evident. Farm industry representatives remained firmly committed to increased production and productivity as the top priority, while consumer, labor, and environmental advocates sought to limit growth and to protect owners of small farms, consumers, and the "public interest."

The board's executive secretary worked feverishly to develop working compromises. With swing votes from liberal farmer and farm science appointees, the board ultimately supported most "new constituency" goals, while retaining a strong commitment to farmers, farming, and the economic well-being of farm families. To facilitate compromise, the board decided to include "separate views" in its formal reports, in which board members could express particular concerns while still supporting the overall consensus.

The UAB's 1979 report to the secretary of agriculture identified

[274]

nine broad research and extension topics for priority attention: (1) basic research in agricultural science, (2) integrated pest management, (3) food security, (4) the structure of the food and agriculture system, (5) water and agriculture, (6) agricultural transportation and distribution, (7) energy and agriculture, (8) competition in the food and agriculture system, and (9) research on human nutrition. The report also contained a "separate view" calling for additional emphasis on providing human nutrition information for urban consumers. The report did not, however, include any "minority opinions" that contradicted the board's overall recommendations.

The UAB's recommendations reflected the liberal agricultural policy agenda, particularly in its concerns about limiting growth, conserving resources, assuring equity, and broadening participation in agricultural science. Although most of the board's priorities were at least partly reflected in ongoing research and extension activities, the board gave them a much stronger emphasis. Few agricultural scientists, for example, disagreed about the importance of basic research, but the UAB argued that past research was inadequate; that research priorities were too greatly influenced by the needs of agribusiness; that emerging fields like biotechnology, organic farming, and farming systems research were being insufficiently funded; and that non-land-grant scientists should be more involved. The board's call for more research on integrated pest management, food security, and on-farm energy use reflected a new emphasis on improving and maintaining what was perceived as a limited agricultural resource base. The board's emphasis on studying the structure of agriculture and competition in the food and agricultural system reflected concerns about the concentration of wealth in large agribusinesses and the limited opportunities for minority farmers and small-farm owners. Similarly, the emphasis on human nutrition focused on the needs of urban consumers, rather than the needs of research and extension's traditional farm clients.

The UAB's 1979 report provoked widespread controversy. Federal, state, and local research and extension agencies produced voluminous data documenting the special needs of their rural constituencies, while arguing at the same time that the board's recommendations were already being largely fulfilled. Public interest lobbyists, on the other hand, demanded more radical change and more rapid action. The board itself began traveling around the country holding largely symbolic public forums to dramatize its commitment to public par-

[275]

ticipation. In the end, however, research and extension policies changed very little, and all but the least controversial of the UAB's recommendations were watered down or ignored.

## The UAB's Influence

Federal research and extension programs are approved through a formal bureaucratic process in which budgets are proposed, defended, and implemented. Although ultimate responsibility for administering programs rests with the White House and responsibility for approving programs rests with Congress, most decisions about federal programs are made by middle managers at the USDA. These managers rely on lower-level state and federal bureaucrats, who have a major influence on the content of federal research and extension. State and local partners have primary responsibility for the bulk of research and extension activities that are conducted at the state and local level.

The UAB's main vehicle for influencing research and extension programs was its formal reports. But because the USDA provided the data, defined the framework, and translated the board's recommendations into budget proposals, the UAB's influence was limited. Although the UAB's reports were sent to the president and Congress, the UAB could not initiate new programs and policies. In the end, the UAB's primary role was as a symbol of the administration's commitment to new constituencies.

An examination of a seemingly uncontroversial proposal to create a competitive research grants program should make the UAB's limited role clearer. Most USDA funding for state institutions is provided through demographic funding formulas and then reallocated to researchers by the land-grant universities and state experiment stations. Universities outside the land-grant system, despite their preeminant role in such fields as molecular biology and human nutrition, receive little or no USDA support. Even within the land-grant system, there is no assurance that the scientifically "best" research projects will be funded.

As part of the 1977 farm bill, Congress authorized a modest "competitive research grants" program which the UAB's 1979 report strongly supported. This program was intended to fund the scientifically best proposals from both land-grant and non-land-grant re-searchers. While the state partners endorsed the idea of competitive funding in principle, they fought it in practice, lobbying hard to en-sure that the program remained small and that its funding was added to the federal research budget, rather than reallocated from existing land-grant funding. In the end, the bulk of the competitive grants were in fact awarded to researchers at land-grant institutions.

The UAB's call for more research on "the structure of agriculture," more urban extension services, better human nutrition guidelines, and more attention to conserving the agricultural resource base had even less influence. While senior USDA managers publicized the UAB's recommendations, most farm groups opposed them. Indeed, when the secretary of agriculture publicly suggested that the depart-ment might decrease its support for research on agricultural mecha-nization (a UAB recommendation), the uproar was so great that the proposal was quickly shelved.

After the controversy provoked by its 1979 report, the board's sub-sequent recommendations grew blander. While the board continued to provide symbolic recognition of new constituencies, it could not by itself increase their influence. To function effectively, the board re-quired at least the acquiescence of traditional agricultural interests. The board in turn acquiesced to the traditional division of agricultural science spoils.

The UAB's limited role became even clearer after the 1980 elec-tions. Its rhetoric began changing even before President Reagan was inaugurated. The board's 1981 report, for example, emphasized the importance of production and productivity, technological change, and agricultural exports. Limits to growth and the importance of national research needs were quickly forgotten. The board was fighting to survive.

The Reagan administration had little desire for an advisory board that symbolized the Carter administration's commitment to "new con-stituencies." Board vacancies were quickly filled with members who were more strongly tied to traditional agricultural institutions. To ensure that the changes would stick, a new farm bill was passed that doubled the number of agricultural producers on the board. A sup-posedly independent advisory board, established to democratize pol-icy making, had become simply another forum for the bureaucracy's traditional clients.

Gerald M. Britan

## The Science and Education Administration

Like the UAB, the Science and Education Administration (SEA) was created to make previously separate agricultural research and extension agencies more responsive to "new" agricultural science priorities. An important element in this centralization was the creation of a Joint Planning and Evaluation Office (referred to as JPE) responsible for developing a science and education budget and for assessing the social, economic, environmental, technological, and other impacts of agricultural science and education policies and programs. The JPE also coordinated the citizen and scientist advisory panels created by the 1977 farm bill.

When I joined JPE in 1980, its program analysis activities were just beginning. New staff members were being hired, and ambitious studies of research and extension programs were being planned. But it quickly became apparent that the traditional research and extension agencies retained the power to define their own agendas. After intensive lobbying by the state partners, senior USDA administrators decided that federal agency managers and state research and extension administrators must give approval before any programs could be analyzed or changes proposed. The targets of policy reform had become major actors in the policy reform process.

JPE's program analysis staff had, for example, proposed studies of human nutrition, farm mechanization, soil conservation, and competitive research grants. The obvious political goal was to justify more federal and state emphasis on "new constituency" issues. In the end, none of these studies was conducted as planned. Instead, the program analysis staff documented the achievements of research and extension agencies in their own terms: Rather than considering the negative impacts of agricultural mechanization, staff members calculated the contribution of mechanization to increased production. Rather than studying the changing role of extension programs in technology transfer, staff members prepared case studies of the most successful technology transfer projects. Rather than assessing the participation of minorities in agricultural research, staff members documented a single minority apprenticeship program.

Like the UAB, the Science and Education Administration sought to refocus agricultural research and extension programs on "high priority national issues," but to do so would have required control over previously independent federal agencies and their state partners. It is not very surprising that the state partners and their agency allies resisted. It is only a bit more surprising that they resisted successfully. Although the Carter administration restructured the bureaucracy, the structure of power was unchanged.

The 1980 Republican platform emphasized the needs of agricultural producers and stressed the importance of a decentralized research and extension system. Soon after Reagan's election, the Science and Education Administration's rhetoric also began to change. The demand for greater federal control became a desire for improved coordination. The emphasis on targeting programs at national needs became a concern for avoiding program duplication. The fear of environmental degradation became a concern for maintaining the resource base for agricultural production. The desire for a better understanding of social and economic impacts became a call for more state and local involvement in decision making.

But the change in rhetoric was to no avail. By March of 1981, SEA's program analysis staff had been moved to isolated satellite offices in Virginia. By June, the Science and Education Administration was disbanded, and the Federal Extension Service, Cooperative State Research Service, and Agricultural Research Service were reestablished as separate agencies. By the summer of 1981 the joint planning and evaluation staff had been eliminated entirely and its staff members dispersed to the newly decentralized research and extension agencies. Power was being symbolically returned to the federal agencies and state partners that in fact had always retained it.

## Conclusions

While policies can sometimes be altered by fiat, policy change is usually more complicated. The Carter administration believed that the needs of newly emerging consumer, environmental, labor, minority, and urban constituencies could be addressed by a democratized policy-making process with a more prominent role for new interest groups. Thus the Carter administration created numerous policy advisory boards and reorganized federal agencies in an attempt to ensure that the influence of these boards was felt.

The National Agricultural Research and Extension Users Advisory Board was such a policy board and the Science and Education Administration was such a reorganized bureaucracy. But the programs and policies that the UAB and SEA attacked were supported by powerful interests and by long-standing and politically well connected state extension services, experiment stations, and land-grant universities. They were also supported by existing federal research and extension agencies that were tightly tied to the state, local, and private institutions they served.

In the end, the UAB and SEA had little effect on agricultural science policy. As a result, many of the issues they raised remain unresolved. Research and extension programs still emphasize larger and more capital-intensive farming. Problems of human nutrition, agricultural laborers, and family farms may be ignored, but have not gone away.

The experience of SEA and the UAB suggests that successful changes in agricultural science policy will only rarely be initiated by the federal government. Given the current research and extension structure, most decisions will continue to be made at the state and local level, and it is through action at the state and local level that changes should be sought.

## References Cited

Brazzel, James M., and Jim Nielson. 1980. *Evaluation as an Aid to Decision-Making in Food and Agricultural Sciences.* JPE staff paper no. 80-DD-02. Washington, D.C.: U.S. Dept. of Agriculture.

Carson, Rachel. 1962. *Silent Spring.* Boston, Mass.: Houghton-Mifflin.

Cochrane, Willard W. 1979. *The Development of American Agriculture: A Historical Analysis.* Minneapolis: Univ. of Minnesota Press.

Hightower, Jim. 1978. *Hard Tomatoes, Hard Times: The Original Hightower Report.* Cambridge, Mass.: Schenkman.

Mayer, A., and S. Mayer. 1975. *Agriculture: The Island Empire.* Lincoln: Univ. of Nebraska Press.

Paarlberg, Donald. 1980. *Farm and Food Policy.* Lincoln: Univ. of Nebraska Press.

U.S. Dept. of Agriculture. 1979. *Structure Issues of American Agriculture.* Economics, Statistics and Cooperative Service. Agricultural Economic Report no. 438. Washington, D.C.

————. 1981. *A Time To Choose: Summary Reports on the Structure of Agriculture.* Washington, D.C.

# Afterword

## Michael Chibnik

Most of the papers in this volume are based on fieldwork conducted in the late 1970s and early 1980s, when there was a strong international demand for American farm products and land values were high. The authors' ethnographic analyses show how the increasingly capital-intensive nature of American agriculture affected household economic strategies and rural social structure. Tenure patterns, conservation behavior, and household labor division are all discussed in a context in which land is expensive, capital scarcer than labor, and agribusiness powerful.

In the past five years, however, American farmers have operated in a worsening economic environment. Exports have dropped, land values have plummeted, and government planners are attempting to dismantle price support programs. These recent developments have some interesting implications for the structure of American agriculture and for future anthropological research and analysis.

The strong dollar is the most important reason American farmers are exporting less in the 1980s. Because foreign buyers must pay more than they have paid previously for American products, many now prefer to purchase from countries with weaker currencies. There are numerous other causes of the drying up of world markets. Three important ones are the impoverishment of debt-ridden Third World nations, greater food self-sufficiency in many foreign countries, and a reduction in the number of trade agreements between the United States and the Soviet Union.

The decrease in export demand has led directly to falling land values. The many farmers who used land as collateral to borrow heavily in the 1970s now find themselves in a precarious financial position. The economic difficulties of American farmers are likely to continue. Ever-increasing production and a stable domestic demand will keep prices low unless exports unexpectedly increase dramatically. Input costs will probably rise as fossil fuels become scarcer and soil degradation continues.

The Reagan administration's reaction to the farm crisis has been to seek the elimination of price support programs. Because growers have no incentive to accept a lower price from a foreign buyer than they can get from their own government, supports are thought to help keep the world market prices of American foods high. Although government planners concede that the absence of price supports would result in the failure of many farms, they argue that farmers who succeeded would be more efficient and better able to compete with foreign growers. The administration's position is consistent with its stated free market approach to economic matters and its view that farms should be treated as businesses.

Opponents of the Reagan administration's plans think that farming is not just another business. Their arguments are partly based on certain economic characteristics of agriculture. Unlike the demand for most other products, the demand for food does not increase much in a growing economy. Farmers therefore often suffer in generally prosperous times, and measures that stimulate most industries are likely to have little effect on agriculture. Furthermore, individual farmers have very little economic power compared to producers in many other industries. The actions of large electronics or automobile firms, for example, can greatly affect the costs, quantity, and quality of products offered; the equivalent power in the food industry is wielded by agribusinesses concerned with processing and distribution.

Those who feel that federal and state governments should protect medium-sized farms, however, are fundamentally moved by humanitarian concerns. In her contribution to this volume, Sonya Salamon compares a rural community composed of "yeoman" farmers to one in which "entrepreneurs" are predominant. The yeomen, who seek to ensure that their farms will be passed on to their children and grandchildren, live in a socially cohesive area with small farms and many community organizations. The entrepreneurs, who stress individual economic efforts, live in a socially fragmented community with larger farms and fewer organizations. Laissez-faire agricultural policies, many fear, will result in more "entrepreneurial farms" and fewer yeoman communities. Free-market enthusiasts dismiss such arguments as being sentimental and ignoring economic reality.

Perhaps because their research usually focuses on only one or two communities, ethnographers are ordinarily reluctant to enter such general policy discussions. Nevertheless, anthropologists already have contributed to the current debate over appropriate farm policy by describing how the increasing capitalization of agriculture has affected household organization and community structure. Goldschmidt's famous study in the 1940s of two California communities is an early example of such research; several of the chapters of this book are in a similar vein. Although the effects of capital intensification are tremendously important, future anthropological research should also investigate other related processes relevant to agricultural policy making. Here I will briefly discuss three of many promising research directions.

Agriculture has not escaped the bureaucratization characteristic of modern industrial society. The economic position of family farms is profoundly affected by the activities of agribusiness, government agencies, and legislative assemblies. Anthropological examinations of industrial agriculture, however, have concentrated almost entirely on the productive end of the food chain. This may be because it is more difficult to apply traditional ethnographic techniques to the study of the bureaucracies dominating food processing and distribution, equipment manufacture, governmental policy making, and agronomic research. Nevertheless, Gerald Britan's contribution to this volume demonstrates that anthropologists can provide insights into the formal structure and informal cultural understandings of these organizations. Britan shows how conflicts between competing interest groups can affect bureaucratic structure and policies. Future research on agricultural bureaucracies can provide additional ethnographic details about their daily activities and decision-making processes.

Anthropologists might also focus more on changing land tenure relations. Many farmers can no longer be categorized simply as "owners" or "renters" because a growing number use both their own and rented property. Landlords include close kin, neighbors, and strangers living in distant cities. Rental arrangements vary considerably. Although some entail detailed written contracts, informal oral agreements are also common. Many involve complex crop-sharing arrangements through which the renter provides labor and the owner provides land and some capital. Others are uncomplicated cash rentals.

Many of the contributors to this volume discuss land tenure, and I would not argue that anthropologists have ignored the subject. Nonetheless, much more research can be done. Little has been written about either the form of rental arrangements or the negotiations leading up to their establishment. Another neglected topic is conflict over land use rights and obligations. Disputes over land are perhaps the biggest single source of family tension and intracommunity dissension in rural areas.

As land values continue to fluctuate, tenure relations can be expected to change. Low land prices, tax laws favoring agricultural investment, and the economic problems of many farmers may result in more rural property being owned by nonlocal residents. Since land tenure is a central feature of rural social structure, anthropologists interested in American agriculture should pay careful attention to such developments.

Finally, anthropologists might examine Americans' contrasting perceptions of farmers. Many Americans regard agriculture as similar to other businesses and think that farmers are not much different from other members of the middle class. This view is shared by Reagan administration policy makers urging free market economics, "entrepreneurial" farmers proud of their business acumen, and some urban radicals convinced that all their food is produced by giant corporations. Others regard family farming as a cherished but threatened way of life fundamentally different from that in other segments of American society. This view is held by many rural residents, some of their representatives in Congress, and urban romantics appalled by the impersonality of city life.

Such perceptions clearly influence public policy. If the several million farmers are regarded as just another special interest group, legislation designed to preserve the relatively small number of family farms will not receive much support. However, if farmers are regarded as a unique and valuable group, such legislation might gain favor among suburban and city residents.

Anthropologists can add to our knowledge of the perceptions and self-images of farmers and nonfarmers and show how they are influenced by the place of farm life in American culture. They can also examine how perceptions change as the structure of American agriculture is transformed.

Most important, ethnographers can provide evidence refuting stereotypic perceptions of agriculture. The contributors to this volume show that American farms are varied and cannot be neatly pigeon-holed as either conventional businesses or unique family enterprises. The major contribution of anthropology to the understanding of American farming may well be its documentation of the diversity and complexity of rural life.

# Index

**Library of Congress Cataloging-in-Publication Data**

Farm work and fieldwork.

   (Anthropology of contemporary issues)
   Includes index.
   1. Farmers—United States—Congresses.  2. Agricultural laborers—United
States—Congresses.  3. Agriculture—Social aspects—United States—
Congresses.  4. Farms—United States—Congresses.  5. Ethnology—United
States—Congresses.  I. Chibnik, Michael, 1946–   .II. Series.
HD8039.F32U635    305.5′55′0973      86-19960
ISBN 0-8014-1978-6 (alk. paper)
ISBN 0-8014-9446-X (pbk.: alk. paper)